Ralph Ellison

AND THE GENIUS OF AMERICA

Ralph Ellison

AND THE GENIUS OF AMERICA

Timothy Parrish

UNIVERSITY OF MASSACHUSETTS PRESS · *Amherst & Boston*

Copyright © 2012 by University of Massachusetts Press
All rights reserved
Printed in the United States of America

LC 2011044230
ISBN 978-1-55849-922-5 (paper); 921-8 (library cloth)

Designed by Jack Harrison
Set in Adobe Caslon Pro by House of Equations, Inc.
Printed and bound by Thomson-Shore, Inc.

Library of Congress Cataloging-in-Publication Data

Parrish, Timothy, 1964–
Ralph Ellison and the genius of America / Timothy Parrish.
p. cm.
Includes bibliographical references and index.
ISBN 978-1-55849-922-5 (pbk. : alk. paper)—
ISBN 978-1-55849-921-8 (library cloth : alk. paper)
1. Ellison, Ralph—Criticism and interpretation.   I. Title.
PS3555.L625Z84 2011
813'.54—dc23
2011044230

British Library Cataloguing in Publication data are available.

For Ralph Ellison,
From the Territory He Dreamed a Nation

Contents

Preface

This book began in part as a response to Arnold Rampersad's 2007 biography of Ralph Ellison. It seemed to me that Rampersad's book had exhausted a line of thinking that began with the early reviews of *Invisible Man* which criticized Ellison's presentation of American black experience. This view of Ellison is rooted in the assumptions of the pre–*Brown v. Board of Education* world which had inspired *Invisible Man* but which Ellison's career ultimately worked to dismantle. This vein of response continued through the 1960s and '70s as some readers questioned Ellison's authenticity as a "black" intellectual, while others suggested that Ellison had failed of his promise because he did not publish a second novel. The dubious achievement of Rampersad's book was to combine these two strains into one. Rather than highlighting Ellison's extraordinary, unique achievements as a novelist and intellectual, his challenging post-*Brown* vision, Rampersad tried to draw attention to what Ellison had not achieved and had not written. Although this seemed to me a counterintuitive way to go about a biography, I recognized that the perspective Rampersad advanced to define Ellison's life was in fact a common one in the voluminous writing that Ellison's work and life inspired and continues to inspire.

At first, my aim was simply to re-imagine Ellison's career in terms of what he achieved rather than what he did not achieve. Thus, instead of speculating about why Ellison did not publish more than one novel in his lifetime, I tried to show what a truly revolutionary, wide-ranging intellectual figure he was. Having written one of the handful of classic American novels, Ellison had a career as a public intellectual no less remarkable than that of Emerson or Thoreau, his closest peers as a theorist of American possibility. As my version of Ellison moved beyond the highly policed areas of English and African American studies departments, I realized that I was not alone in following Ellison's long shadow to unlikely places. The political scientists Danielle Allen and Lewis Morel, the historian Leon Litwack, and the social historian Richard Kluger had all been working to establish Ellison's importance as something more than the author of one well-regarded novel whose personal example offended some of his readers.

Then, as I was close to finishing this book, something remarkable happened. Ellison's second novel, never titled but long labored over, was published by John Callahan and Adam Bradley as *Three Days before the Shooting*. Suddenly, nearly sixty years after *Invisible Man*, the published works of Ralph Ellison had nearly doubled. Though unfinished and difficult to absorb quickly, Ellison's book is clearly a major work of American literature, just as Robert Musil's unfinished novel *The Man without Qualities* or Franz Kafka's *The Trial* and *The Castle* are major works of German literature. Like Musil's work in particular, Ellison's novel has seemingly countless variants and will likely exist in multiple forms. Its publication, like a message from beyond the grave, tells us that Ellison's legacy remains to be confronted and that his future place in American letters and cultural history is not the one that was prepared for him during his lifetime. Numerous brilliant readings of *Invisible Man* exist, and there are many more to be written, but I think we are far from coming to terms with the meaning of Ellison's career largely because he was misunderstood during his own time. As the publication of *Three Days* reminds, Ellison was forever addressing an America that is still unrealized. His ideal readers most likely never knew the world he knew and live closer to the future America he addressed.

Like his unfinished second novel, Ellison's career was gigantic and protean. During his life, he went from being Richard Wright's apprentice to being the confidante of Robert Penn Warren and an adviser to President Lyndon Baines Johnson. Arguably no one in American letters, except perhaps Frederick Douglass, has traveled as far as Ellison did. With Wright, Ellison had despaired of the position of blacks in American society. Together they dreamed of integrating the American literary canon and worked to improve the position of blacks in American life. With Warren and Johnson, Ellison endeavored to realize the potential of the Civil Rights movement. Together they broadened notions of American culture and society so that Americans would understand that, as Ellison's famous narrator declared, "our fate is to become one, and yet many—this is prophecy, not description." The election of Barack Obama as president of the United States was, in a limited way, the symbolic fulfillment of Ellison's journey.

Every act of Ellison's imagination was inspired by his commitment to a vision of American history and possibility. Yet, Ellison also demanded something more from his life than simply struggling for the improvement of the American *polis*. He wanted to be and was an artist. He aspired to write literary works that added to the Western literary tradition that comes from Homer and Virgil, goes through Dante, Shakespeare, Milton, and Cervantes, before making its way through the genre of the novel. To Ellison, *Invisible Man* was the definitive reply to and summation of the nineteenth-century American tradition of Stowe, Hawthorne, Melville, Twain, James, Crane, and, finally, Faulkner.

Of all the great American novelists, Ellison was probably the most well read, most gifted student of literature. He read and absorbed everything, seemingly, from Homer to Faulkner. Not even Henry James had a more refined sense of literary possibility than Ellison. Yet, despite the numerous famous literary friends Ellison made during his life, his studies were pursued from an isolated position within a library that had been segregated according to race. Neither James nor Ellison graduated college, but Ellison had to earn and to steal his education in a way that even James, who fled America in order to write, likely could not have imagined. Ellison's stolen education speaks to his isolated place in American letters but also to his commitment to join and transform this tradition come hell or high water.

Ellison was an outsider to the Western literary tradition that inspired him, and that knowledge complicated his every literary gesture. Always, whatever Ellison read or wrote and whichever audience, present or future, he addressed, he did so from the perspective of being a *black* American during a particular era of American history. Despite his admiration for the many gifted black American writers who preceded him, writers who came from the same historical position that he did, Ellison believed that no one with his particular history had contributed to world literature in the way that Melville, Twain, or Faulkner had. Other than Richard Wright, Ellison recognized no one "like him" who had tried to do and come close to achieving what he hoped to do with his own work. With *Invisible Man*, he came as close as he could to achieving his aim of writing "a classic" work that told the story of his particular experience as a "black American" and did so in a way sufficiently ingenious that people who did not understand what it meant, or means, to be a black American could also recognize their story in his. Cervantes is remembered as the author of *Don Quixote*; Twain is remembered as the author of *Huckleberry Finn*; Ellison will be remembered as the author of *Invisible Man*.

Before Rampersad's book appeared, I had been teaching *Invisible Man* to undergraduates at Texas Christian University, a predominantly white institution where most of the students are religiously devout. On the surface, the relevance of Ellison's work to students of this politically and socially conservative university may not seem obvious. Yet, I found that along with William Faulkner, no American novelist excited the imagination of TCU students as greatly as Ellison did. I recall especially one memorable class of *Invisible Man* readers which consisted almost entirely of young women, nearly all of whom belonged to one sorority or another. Initially, Ellison's conception of invisibility seemed foreign to them. Suddenly, though, a breakthrough occurred when one student observed, with considerable excitement, that Ellison's metaphor spoke to life as a sorority sister at TCU. "Come on, girls, think about it," the student exclaimed, "this book describes our life here. All of us desperately want to join a sorority—to have a place and be a member of a community within the larger, sometimes alienating place that is TCU. And what allows or enables us to join *this* sorority but not *that* sorority? And how will we be known once we have been pledged? Isn't the answer 'by our face'? Each sorority has *a look*, and that *look* is what we wear as our faces. So, girls, the face you wear, the look you have, *that* more than anything determines how you will be known and who people think you are. It's the same as in this book. This 'invisible man' is judged again and again by the color of his face. That's it. The brown or whatever shade he wears. His chances of being known as something different, something more complex, do not stand a chance against the plain fact of how his face causes him to be judged. I understand that he has other problems that most TCU students do not have, but his basic problem is that he lives in a society that knows him only on some surface level and refuses to know or even imagine him as he really is." Though some may find this story merely amusing or even quaint, it struck me as a necessarily particular incidence of the universality to which Ellison's work aspired.

Years after this episode, I was at the Library of Congress reading Ellison's correspondence when I came across a letter that Ellison had written to Richard Wright in which he said that he was tutoring a Bennington student who had been reading Wright's works. Ellison was pleased to tell Wright how his work had affected this young, presumably socially well off, white woman. Confronting Ellison's clear delight with this student's encounter with Wright, I was struck by Ellison's utter faith in the potential of great literature to transform readers' imaginations and lives. I thought that he likely would have been delighted and gratified by the impact his novel had made on TCU students and that he had committed his life to making such unlikely encounters possible.

I wish now that I had kept track of the countless students who have told me that their lives had been changed by reading either *Invisible Man* or one of Ellison's essays. What a story their stories would tell. Literary critics define influence in terms of how the traces of one book may be found in another. How do we account, though, for the influence of Ralph Ellison? His words and acts have illuminated so many invisible places, galvanized so many lives otherwise invisible, and his very example stands as a continuing challenge to meet life with the stern discipline that only a commitment to the noblest ideals can raise. I am sorry that this book cannot do him or his example justice.

Thanks to the generosity of Thomas Schaub and Mary Mekemson, I was able to publish an essay that responded to the exhausted tradition of thinking about Ellison that Rampersad's book embodied and that my book tries to redirect. That essay is not included here, but the response to what I wrote emboldened me to attempt this book. Without the encouragement and advice of Ross Posnock, Stanley Crouch, John F. Callahan, and Adam Bradley this book could not exist in its present form. To Ross, especially, I owe a mounting debt of thanks for his continuing support, and his own august example, since I was a graduate student under his direction at the University of Washington. Marc Conner's support was also most welcome, as was the counsel of Donn Zaretsky. While writing this book I exchanged correspondence with Roseanna Warren, and her blessing has meant more to me than she could ever realize. Todd Holmes was my assistant at the Yale University Library and provided invaluable help. My Florida State University colleagues Ralph Berry, Andrew Epstein, and Barry J. Faulk provided friendship and intellectual support. I am also obligated to Dr. Alice Birney and her staff at the Library of Congress who helped to make reading in the Ellison Papers such a pleasure.

At the University of Massachusetts Press, Clark Dougan, Bruce Wilcox, and Carol Betsch have been wonderful in their attention and care that I write the best book that I can. I am fortunate to work with each of you.

In diverse ways impossible to specify, Vicki Aarons, John Ballard, Brian Evenson, Katy Garrison, Marleena and Quinn Huckaba, Jane Menton, Tim Murray, Cindy Phillips, Robert Rodriquez-Lawson, Mark Wiebe, Aimee Wilson, and Brett Zalkan helped me to write this book.

In 1996 my brother, Jon, and his wife, Edna, gave me the Modern Library editions of *Flying Home* and *The Collected Essays of Ralph Ellison*. Now the bindings of those books are broken and their pages are slipping out. I do not recall if I thanked you two for those books then so let me thank you now. If you could see all the places they have been.

Recently, my son, Matthew, the family's prize-winning history student, completed a project on the Punic Wars that was exhibited at the Florida

State Fair. How proud I was to see you seeking to understand the past. I thought of how closely your efforts resembled mine. But be careful, Matthew, an interest in the past may take you anywhere, even to writing more about it. My daughter, Samantha, the prize-winning fiction writer in the family, has inspired me with her stories, poems, and essays. I think that writing is a habit that you will find hard to break. I will always want to read what you write, Sam, and I hope you never stop.

To my wife and partner, Elizabeth, this is our fifth book together. You have touched every page and read every word in this book, as I have touched every page and read every word in your books. I recall often the first time you read and revised an essay I had written. I wanted to embrace you on the spot. I never let go.

Finally, this book is dedicated to the memory of Ralph Ellison, whose living spirit mingles with Emerson and Lincoln, among so many others, and whose example continues to inspire whoever will venture to meet it.

Ralph, I have tried.

Chapter 1 is a significantly revised version of "Ralph Ellison: The Invisible Man in Philip Roth's *Human Stain*," *Contemporary Literature* 45.3 (2004): 421–59; reprinted with the permission of the University of Wisconsin Press.

Ralph Ellison

AND THE GENIUS OF AMERICA

Ellison Reconstituted

Beyond *Invisible Man*

Now mind! I recognize no dichotomy between art and protest.

Dear Irving, I am still yakking on and there's many a thousand gone, but I assure you that no Negroes are beating down my door, putting pressure on me to join the Negro Freedom Movement, for the simple reason that they realize I am enlisted for the duration.

I wish that we would dispense with this idea that we [Negroes] are begging to get *in* somewhere. The main stream is in oneself. The main stream of American literature is in me, even though I am a Negro, because I possess more of Mark Twain than many white writers do.

RALPH ELLISON

In 1903, in the pitch dark of the nearly one-hundred-year-long Jim Crow night, W. E. B. Du Bois defined the status of black Americans through the ironic inflection of a too familiar question: "How does it feel to be a problem?" (3). In 1952 Ralph Ellison gave perhaps the definitive answer to Du Bois's question with his classic novel, *Invisible Man*. Along with articulating the many complex ways in which it was problematic to have been born black in America, Ellison insisted that the implied premise of Du Bois's question addressed all Americans, not just black ones. In other words, the "problem" of being black in America was not peculiar to black Americans but was shared by every American. For blacks, the "Negro problem" meant that they were denied their proper status as equal citizens; for whites, the problem was more complex in that it meant that their identities depended on either their explicit or their tacit consent in the daily subjugation of others. *Invisible Man* indicated that the "Negro problem" was a collective one that could be solved only by means of a heroic *national* action: one that confirmed that America was committed to democracy in practice and not merely as a beautiful but empty ideal. The publication of

Invisible Man suddenly and shockingly vaulted Ellison into the vanguard of American letters. He would be invited to join the American Academy of Letters and its inner circle, the Century Club. Arguably—and with apologies to Frederick Douglass, W. E. B. Du Bois, Zora Neale Hurston, and, most obviously, Richard Wright—Ellison, within his lifetime, became the first "canonical" black *American* author.

If Ellison's sudden visibility as a great American author made him famous, it was perhaps even more remarkable that the seemingly entrenched historical situation that his book named was visibly changing as well. With the explosion of the Civil Rights movement, and in particular through the extraordinary leadership of Martin Luther King Jr., the invisibility that, for white Americans, had cloaked the humanity of black Americans was disappearing almost as quickly as a plantation house could burn down. Two years after *Invisible Man*, the Supreme Court put a legal end to segregation and Jim Crow with *Brown v. Board of Education*. By 1965, Lyndon Johnson, a white Southerner, had accomplished with the Civil Rights Act and the Voting Rights Act what a Northern president likely could not have done: he had persuaded the United States Congress to ensure that all black Americans were afforded the "equal rights" that the 13th, 14th, and 15th Amendments had promised after the Civil War.

The social contract between blacks and whites guaranteed by those amendments had been rescinded by what Du Bois and Ellison referred to as the "revolution of 1876," which in effect said that in the South old times are not forgotten and that a new slavery as pernicious as any preceding it could be and was made the law of the land. After 1876 the rights of Southern blacks had become so inconsequential that by the 1890s blacks could be imprisoned or even killed at the will of white people. One reason that Du Bois wrote *The Souls of Black Folks* was to protest the exponential increase in lynching that had become so prevalent that people could and did purchase, in Bob Dylan's words, "postcards of the hanging" as tourist souvenirs of places where such acts were tolerated, encouraged, and celebrated. As Danielle Allen argues in *Talking to Strangers* (2004), however, the post-*Brown* era touched off a "reconstitution" of American society that effectively restaged the Civil War as a victory for black Americans by authorizing their official and legal status as American citizens. *Invisible Man* was hailed by literary critics as a type of modernist masterpiece written by the black heir of James Joyce, but it was more fundamentally a shot fired in the long battle for blacks' equal rights and harbinger of imminent victory—a flag that heralded the movement's arrival.

To see the walls of segregation coming down from Selma, Alabama, to Washington, DC, to see the violence that had since the Civil War supported those walls being "peacefully" turned around ("they ain't going to turn me around / turn me around / turn me around," sang the Civil Rights protesters during their marches) so that white Americans were now horrified to witness the "savagery" that other white Americans were willing to commit against black Americans, to see the history of black invisibility that *Invisible Man* had brought to literary light being turned inside out almost as if in response to his literary labors—these were shocking and exhilarating processes for Ellison to witness. Throughout the post-*Brown* era he was writing another novel, but it turned out that for him the history that was happening all around him was possibly more enthralling and more meaningful than the novel he was writing. As a voice remarks in his unfinished second novel, "Nine owls have squawked out the rules and the hawks will talk, so soon they'll come marching out of the woodpile and the woodwork—sore-head, sore-foot, right up close, one-butt-shuffling into history but demanding praise and kind treatment for deeds undone, for lessons unlearned. But studying war once more" (*Three* 409). Ellison was transfixed by this "war," and his published essays and unpublished novel constituted his studied response during this period to the social cataclysm it had touched off.

Ellison understood his post–*Invisible Man* career to be intimately connected to the history that was changing around him. In 1954 he confided to Morteza Sprague, his former professor at Tuskegee, that "the whole road [of post-segregationist] America stretched out and it got all mixed up with this book I'm trying to write and it left me twisted with joy and a sense of inadequacy" (*Three Days* ix). Here I think that Ellison is talking not about his second novel but about feeling personally challenged as a black American intellectual to meet a historical moment that was suddenly so different from the one he had been born into. He conveys this sense of joy in another 1954 letter, this one to Albert Murray, a friend from Tuskegee and, along with Richard Wright and Robert Penn Warren, one of three great literary friends in Ellison's life. Writing a few months before the *Brown* decision but in the spirit of his own triumph as the author of *Invisible Man* and the vistas that he saw opening up for blacks, Ellison warned Murray that "the world is changing so fast that most of these studs are going to crumble up before the very complexity of the freedom they thought they wanted and didn't." In that same letter Ellison had advised Murray that as an aspiring artist he should "stick to Mose. Man. He's got more life in his toenails than these zombies have in their whole bodies" (*Trading* 68). The letter expresses Ellison's supreme confidence in himself and in the cultural resiliency of blacks—of "Mose"—because for him, one was the expression of the other. Moreover, history in the 1950s and 1960s was bearing him out. Mose was winning. Yet within this exhilaration Ellison was also sounding a note of disquiet concerning the challenges that the "complexity of freedom" of the post-segregation era was going to expose. He feared that not all Americans, black or white, would be prepared to meet this complexity, and he knew that the stakes would be high for everyone. For Ellison, *Invisible Man* had both named and raised those stakes. When *Brown* and later the Civil Rights movement made evident that the themes of *Invisible Man* had become national concerns of the highest public importance, Ellison, as a black intellectual, was ready to meet the challenge—in his own way—head on.

Of his two biographers, Lawrence Jackson in *Ralph Ellison: Emergence of Genius* (2002) best captures the sense of Ellison's ferocious commitment to "stick to Mose" and his intense and varied efforts to find both a cultural and a political solution to the "Negro problem." Better than any other commentator on Ellison's career, Jackson documents his numerous and various efforts to advance the political cause of blacks. For instance, Jackson shows that Ellison's involvement with the Communist Party was sincere, since at that time the Communists were the only American political party working for Negro equality. More recently, Barbara Foley has reclaimed Ellison's apprentice efforts as a writer to demonstrate that his repudiation of his Marxist origins was not as categorical as he subsequently led people to believe.[1] Ellison's rejection of the Communist Party, though, reflected both a commitment to his own individual artistic conscience and his political desire to see blacks achieve a greater visibility in American society than the Party could make happen. By Jackson's account, the "emergence of genius" that *Invisible Man* announces is the realization of Ellison's aesthetic vision as a black American writer. Because Jackson's biography ends with the publication of *Invisible Man*, however, its strong if not explicit implication is that Ellison's creative life and political commitment ended in 1953 when he won the National Book Award.

The other major biography, Arnold Rampersad's *Ralph Ellison: A Biography* (2007), treats *Invisible Man* as if it were a brilliant anomaly in an otherwise sad story about a black man who lost his way upon reaching the bright lights of American life. Rampersad's book is rooted in the second half of Ellison's life and works to diminish Ellison's political commitment and his aesthetic achievement by portraying him as a social parvenu. Where

Jackson recounts a life that inevitably leads to the triumph of *Invisible Man*, Rampersad details a life that was a perpetual falling-away from that triumph and, ultimately, a tearful failure. (Rampersad leaves Ellison on his deathbed with a tear in his eye in the book's final pages.)

Rather than clarifying Ellison's importance as a twentieth-century American intellectual, the effect of these two biographies is to cause the reader to wonder what happened to Ralph Ellison. At best, Ellison comes off as a one-shot genius; at worst, as a literary operator more famous for the novel he did not write than for the one he did.[2] The true tragedy of Ralph Ellison is not that he never published another novel but that the scope of his extraordinary and arguably singular achievement as an American intellectual still goes unrecognized. When one actually confronts the body of Ellison's work, his fiction and nonfiction, the work he published and the work he left for others to publish, one confronts a legacy that is as complex and rich as any in the canon of American literature—as if the same mind had written *Moby-Dick* and "The American Scholar." William Faulkner, along with Henry James, wrote more "great" novels than any other American novelist, but no one, including Ellison's namesake Ralph Waldo Emerson, has ever told us more than Ellison did about what it means to be an American and to be committed to democracy as a living civic ideal.[3]

To Jackson's credit, his biography shows why Ellison might well be called the "African American Thoreau."[4] Jackson (like Foley) excavates the enormous labor that was required to write *Invisible Man*. Rampersad's biography, however, undermines Jackson's achievement by turning Ellison into a kind of curiosity of American letters and in so doing crystallizes a critical subtext present even in positive accounts of his career. Rampersad's book would canonize Ellison as a "problem" in American literary history who, despite one burst of obvious genius, failed his talent and did not live up to the demands of his historical moment. Without offering a reading of Ellison's second book manuscript, Rampersad directs the reader's attention to its persistent absence as a cultural fact and tacitly questions how Ellison could be so "successful"—in terms of academic appointments and seats on prestigious boards, and as a much-in-demand speaker—when he was the author of "only" one novel. Rampersad gives an exhaustive accounting of the dinner parties Ellison attended, often among other impressive guests and prominent intellectuals, but cannot tell why he was such a polarizing figure for so long. If Ellison's life is as inconsequential as Rampersad's book implies, then why does it deserve a long biography or continue to provoke passionate debate? A reader of Rampersad might think that one becomes a major American writer not by writing a classic novel, producing two books of essays that are in their way just as impressive as the novel, and persistently challenging Americans to live up to their professed ideals, but simply by promising to write a novel that one is not even working on.

That Ellison never published a second novel is an obvious historical fact. Anyone can observe it, and Rampersad does—over and over. What makes his book so disquieting, however, is not only its implication that what Ellison did not achieve is more important than what he did achieve but the suggestion that the drama of the second novel was due to a writer's block brought on by Ellison's alienation from other blacks. Thus, rather than regarding Ellison's canonization as a great "American" author as an achievement consistent with the aims of Civil Rights movement, which Ellison understood it to be, Rampersad downplays Ellison's lifelong political commitment to black equality and structures his career so that it sinks into a "second-novel-as-black hole" from which even the author of *Invisible Man* seems unable to escape.

Ralph Ellison and the Genius of America attempts to restore the urgency and ongoing vitality of Ellison's career. This book builds upon the work of scholars from a variety of intellectual disciplines to argue that Ellison, perhaps more than any other American writer, was the essential visionary of post–Civil War America. In *Invisible Man* he portrayed the despair and the rage that characterized the pre-*Brown* African American experience. After *Invisible Man* he seized upon the Civil Rights era as a chance to remake American society as if it were to undergo a second revolution. Moreover, Ellison, not Richard Wright or James Baldwin or Amiri Baraka, was the black intellectual who could envision an America that would, within a generation of Martin Luther King Jr.'s death, elect and celebrate the election of a black president. Finally, Ellison's work can be read to identify the challenges and compromises that any president, though perhaps especially a black president, would have to encounter. The election of Barack Obama does not by itself justify Ellison's vision, but it does suggest the prescience and vitality of that vision. In rehistoricizing Ellison's career, I argue that his legacy includes not just *Invisible Man*, not just his underappreciated essays and speeches, not just his rich and dense and multilayered—though unfinished—second novel but also his achievements (at once political, personal, and human) as a representative black figure enlisted, as he told Irving Howe, for the duration.

Ellison's story cannot be limited to a single novel, and in fact his life was an attempt to live up to the implications of *Invisible Man* as an aesthetic achievement and as a symbolic act of history. His career did not begin in 1952 but at least as early as 1937 when he met Richard Wright, and that career continued uninterrupted until his death in 1994. That career manifests itself in his speeches, in his appearances at public symposia, and in his public friendships and literary relationships. The work that Ellison pursued as the logical reaction to the success of *Invisible Man* represented his attempt to make *Invisible Man* answer, as it were, the Civil Rights movement that the novel had foreshadowed.

In proposing to restore urgency to Ellison's career, I am not suggesting that he has quite been buried. Despite the inevitable arguments regarding the legacy of his unprecedented career, the continued interest in *Invisible Man* testifies to Ellison's enduring importance as an American author. Probably no book is assigned more often in American and African American literature classes. The novel has proved remarkably resilient to changing literary fashions; that it has never fallen out of critical favor is reflected in the consistent attention Ellison has attracted in academic journals and conference papers. Prominent recent critical anthologies, Ross Posnock's *The Cambridge Companion to Ralph Ellison* (2005), John C. Callahan's *Ralph Ellison's Invisible Man: A Casebook* (2004), and Steven C. Tracy's *A Historical Guide to Ralph Ellison* (2004) confirm Ellison's continuing importance—despite his status as a one-book author—as perhaps the most consistently read and taught post–World War II American writer. Moreover, as Adam Bradley's *Ralph Ellison in Progress* (2010), Barbara Foley's *Wrestling with the Left* (2010), Jerry Watts's *Heroism and the Black Intellectual* (1994), Kenneth Warren's *So Black and Blue* (2003), and John S. Wright's *Shadowing Ralph Ellison* (2006) make clear, Ellison remains an essential figure in trying to assess the evolving role of the black American intellectual since the end of segregation.[5]

John S. Wright makes a crucial statement when he notes that Ellison's work was "canonized, in part as quiet counterpart to the discordant literature of Black Power," at the same time that "the WASP literary sensibility had almost invariably blunted any wrenching confrontation with Ellison's world by dissolving his novel's specific angers into an abstract statement about Man" (16). Wright is correct to point to the "novel's specific angers," and in a very significant sense those angers have still not been fully elucidated, in part because Ellison himself tempered them as the historical situation of blacks improved during his lifetime. Ellison is sometimes presented as a Cold War writer, but in fact the Cold War was of little interest to him except as a matter of personal political safety.[6] Those "specific angers" that Wright identifies were largely the expression of a "black" point of view largely unavailable to the WASP literary establishment that canonized Ellison. History may have seemed "static" or "repressive" to white intellectuals of the 1950s (especially to Marxist ones), but for most black Americans, history was changing with a rapidity unimaginable since Reconstruction. Ellison, a lifelong, committed Negro-ist, was thrilled by the Civil Rights movement, and he feared Richard Russell, the Georgia senator who wanted to overthrow *Brown*, more than he feared Joseph McCarthy. From his Negro-ist perspective, Ellison decided that the next historical challenge facing Americans, black and white, was to overcome the legacy of Jim Crow thinking.

Ellison's novel did not simply identify a tepid Cold War ambiguity, nor was it written to be celebrated as if it were a well-wrought urn. *Invisible Man* identified and criticized a tradition of historical paralysis (and sadism) that was rooted not merely in the post–World II era but in all of American history, and it had everything to do with the status of blacks in American society. Yet, as Wright suggests, the "specific angers" that drove *Invisible Man* were overshadowed by the celebration of Ellison's success as an individual (black) author. Instead of being seen as a black writer advancing the cause of blacks through literature, Ellison was seen as the black author who had transcended his blackness. This view allows his aesthetic vision to be celebrated while denying one of his crucial motivations for writing. Only a "diverse" culture paralyzed by racial fear could contort such a justification of a book's appeal. Thus, there is a sense in which the work has never been fully understood, despite the lavish attention and praise it has received, because its critical reception has never adequately escaped the Jim Crow origins of its response. The canonization of the "Great Black American Author" carries with it a lasting and unresolved irony: Ellison's critical reception among intellectuals has been segregated into divided factions of black and white readers who preserve and reenact the Jim Crow logic that Ellison had hoped his work would destroy. For the most part, white readers have praised Ellison's literary mastery, while black readers have expressed disappointment in Ellison's career and worried that he was raising himself in American society at the expense of other blacks.[7] The truth, though, is both simpler to state and harder to understand: Ellison was a black writer who happened to write one of the very few essential novels of American literature.

In his excellent 2004 "Bibliographic Essay," Robert J. Butler observes that "the first fifty years of Ellison scholarship have produced an enormous body of criticism which has firmly established Ellison as a major writer," but "much serious work needs to be done if we are truly to gain a comprehensive understanding of Ellison's remarkable achievement" (Tracy 249). Butler correctly suggests that this will require coming to terms with his posthumously published writings. Perhaps more crucially, it will also require Ellison's readers to abandon the false premises concerning his career—most having to do either with the second novel or with Ellison's status as a "black" and hence "problem" intellectual—left over from the misperceptions accumulated during his life. Ellison was the consummate novelist of black experience who nonetheless was dedicated to a broad understanding of American life, of which black experience was a crucial component (and vice versa). In a Jim Crow world, this was an untenable position. As the author of *Invisible Man* and two classic books of essays, though, Ellison's career as an intellectual is one of the amazing success stories of American literature. Neither his complicated stance as Negro American intellectual in a racist society nor the convoluted saga of his second novel—much confused by Ellison himself—makes him a failure.

Adam Bradley, who with John F. Callahan spent years reading and editing Ellison's second novel, has recently tried to challenge the mistaken though prevalent view that Ellison somehow failed in his mission. "The story of Ellison's literary life seems like a tragedy," Bradley acknowledges, but although "such a narrative has the virtue of simplicity, it is finally insufficient" (7). When Ellison—bursting with pride about the success of *Invisible Man*—wrote to Murray about the "studs" who might "crumble," I suspect that he had little doubt that he would one day publish another novel. This next novel, and perhaps others to follow, would "stick to Mose" and, as *Invisible Man* had done, convey the "complexity of freedom" that Ellison perceived in American society. Even as Ellison was writing to Murray, he was hard at work on that second novel and beginning, for many, the tragic arc that Bradley questions. From his interviews over the years, Ellison indicated that he wanted that novel to portray and perhaps define the postsegregation era. The letter to Sprague hints that as early as 1954 he worried that history was outpacing and outwitting his ability to write his book. In his 1982 interview with John Hersey (*Ralph*), Ellison was still lamenting his sense that history had overtaken his ability to finish. By the time he died in 1994, he had written thousands of pages of a novel that he would neither finish nor publish. Why the second novel was never finished to his satisfaction is a mystery that cannot be solved. As one of its characters remark, a miss is a mystery and a hit is history (*Three* 814). With the publication of *Three Days before the Shooting* (2010), however, Ellison's second novel is now, finally, history as well as mystery, though it may be a hundred years before this fact is assimilated into the collective understanding of Ellison's achievement.

Those who believe that the only appropriate response for one who has written one great novel is to write another novel, and then after that another one, and so on until death, became fixated upon Ellison's novelistic silence—a silence punctuated by his periodic promises that the book would soon be finished and out. Bradley captures the fascination that Ellison's silence provoked in his admirers and his critics: "For all the thousands of pages of fiction Ellison wrote in the last half of his life, the discussion of Ellison's literary career after *Invisible Man* is most subsumed in a single question: How could Ellison have written for forty years without completing a second novel?" (14). Yet this question is misleading and always was, since it does not allow for and in fact conceals what Ellison did accomplish. No doubt he hoped to publish another novel and worked hard to do so. My view is that one reason he did not publish the book is that he did not think it surpassed *Invisible Man*, and this was because, as he said, it was so tied (in his mind) to the historical moment that it was portraying. The second novel begins on the eve of *Brown* and was rooted in the same historical situation of political paralysis as *Invisible Man*. Where *Invisible Man* ends by challenging the reader to change history, *Three Days* implies no ending that allows for historical change, even though its drama centers on the assassination of a "white" U.S. senator by a "black" gunman. In *Invisible Man* the conclusion implies the possibility of revolt, but in the second novel black revolt comes out in the open, into the very chamber of the Senate. Beyond the book, though, in the streets and on television, peaceful black revolt was in fact helping to destroy Jim Crow. Ellison kept revising the book to meet the changing times, but the violence at the center of the book's conception seemed at odds with the history he was witnessing.

Three Days before the Shooting reveals Ellison's typical preoccupation with the intersection of Negro experience and American possibility.[8] It is both a record of his "involvement" with the political changes of his era and, surprisingly, an accounting of his doubts about it. Like *Invisible Man*, the book portrays a variety of the conflicting political positions that blacks could plausibly take in response to their history. Where the first novel uses psychology to critique whites' vision of blacks, the second novel more explicitly attacks the moral bankruptcy of white Americans. There is no certain sense that the "white" Senator, despite having been raised by blacks, is worth saving. The death of the Senator may or may not be a tragedy—it depends on whether one wants to invest him with having had the potential to be another Lincoln. Either way, the book, despite its comedy, suggests that any hope for a truly "equal" America is perversely optimistic. Adding the second novel to our understanding of Ellison shows just how insufficient the "tragic arc" line is to understanding what Ellison chose to do with his career: it reveals a different perspective—one that Ellison chose not to endorse—on the preoccupations that dominated his life after *Invisible Man*.

The second novel more obviously recalls his 1940s letters to Richard Wright in which he consistently expresses his bitterness about the place of blacks in American society. In those letters he even mocks black newspapers for agitating to get black soldiers killed side by side with white soldiers, since they would thus be sacrificing themselves for a Jim Crow society. After those "studs," the "master strategists, the N.A.A.C.P. legal boys," managed to "dry-run the Supreme Court of the U.S. and (leave it to some moses to pull that one)" to win *Brown*, though, Ellison's stance regarding the potential of blacks to rise in American society drastically changes (*Trading* 132). His 1950s letters to Murray are ebullient concerning the social changes he sees. Any bitterness he expresses comes when he fears the legal victories may be a mirage. One may say that what has changed since the 1940s is that Ellison has become a successful novelist, but I do not think that alone explains his optimism. Arguably, in his letters to Murray he seems more enthusiastic about the burgeoning Civil Rights movement than he does about his second novel (which is also clearly exciting him). The novel is something he is playing with, but the Civil Rights movement is "real": history's boomerang in stunning flight before his watchful eyes. Seeing in these letters Ellison's sheer fascination with what was going on in the world beyond his study renders plausible the claim that he felt his fiction was inadequate to express what was happening. Meanwhile, he did share in public his opinions concerning the relationship of black experience to American history, and he became a figure of controversy for it.

Nonetheless, *Three Days* makes clear that Ellison was not a case study of a blocked author but was courageously trying to name and meet the challenges of the post-*Brown* era. History had answered the challenge with which Ellison had ended *Invisible Man*, and suddenly Americans were busy tuning in to the frequencies that connected them beyond color. What does a writer whose will to write comes from his desire to see American society transformed do when his most searching questions are heard and are being answered? Does he write another novel with its requisite need to follow Sidney's credo that the artist "nothing affirmeth," or does he engage as clearly and straightforwardly as he can the implications of what is happening in a society that is finally shaking off the shackles that had oppressed so many for so long? Ellison tried to follow both courses but in the end, whether intentionally or not, he chose the latter one.

Beginning with Irving Howe's famous 1963 attack ("Black Boys"), Ellison has been castigated for situating himself above the political fray, but in retrospect it should be clear that he was among the most politically engaged authors in the American literary canon. To see this Ellison requires surrendering the fascination with the forty-year performance in which he kept promising the novel that was indeed secreting pages above, below, and around the desk in his apartment office but was never brought out where others could read it. The usually adroit Ellison helped to establish such a denuded critical context for his work when he acknowledged to Howe that he had been "remiss and perhaps vulnerable" in not writing more novels (*Collected* 188). Eventually, his long-promised second novel became the most famous mystery in American letters (the other candidate is the long-missing but eventually delivered sequel to Henry Roth's *Call It Sleep* [1934]). Still, as irresistible as any purported mystery may seem, there is something deeply wrong with a literary history that obsesses over what an author chooses not to publish and then renders its judgment on the author's career without ever reading the actual pages that author did in fact write but just did not share. It suggests some powerful if not quite namable fear to come to terms with what the author did accomplish.

In his review of *Three Days*, Stanley Crouch confronts the strangeness of Ellison's reception history. Crouch suggests that instead of clarifying Ellison's career, the publication of a version of the second novel may only have further obfuscated it. For Crouch, one of Ellison's staunchest defenders, Ellison became obsessed with writing the Great American Novel, one that would encapsulate its age in a literary form that would be a worthy successor to Melville and Faulkner. Crouch suggests that Ellison had "to hit a grand slam" and would settle for nothing less, so that in laboring over the book endlessly rather than publishing it, he "betrayed the national ethos of money and self-obsession expressed through career ambitions" (1). Had Ellison simply published what he could, accepted his critical lumps, and moved on to the next book, his career might have been different. This is what a working novelist normally does. Crouch does not discuss why the novel fails to enhance Ellison's reputation; he just takes it for granted that despite some excellent pages, it does not quite constitute an important contribution to Ellison's legacy.

Crouch says of the second novel that "in its best sections, this mysterious draft is full of wit, satire, and the chaos that Ellison concluded was so central to the ongoing surprises of American life"—but so what? (3). Despite his lavish praise of the author, Crouch indicates that the second book lies somewhere just beyond the Ellison canon. The fact that elsewhere the book scarcely was noticed at all—invisible in plain sight, as if its appearance could only confirm its nonexistence—reinforces this view, or non-view. Whether because of its length or because it was understood to be unfinished, *Three Days* did not receive the attention that one might have expected a fifty-year literary obsession to attract in the places where one expects to see new literary works discussed. Indeed, in the very magazines and newspapers where Rampersad's life of Ellison as a failed second novelist had been prominently reviewed and largely praised, there was hardly a word to be found that might offer even a preliminary judgment concerning the thick volume that represented so much of Ellison's life's labor. In the immediate wake of *Three Days*' appearance, one could search the archives of the *New York Times*, the *New Yorker*, and the *New Republic* and find nothing of substance about it.

It is tempting to say that so powerful was Rampersad's biography that in effect it foreclosed consideration of the novel, except that the editors of *Three Days*, against what one takes to be their intentions, had in effect already risked such a reaction by virtue of their hesitant presentation of Ellison's labor. John Callahan, whom Ellison had named as his literary executor, was, by his account, astounded when he saw what the author had left him. Taking Ellison at his word that he was near completion (as he had said publicly for the last twenty-five years of his life), Callahan remarked that "it was a jolt realizing that what he left behind was not nearly finished. There was not one coherent, continuous narrative. I suspect there never was" (Bradley, *Ralph*, 38). In their "General Introduction" to the book, Bradley and Callahan wrote that it was "not the novel readers were waiting for at the time of Ralph Ellison's passing" (*Three* xxviii). True enough, but what could be?

If readers have persistently asked the question why Ellison did not publish a second novel, then we now have to admit that he wrote more than one novel—he wrote *several versions* of a multivolume novel. Even the 1,101 closely printed pages contained in *Three Days* do not make up the complete manuscript, and one can well imagine other editors coming up with different versions. From the 1950s on, according to Bradley and Callahan, Ellison had composed significant chunks of a novel that, judging by his letters, he was always on the edge of publishing—even as he was continually revising it. Apparently, he could have published some version of it almost any time after 1958. Saul Bellow says he read 200 pages of a novel in progress in 1959, and the year before, Ellison was telling Murray that "Bellow has read book two and is to publish about fifty pages in a new mag which he is editing" (*Three* xi). Those fifty pages would appear as "And Hickman Arrives" in 1960 in Bellow's journal *Noble Savage*. In fact, before *Invisible Man* was even finished, Ellison told Murray that he was "trying to get going on my next book before this one is finished, then if it's a dud I'll be too busy to worry about it" (*Trading* 21). *Invisible Man* was anything but a dud, and as Ellison's career developed (or did not develop, depending on one's point of view), he became "too busy" worrying about, or perhaps just writing, his second novel for him ever to finish it. Or perhaps he decided he did not need to publish it to enhance his achievement.

Bradley and Callahan characterize the book as "serpentine fragments," some of "which extend to over three hundred manuscript pages" and are "related" but lack "the necessary connective episodes that could have made his fiction whole" (*Three* xvi). Yet the question of what renders a fiction "whole" is extremely problematic, since it may raise more questions than it closes off. Such a judgment, it seems to me, is first the artist's to give, and apparently Ellison shared it, but if the author cannot render something whole to his or her satisfaction, then readers still might. Over time, Ellison's novel will presumably be read and will likely acquire a significant place in American literary history. Virgil asked that his *Aeneid* be destroyed because he did not complete it: Chaucer never finished or published his *Canterbury Tales*; Petrarch's *Canzoniere* was not published in his lifetime; T. S. Eliot's "The Wasteland" required the assistance of Ezra Pound to achieve its celebrated form; Thomas Mann published *The Adventures of Felix Krull* unfinished. One can well imagine a different version, or even versions, of Ellison's second novel called "The Adventures of Alonzo Hickman," not to mention others called "Severen's Story," "The McIntyre Files," and "Birth of a Nation." The fact that the book is technically "unfinished" does not detract from the sense it gives of being a powerfully imagined work. It is unfinished mostly in the sense that it does not have an ending—Ellison never finishes killing the Senator. If the Senator were to die, as Alonzo Quijano finally dies at the end of *Don Quixote*, then one could more easily imagine a version of the book which, like Robert Bolaño's *2666*, was "all but complete" except for a handful of author's adjustments.[9]

Ellison was a demanding and even finicky writer. He did not want to publish something that he did not think was right and, despite his obvious gifts as an episodic and improvisatory writer, was committed to an ideal of the "whole" which he could not realize. Bradley, though, reminds us that Ellison wrote much more of *Invisible Man* than he published; alternative versions exist in the files at the Library of Congress. Reading Ellison's career through the drafts of the second novel, one might regard it as a miracle that *Invisible Man* was ever finished and published. In 1961 he said that he had "the feeling that it stands on its own if only as one of those pieces of writing which consists *mainly* of one damned thing after another sheerly happening" (*Three* xxii). At different points in his life Ellison did regard the second novel as close to being finished. According to Bradley, the novel was probably nearest to publication by Ellison in 1970. Bradley further suggests that Ellison became sidetracked by his acquisition in 1982 of a word processor, which allowed him to revise the same few passages over and over again. Yet as early as 1958, with apparently two books of a projected three-book opus mostly drafted, Ellison opened a letter to Bellow with the words, "things ain't coming worth a damn" (*Three* xi). Although the letter itself is comic, and these words may not reflect an accurate self-judgment, one may still wonder whether Ellison suspected even in 1958 that the novel was not going to work out. Who knows? If he had not published it by 1961 or 1970, why would it be logical to think that something that happened in 1982 was the book's fatal stroke? Perhaps Ellison intuited a book he could envision but could not convert to reality. As Bradley and Callahan suggest, Ellison's notes for the novel seem to refer to passages or events that he apparently never wrote or related (xxi). Perhaps the book meant so much him that he could not bear to let it go.

There is no answer to the question of why Ellison did not finish. He simply did not. Even if there were an answer, it could not be found in the manuscript. You cannot find in the manuscript what it was about the manuscript that makes it unfinished. You can only guess. Did he not publish the novel because he could not finish it, or did he not finish the novel because he could not bring himself to publish it? I think the answer is the latter, but one can only guess—which is to say that one can only answer the question speculatively and make Ellison the subject of a story that he did not write. Inevitably, people will look for psychological explanations. Yet the problem with psychologically oriented explanations, as *Invisible Man* might remind readers, is that by their very premises they may reveal more about the interpreter than the interpreted. In the case of Rampersad, for instance, his charge that Ellison could not write because he was alienated from other blacks constitutes the apotheosis of a line of thinking about Ellison that goes back to the first reviews of *Invisible Man*, mostly by black readers who worried that Ellison was somehow "betraying" black experience through his portrayal of black life. These early readers were clearly angry that the book had been published. From their perspective, *Invisible Man* was published precisely to express Ellison's alienation from other blacks![10] By this logic, everything Ellison wrote or did not write expressed the same intention, and, ultimately, what he wrote did not matter at all, since one knew what he was going to say anyway.

With the publication of *Three Days* and the recent opening of the Ellison papers housed at the Library of Congress, readers now have access to what Ellison did not publish and will have to reorient themselves in Ellison's work. Bradley suggests that because of its multiple versions and its obsessive concern with the shifting nature of American identity, Ellison's manuscript is perhaps the quintessential candidate to be declared the elusive "Great American Novel" (*Ralph* 214). There is much to recommend Bradley's assertion, because *Three Days*, rich in conception and in execution, adds immeasurably to the fascinating section that Callahan published as *Juneteenth* (1999), and there is arguably more to be experienced from it than from most of the finest novels of Ellison's distinguished American contemporaries. Bradley makes the interesting observation that "at times one wonders whether Ellison could have written the novel in perpetuity" (36). As I suggest in chapter 1, writing a novel in perpetuity is in fact what Ellison was doing. Moreover, the unfinished state of the book accurately reflects Ellison's sense that history, having been unsettled by *Brown*, was still up for grabs.

In their introduction to *Three Days*, Bradley and Callahan reiterate Ellison's anxiety that the book did not and could not cohere. By making this claim, they are following Ellison's lead, but it may be a case where the book's power outwits the author's ability to control it. Despite an admirable attentiveness to what they perceive to be Ellison's intentions, they may only have erected a formidable barrier between what Ellison wrote and the patient, engaged critical attention it deserves. After Kafka tried to write what later became published as *The Trial* and *The Castle* and (like Ellison) read portions of these works aloud to admiring friends, he asked Max Brod to see that these unfinished books were destroyed. Fortunately, Brod ignored him. Ellison, by contrast, who may have considered his work more unfinished than Kafka believed his to be, and who, as an admirer of Kafka, certainly thought that his own work was more unfinished than Kafka's posthumous novels, did not ask that his manuscripts be destroyed.

Presumably, Ellison made Callahan his executor and left his papers behind so that interested readers would encounter a version, or versions, of what he had done. Ellison's numerous interviews, speeches, and essays undoubtedly helped to shape the reception history of *Invisible Man*, but with this novel his judgment should influence only the incurious. Seventy-five years passed before *Moby-Dick* began to get its due, and in time Ellison's second novel should compel readings not bound by the misguided assumptions pinned on Ellison's career while he was alive. As the existing barriers set up against his entire work are allowed to crumble, his career will eventually take on a shape significantly different from the one it currently has.

Throughout *Ralph Ellison and the Genius of America*, I discuss Ellison's second novel, but I do not propose to offer a definitive view, nor do I wish to suggest that my primary goal is to elevate *Three Days* to the importance of *Invisible Man*. They are different achievements, and the terms that make one successful cannot apply to the other. What matters is that both works express the "genius" of Ralph Ellison and are worth sustained encounter on that basis. I discuss *Three Days* in the context of Ellison's dilemma as a public intellectual committed to presenting a view of American history and culture that brought to light the invisible but essential contributions made by African Americans. As I have already suggested and discuss further in chapter 1, I think the intention of Ellison's second novel is evident and that a possible reason why he never finished or published it is that the novel arguably contradicted the public stance of a post–Civil Rights black intellectual, which he was working through in the essays he published and the speeches he gave after *Invisible Man*.

Invisible Man became for Ellison an elastic text that he could interpret and reinterpret to fit the changing times. It became the novel he was continually revising in public, while the second novel was the one he was continually revising in private. When Ellison began *Invisible Man* in 1945, he was writing in part to protest the same historic conditions that compelled Du Bois to write *The Souls of Black Folk*. Through his reading of Lord Raglan, however, Ellison structured the book so that it would not be merely an artifact of his times. The anonymous "hero" of the novel could be seen as the black people of America, or as the democratic principle of equality, or even as any "American" in the way that Franklin's *Autobiography* proposed to speak for the nation. This elasticity is in part why the book can be read, as I read it in chapter 4, as a template for the heroism of Martin Luther King Jr. and as a kind of primer for the Civil Rights activists' actions of the 1950s and '60s. In any and each of these interpretations, Ellison's book ties its meaning to a mythic interpretation of American history, written in the tradition of the epic and thus meant to connect the past to the future. One can make the case that *Invisible Man* is *the* canonical American novel; it will last as long as America survives as a nation. At the very least it stands, along with Faulkner's works, as the answer to the nineteenth-century tradition of the American novel represented by Stowe, Hawthorne, Melville, Twain, and James.[11]

Three Days, by contrast, lacks a single narrative perspective to unite its disparate episodes, though this fact may enhance rather than qualify its interest. One could argue that Lincoln holds the book together as the contradictory episodes play out beneath his shadow and take up the meaning of the Civil War. However, this observation applies to the rest of Ellison's work as well. Bradley makes the provocative suggestion that "*Invisible Man* was Ellison's masterpiece, but the second novel was his life's work" (*Ralph* 8). Yet although *Three Days* is a wonderful addition to the Ellison canon, I do not think it can be described as Ellison's life work any more than *Invisible Man* can. Better to say that *Invisible Man* was his life's major achievement and that living up to its implications became his life work. Although he perhaps too often called attention to the formal, literary mastery that *Invisible Man* sought to realize, the book was much more to him than the phrase "literary achievement" ordinarily conveys. As a pragmatist reader of Emerson and Kenneth Burke, Ellison understood words to be acts (and was careful with the words he did authorize). He understood his novel to be a form of social and political action, just as he understood Jefferson's Declaration of Independence or Lincoln's Emancipation Proclamation to be living acts that continued to structure the acts of Americans and through them the processes of democracy.[12] Although "only" a novel, *Invisible Man* was for Ellison a living act just like those of Jefferson or Lincoln, but it seems that he could not authorize *Three Days* in those terms. Ideally, *Invisible Man* could be used to shape a nation: that is the narrator's fantasy in the book's Prologue and Epilogue. And if *Invisible Man* is, as a novel, something more than a political pronouncement, then it also remains at bottom the affirmation of the eloquence and the dignity of those whom society has ignored, undervalued, and oppressed.

As Barbara Foley's work points out, Ellison became a writer as a political agitator. Although he distanced himself as an artist from his Marxist origins, he never lost his will for the cultural troublemaking that had everything to do with the status of blacks in American society. When Ellison wrote *Invisible Man*, blacks for the most part could not speak out in public;

in many places they could not even eat a meal or use the public restrooms. Ellison began *Invisible Man* at a time when the United States was engaged in a world war but remained so committed to demonizing its black citizens that it would not even allow them to die by the side of whites in battle. *Invisible Man* captured and critiqued the pathological will to segregation that had defined American society up to that time, but it did not do so to render its protagonist, its reader, or, especially, its author immune from the historical conditions that inspired its creation. To some readers, Ellison's protagonist may seem to escape the society that cannot see him, but for Ellison *Invisible Man* was the continuation of a collective Negro struggle for equality as well as a supreme aesthetic achievement. His readers and critics have understood the latter point better than the former. The novel's success became Ellison's entry into the very public and previously forbidden world of social engagement and political debate. Once he had arrived, he challenged his audience at every turn and became during the late 1960s the most controversial figure in African American letters. Ellison was controversial not for what he had failed to write but for the public stances he took as a black intellectual. An essay he published in *Time* magazine and one remarkable response that it provoked reveal volumes about the neglected meaning of his career. They also tell us that despite all his wrestling with a second novel, Ellison knew very well what he had accomplished, and it was enough for him.

Ellison's Answer to Claghorn

In 1970, when his second novel may have been as close to publication as it ever would be during his lifetime, Ellison wrote an extraordinary letter that he never sent. This letter probably says as much about his career, and his own sense of his career, as the novel he never published. I would go further and say that if any single anecdote could stand in for Ellison's career and how he wanted it to be understood, it would be this one. The letter Ellison wrote was not addressed to Richard Wright, Albert Murray, Saul Bellow, John Cheever, Robert Penn Warren, Lyndon Baines Johnson, or any of Ellison's other famous correspondents. The letter was brief, and it was to someone named S. D. Claghorn. The occasion for the letter was Ellison's recent essay in *Time*, "What Would America Be Like without Blacks?" (*Collected*). Claghorn had read the essay and had written to tell its author what he thought of it—in short, he found it offensive, dangerous, and threatening. His response proves that black intellectuals were not the only ones who considered Ellison's work problematic at this time. Some white readers did not like it either.

Claghorn was provoked because Ellison's essay presented an incendiary view of American history, one that consolidated and pushed forward the logic of the Civil Rights movement. Written during the same time that Ellison was being attacked by black writers for what they took to be his political quietism, this essay advanced the perspective that the founding of the fight for democracy was largely an African American achievement. It was a persistent theme for Ellison, but writing the essay had not originally been his idea. *Time* had asked him to write something that answered the question posed by the title. The *Time* editors presented the essay as an opportunity to celebrate the achievements of American blacks, but Ellison suspected that the suggested question implied a hope: the wish of white Americans that the "Negro problem" had never been a part of the nation's history. Despite or because of his misgivings, he wrote the article in order to address what he called the "free-floating irrationality—indeed, a national pathology" that made so many find the question worth asking. It took this famously blocked writer less than a week to compose masterly essay worthy of Emerson or Thoreau.

The answer Ellison gave was that there would be no America without blacks—that even to ask the question was inadvertently to betray ignorance about one's cultural origins. The insistence that blacks were an essential component of American history and democracy had been one of the messages of *Invisible Man*, though the political context for making this point had changed radically since that book was published. Obviously, says Ellison, there would have been "no slave economy, no Civil War, no violent destruction of the Reconstruction, no K.K.K. and no Jim Crow system," and thus the political history of the country would have been "almost impossible to conceive" (*Collected* 582). Not only had the systematic disenfranchisement of blacks come at a great cost to whites and blacks, but the pathological obsession with the impossible task of "getting shut" (*Collected* 578) of blacks had concealed "the tragic knowledge" that "the true subject of democracy is not simply material well being, but the extension of the democratic process in the direction of perfecting itself" (582). The burden and the necessity to carry this "tragic knowledge" so that all Americans could understand its implications was taken up by black Americans. The "democratic process" Ellison invoked was one that would repudiate the moral abomination of slavery and its aftermath and accept the former slaves as equal American citizens. Otherwise, the claim that America was a democracy was a lie.

Ellison asserts that "materially" and "psychologically" "the nation's heritage is Negro American" (583). It is not just that the slaves helped to build the United States but that a Negro sensibility has also permeated virtually every dimension of American culture. "Without the presence of Negro American style, our jokes, our tall tales, even our sports" would not have the effect that they do. Ellison describes how the art of Whitman, Twain, Crane, Hemingway, and Faulkner would be unimaginable without the aesthetic and moral example blacks had provided. If, as Ellison suggests, "whatever else the true American is, he is also somehow black," then it is also true that "most American whites are part Negro American without even realizing it" (583, 580). Deftly, through a remarkable range of historical detail, the essay spells out the monumental—almost unfathomable—implications of "what the nation would have become had Africans *not* been brought to the New World" (580). Written after King's assassination and Nixon's election and while the Civil Rights movement had fragmented, the *Time* essay places the achievements and perspective of black Americans at the moral center of American culture and politics. In a time of intense political strife, Ellison declares that "today it is to the black American who puts pressure upon the nation to live up to its ideals" (583). The protagonist of *Invisible Man*, an aspiring Negro leader, had offered a version of this stance when he suggested that "the invisible victim is responsible for the fate of all" (14). In 1970, with far more authority than his fictional narrator could claim, Ellison was framing this argument no longer from the perspective of the black victim but from that of the black leader whose presence in American public life was no longer invisible.

One cannot imagine *Time* magazine publishing such an essay in 1952, but Ellison had been preparing all his life for a time when such a declaration would be possible. Bradley correctly notes that "at a time when black power was the word, it is hard to imagine ascribing more power to the blackness than Ellison does here, endowing black Americans with the capacity to shape a nation" (70). Nonetheless, not every person who read this essay or heard Ellison make similar arguments in addresses at universities shared his point of view. That he was attacked by other black intellectuals such as Addison Gayle or Clifford Mason during this period is a well-known part of Ellison's story, but the truth is that there were many more white Americans uncomfortable with this message than most black Americans could possibly be. If, as Ellison once said, *Invisible Man* was written primarily with black readers in mind, then this essay in *Time* was addressing white Americans in the same way that King had targeted white Americans during the Civil Rights marches. Where King promised to love his white "brothers" even when they struck him, however, Ellison in this essay, in effect tells whites they are part black and that blacks are 100 percent American, whether whites like it or not. His essay is a calculated blow against any assertion, veiled or not, of white supremacy in American culture. When Ellison notes that "since the beginning of the nation, white Americans have suffered from a deep inner uncertainty as to who they really are," he is alluding to a deeply ingrained cultural pathology in which white Americans cannot accept that their sense of themselves is bound to black Americans in ways that cannot be undone (*Collected* 582). Bradley speaks of "the hopeful notes of coexistence and connection" that the essay tried to strike, but "coexistence and connection" with blacks was something many Americans wanted to deny at all costs (72). This group did not want to be assured that "most American whites are culturally part Negro without even realizing it" (*Collected* 580). Mr. Claghorn certainly did not desire such assurance when he wrote to express his disdain for Ellison's argument.

Bradley, who first found Claghorn's letter in the Ellison files at the Library of Congress, describes it as a "racist screed," but the letter also expresses a sense of identification with what Claghorn takes to be Ellison's position. In the essay Ellison says that to perfect their democratic experiment, Americans merely needed to "include" not "assimilate" black Americans into its civic processes. What this inclusion meant tested the democratic experiment to its core. Claghorn, who wished to preserve the integrity of his white American identity, affirms Ellison's claim by denying it: "You are a black bigot—I am a white bigot," he states (71). Ellison is not a black bigot, but Claghorn discerned the pride that Ellison conveyed as a black American and responded in kind. I doubt that Claghorn would have found the rhetoric of Malcolm X or the Black Panthers to be as threatening as he finds Ellison's argument, since Ellison's language allows for no meaningful separation between whites and blacks as Americans. If Ellison implies that blacks have had the superior moral position, then whites, ironically, can take that away from blacks by "including" blacks within the public processes of democracy. For Claghorn, however, the very existence of blacks within American society constitutes a threat to white American society. Where Ellison says it is the "black American" who "gives creative tension to our [American] struggle for justice," Claghorn, presumably referring to the Civil Rights movement but perhaps also to Malcolm X, notes the "pure hell your people have raised in this country" (71). Claghorn's letter means to strike Ellison as Ellison has struck Claghorn, though it pays Ellison the grudging respect that a worthy adversary merits. "You will not agree," he tells Ellison, "even as I do not agree with you, so we are going to have an explosive collision" (72). The nature of that collision Claghorn does not specify, but the implication is that for Claghorn the rising tensions in American society had come to a point where either the blacks wanted to eradicate the whites or vice versa.

From Claghorn's perspective, Ellison's essay—appearing in *Time* magazine, the epitome of a mainstream voice in matters regarding American culture—was proof that blacks were winning the cultural war against white Americans, which for Claghorn meant that the racial End Times were near. Thus, his statement that "black is not beautiful—if you don't like black," reads, depending on one's perspective, either as a wish for an American society without blacks or as a promise to make such a wish come true (72). Either way, Claghorn's letter sought to deny Ellison's premise on every level probably because the essay was so effective in abolishing the racist fantasy its title raised. Even though Claghorn reasserted this racist fantasy as a prophecy, his logic, ironically, confirmed Ellison's thesis. Just writing Ellison to deny his argument demonstrated how integral the existence of blacks was to Claghorn's sense of himself.

Rather than accepting Claghorn's response as proof of his own essay's effectiveness, however, Ellison drafted a reply that reinforced the irony of Claghorn's position—and of his own as well. Of course, replying to such a letter would raise a further difficulty. How does one respond to a pathology? The outset of *Invisible Man* raises this very question when the protagonist is called an insulting name by a white stranger. His first response is to demand an apology; when that request is not met, he starts to kick his antagonist and even gets out a knife with thoughts of killing the man before deciding it will be better to walk away. He understands that he can kill his hostile disparager but cannot convert him to his point of view. So he laughs instead. To Claghorn's attack, Ellison composes a reply that is a version of the foregoing exchange in *Invisible Man*:

Dear Mr. Claghorn:
  Thank you for your letter of May 2, written in criticism of my essay which I was invited to write for the April 6th issue of TIME magazine.
  My response is simple: I am willing to admit that I am inferior if you are willing to admit that I wrote *Invisible Man*. Sincerely yours.
                                                                  (Bradley 72)

This devastating reply (had he read it) Claghorn could not have comprehended unless he had read and assimilated *Invisible Man*, but as Ellison well knew, Claghorn almost certainly had not. Nonetheless, let us imagine the impossible. Imagine that Claghorn *had* read *Invisible Man* a number of years before and then forgotten all but the author's name. Reading the essay in *Time*, however, sends him to look for the author's works, and he finds himself with copies of *Invisible Man* and *Shadow and Act*. He reads the later book first and encounters Ellison's complex understanding of American literature. He would perhaps begin to see that he and Ellison shared more than frustration with the racial politics of the day; they were connected in that each of them had an identity that responded to the actions of previous Americans such as Jefferson, Emerson, Lincoln, Stowe, Douglass, Wright, and King. Instead of writing Ellison the "racist screed" that Bradley identifies, Claghorn might have written to say that reading Ellison's work "was like having a sailboat boom swing across the deck and set the boat off on a radically altered course." He would have explained that "your book broke into [my] world like a ball of lightning, Re-enaged, or perhaps, for the first time, engaged, me, with America, with the complexity and the inescapable nature of belonging to it, and to its history of 'ongoingness.'" Possibly, following that course would have sent him back to *Invisible Man* with new eyes and bursting to tell Ellison what was opening before him: "You have opened a world to me, a world which is partly my own and of which I was unwilling to be conscious; I owe you a greater debt than I can possibly explain. And, needless to say, rereading *Invisible Man*, after a lapse of quite a number of years, was a stunning experience." But then he would not have been Mr. Claghorn. He would have been Rosanna Warren, Robert Penn Warren's daughter, who in 1981 did in fact write those words to Ellison after the poet Michael Harper, at Ellison's request, had given her a copy of *Shadow and Act*.[13]

Rosanna Warren obviously never shared Claghorn's point of view, but as an Ellison reader she understands what Claghorn was unwilling to accept: that a black voice had spoken for her as an American and named her condition as an American. Rosanna's father too was deeply moved by *Invisible Man* and *Shadow and Act* and was one of Ellison's most perceptive critics—though he never wrote about Ellison with the sense of ecstatic recognition that Rosanna expresses. Her sense of the "ongoingness" of America and its history, along with the inescapable nature of belonging to this history in all its contradictory permutations, perfectly captures the great theme that pervaded all of Ellison's writings—fiction, nonfiction, and the remarkable collection of personal correspondence now housed in the Library of Congress. I do not know whether Ellison replied to Rosanna, but one may surmise that her response gratified him, in part as the inverse to a response such as Claghorn's. The letters suggest the intense range of response Ellison's work inspired in readers, yet also point to his isolated position in the history of American literature. The Warrens notwithstanding, Ellison often seemed to be writing to people who could not or would not engage him. His isolation was not Joycean; it came not from his unquestionable aesthetic complexity but, I would say, from his commitment to articulating the fact of cultural diversity within American society.

From this perspective, perhaps it is not surprising that one crucial quality of Ellison's career was his keeping so much of it for himself. I have no doubt that he was a demanding artist reluctant to publish until he thought the work was perfect, just as I also think that Ellison's personality was such that he was not interested in publishing book after book in the manner that his near contemporaries such as Wright, Warren, Bellow, and Roth. As one who read widely in history, mythology, and classic literature (his personal library is now housed at the Library of Congress), Ellison was perhaps even more interested in what others could tell him than in what he could tell others. Hence, his one finished novel directly challenges its reader to offer a point of view. Yet as a matter of literary history, the Claghorn letter intrigues because it suggests the extent to which Ellison was addressing an audience reluctant to see things as he did. If Claghorn represented some essential component of his American audience, then how could Ellison argue with an audience that would not "see" his point of view, no matter how eloquently expressed? His best answer to this impossible question was, as he proposed to tell Claghorn but more truly told himself, *Invisible Man*.

Was he right? Did he miss the chance to give other, better answers? At one point Ellison might have conceived *Invisible Man* as a knife directed at the heart of the bigoted white American—as Richard Wright's *Native Son* is sometimes said to be—but the book instead became the remarkable synthesis of what Ellison's *Time* essay describes: a "black" perspective on American life that, as only fiction can, spoke for divergent and even contradictory points of view. Thus, the novel could portray black anger about racism and its effects; it could castigate white Americans for not recognizing the terrible costs of racism in human terms; and it could challenge all readers to overcome their prejudices and their pain to help create a better society. Although other themes can be listed, and the book need not be read by Americans only to be valued as a work of art, the point is that *Invisible Man* portrayed in memorable form all the issues that Ellison's *Time* essay raised.

That essay provided the critical context in which Ellison wanted his novel to be interpreted by future audiences. Claghorn rejected his politics and would likely have rejected his "elitist" novel. Yet for Ellison they were of a piece, and more sophisticated (though no less political) readers have recoiled at his choices. Barbara Foley, for instance, wishes *Invisible Man* had been more "Marxist," but confronting the basis of American racism while retaining aesthetic complexity was a remarkable achievement. For Ellison the "race" problem was deeper than the "class" problem, and the latter could not solve the former. As a committed Marxist, Foley is understandably disappointed that Ellison, a writer with a deeply political vision, turned away from Marxism in his work. Before the government eradicated a viable Communist Party in the United States, though, Ellison had already determined that, like other American political parties, the CP was willing to sacrifice its black members in order to advance party interests. Perhaps more important, Ellison, as an artist, could not bring himself to write a socialist realist masterpiece—the black American equivalent to Fyodor Gladkov's *Cement*, whatever that might be. As Ellison understood, since *Don Quixote* the novel as a literary form has explored the individual's consciousness within society; the novel probes and even portrays society, but it takes its form through its emphasis on the thoughts, experiences, and perspective of individuals. One can much better write a successful Marxist critique of a novel than a "Marxist novel," simply because Marxist premises are not consistent with the novel's formal premises.[14] Although *Invisible Man* takes shape within a black American perspective never before portrayed in American literature, Ellison chose the novel form in order to depict an individual's awakening to the meaning of his experience within a greater history. Ellison's ideal reader will experience his or her own awakening, one that may have to do with "history," but the form that this awakening will take is uncertain. That said, *Invisible Man* explicitly invites its "individual" readers to see their stories in the narrator's story and thus to risk identifying with a class of people heretofore invisible, though present, within American society. In this important sense, one that the knowledge of Ellison's political origins helps to uncover, *Invisible Man* is an imagined act of social revolution.

Claghorn's letter hears but rejects this message, just as Ellison's reply reveals that he understood *Invisible Man* to be his most nearly perfect expression as an oppositional black artist. It took Ellison years to write *Invisible Man*, yet one could argue that he expended as much effort in not publishing a second novel as in writing his first one. How often he must have wanted to put forward a version of what he had written—if only to quiet the carping about his silence. In the long view of literary history, though, one not determined by the consumer-driven fashions of the moment, his decision not to publish another novel could only underscore the significance of *Invisible Man*. He may well have thought, let other American writers surpass *Invisible Man* if they can. And one may well ask, who has?[15]

One thing is certain: *Invisible Man* gave Ellison visibility as a cultural figure, and he seized it according to his situation. In 1971 he said, "I believe that I have contributed more to the general struggle by trying to write the things that I write as well as I can than I could by being a propagandist. I don't want to be a political leader. It ain't my kind of thing. So I leave it to other people" (*Conversations* 201). As an artist and intellectual, Ellison did not understand it to be his task to charge the battlements with King; rather, his essays can be read, as Wynton Marsalis has suggested, as the theoretical justification of the aims of the Civil Rights movement. Although his second novel became mixed up with changes that happened in American society after *Invisible Man*, Ellison's essays and speeches marked his "official" position on what was happening. In this context, Callahan and Bradley make a crucial observation by noting that in the second novel Ellison employs Hickman, the book's hero, "as the mouthpiece for all of what he came to know and think and feel about being African American in America" (*Three* xxiii).

Ellison's editors surmise that he "assuaged" the "demons of self-doubt" about his second novel "by crafting brilliant essays, pieces that mined the same themes of American complexity and restlessness so strongly present in what he had done so far with the second novel" (*Three* xxi). For understanding the seemingly mystifying choices that Ellison made with his post–*Invisible Man* career—which is different from understanding what his second novel means to literary history or meant to him—the equation implied by Callahan and Bradley seems right. Ralph Ellison's essays and speeches replaced, or stood in for, the novel he did not finish or publish. Where his most famous creation went from being a speaker to being a writer, Ellison, in a sense, went from being a writer to being a speaker. The formula is not quite right because in his essays he was still a great writer, even a great creative writer ("Tell It Like It Is, Baby" could be called a short fiction masterpiece), but the essays were for Ellison a kind of speech. Like Emerson's essays, they were addresses that Ellison gave to present and future Americans concerning the democratic responsibilities that constituted the birthright and the obligation of every American citizen.

This equation—the black novelist who trades publishing novels for becoming the conscience of democracy in the wake of the Civil Rights movement—is one that Ellison's critics and readers have had difficulty accepting, but its premise is implied in both novels and, perhaps more directly, in what Ellison wrote privately to Morteza Sprague. In *Invisible Man* the black protagonist seeks a social structure in which his individual humanity can be completely and safely expressed. What he finds is that this is possible only in the world that he creates through his narrative voice. Hickman, as Bliss's guardian, assumes the responsibility for American democracy and never shirks his duty, despite Bliss's betrayal of him. In his letter to Sprague, Ellison indicates that the prospect of black equality means more to him than anything he could write. He says the revolution in rights for black Americans leaves him "twisted by joy," but with that joy comes "a sense of inadequacy." This "inadequacy" may characterize his attempts to translate his feelings into fiction, or it may characterize his own sense of himself as a black man no longer "invisible" behind the veil of segregation. Better to express yourself in life than in a book. I would suggest that, after *Invisible Man*, the most decisive event in Ellison's adult life, the one that had the most bearing on both his career as a novelist and his life as a black American, was the national reconstitution that occurred with what became the Civil Rights movement. With *Brown* and all that came after it, Ellison's life and the life of all black Americans would never be the same again. Nor would *Invisible Man*.

Instead of writing and publishing more novels about the pre-*Brown* world, which is largely what African American literature has done since *Invisible Man*, Ellison chose to confront the suddenly revealed brave new world of equality face-to-face. His legacy as a black intellectual is that he spoke—and continues to speak—to Americans willing to leave the cocoon of racial identity. If some might argue that the narrator of *Invisible Man* can never leave the basement that houses his text, then the author of *Dreams from My Father* (1995) is just one famous example of a reader of *Invisible Man* who took it upon himself to offer a contrary interpretation.[16] This reader chose to leave the Harlem basement (where his own autobiography begins) to become the first African American president of the United States. I make this comparison not to say that the election of Obama has signaled the end of racism in American life but that American history has been working to catch up to Ellison's vision. The possibility that a black man might speak for and represent the interests of all Americans of all colors was a possibility expressed implicitly in *Invisible Man* and then much more explicitly in Ellison's post–*Invisible Man* work. Mr. Claghorn could neither embrace nor imagine such a possibility (though he may have feared it). Ellison's angriest black critics may have wished for such a possibility but lacked the resilient optimism to see that it could happen so soon. Nonetheless, Ralph Ellison's America is the one Obama's election in its most hopeful moment confirmed, and it is the one that Ellison fought for during his long life as a political activist and black intellectual.

Ellison the Political Theorist of Democracy

In his much read and much praised novel *The Human Stain* (2000), Philip Roth tells the story of a black intellectual who passes for white. Although readers have linked Roth's novel to the life of Anatole Broyard, one can also read it as a reflection on the life and career of Ralph Ellison. Ellison never passed for white, but his career has been sufficiently distorted that one could argue that he passed for something that was never wholly accurate. I will say what readers of Ellison and even Ellison himself were reluctant to say: despite writing a great—even a transcendent—novel, Ralph Ellison was not a novelist in the conventional sense of the term. In 1945, when he published "Richard Wright's Blues," Wright wrote him on July 25 to say that it was the best essay he had ever read by a Negro and suggested that Ellison's career might make more sense as a nonfiction than a fiction writer. Ellison, who often seems to have understood novel-writing as a challenging game for his own amusement, replied on August 5 that the thought had occurred to him but that being a novelist was more appealing, since its form is more demanding than that of nonfiction (RWEP LC). Ellison's exchange with Wright predicts his eventual status as a novelist always betwixt and between his chosen form. Though he generally referred to himself as a novelist, he was, almost despite himself, so much more. He was, in fact, novelist, short story writer, memoirist, essayist, music critic, literary critic, lecturer, provocateur, adviser to a U.S. president, and intellectual Jack-the-Bear-of-all-trades. Wearing these myriad hats, he sought to influence American experience, not simply be its transcendent example as the "Negro" author of *Invisible Man*. His interest in the novel was inseparable from his concern to identify and confront the inequities of American racism by arguing for a better America than the one he inherited.

In *The Human Stain* Roth resurrects Ellison—an acknowledged hero to Roth—to test and affirm the cultural ground that *Invisible Man* claimed and the vision that Ellison bequeathed to posterity. Roth's Ellison is less a novelist than "a figure" whose example helps to lead the way out of a static, racist American past to a better, more "equal" American present. Roth's engagement with Ellison depicts a figure whose self-definition was arrested in 1953, when he chose to pass for white because society would not allow him to be himself and "black" at the same time. Ellison never suffered from such a static self-conception, but within the critical writings on Ellison one often encounters just such a static figure. In African American studies departments and English departments, except for the literary analyses of Ellison's fiction, the questions have not changed much since 1963, when Irving Howe criticized Ellison for being insufficiently political in his writing and, tacitly, for having written only one novel. Indeed, one of the great ironies of Ellison criticism is that he is forever chastised for being insufficiently political when the terms of this criticism are so insistently literary. The claim that he failed as a novelist because he published only one novel and that he failed as a black intellectual because he was insufficiently political in his actions seem to be two distinct criticisms. They are in fact manifestations of a single misperception that arises from an attempt to impose boundaries between art and politics, between life and work, which Ellison himself neither recognized nor accepted.

Ellison meant his work to influence not just literary history but history in both its broadest and its most immediate sense. Recently, beyond the lines policed by departments of English and African American studies, scholars from a variety of disciplines have worked to specify the breadth of Ellison's influence as an intellectual intent on changing the course of American society. Historians (Leon Litwack), legal scholars (Richard Kluger), and political scientists (Danielle Allen) have argued that Ellison is essential to understanding, respectively, post–Civil War American history, the role of *Brown* in American society, and the Civil Rights movement and its ongoing aftermath.[17] None of these scholars sees Ellison as a failed novelist or questionable representative of black identity. The unanswerable question of Ellison's second novel does not enter their perspective—though passages from *Three Days* correspond with the logic of their analyses. Litwack's Ellison is a historian; Allen's Ellison is political theorist; Roth's Ellison is arguably the American novelist without whose example Roth's career would not be possible. For each of these intellectuals, Ellison is a central figure, unique among novelists of his era, whose vision helped to envision the American world in which we are now living. Just as Roth suggests that Ellison is the essential American novelist of the past fifty years, so does Allen suggest that Ellison is the thinker who makes sense of the last fifty years of American political and cultural history. Moreover, these two claims reinforce each other.

Understanding Ellison within the broader terms that these recent accounts of him demand means reestablishing his identity as a *black* American or black *American* intellectual. Rampersad, for instance, situates Ellison within a historical moment that seems increasingly distant: that point when Ellison seemed vulnerable to attacks from black critics disappointed that he was not more flamboyantly radical in his critique of American society.[18] In contrast to the "alienated black intellectual" Ellison stands the "cosmopolitan" Ellison presented by Ross Posnock, for whom Ellison's "cosmopolitanism" resides in his refusal to affirm the logic of racial identity.[19] During a 1973 symposium for Alain Locke, Ellison said that the Black Arts movement had succeeded in segregating blacks from whites as effectively as, and perhaps to a more oppressive degree than, the staunchest white segregationist had ever dreamed of doing. More than twenty years before his death, Posnock notes, Ellison discerned and disputed the cultural logic that we now refer to as "identity politics" and that has become, in the years since his passing, even more pronounced and obvious. According to Posnock, Ellison has long been ripe for reconsideration because "the tribal conception of politics founded on a romance of identity" (which has dominated so much of the critical discussion of him and has also been consistent with the postmodern era that followed *Invisible Man*) is "waning" (3).[20] Thus, if Ellison's perceived antiessentialism is part of what makes him seem so contemporary, it was the same stance that had provoked the skepticism of many of his black readers. Yet this too was Ellison's point: surrendering Jim Crow assumptions, which also means trusting other Americans' willingness to accept "equality" as a national ideal, would not be easy.

Horace Porter argues that "Ellison was 'politically incorrect' before the phrase was coined" and suggests that criticism of Ellison's cultural politics misses his essays' "attempt to rescue and restore the image of African Americans from those determined to see only walking personifications of crime and pathology" (137, 135). Moreover, as Harold Cruse pointed out in 1967, the fight over Ellison's status as a black intellectual replays the classic battle between black integrationists and black separatists. Posnock's account of Ellison as a cosmopolitan intellectual is an attempt to get beyond this debate, but there is no doubt that during his lifetime Ellison could not escape it—even as he imagined a different kind of debate. As if to excuse him from the debate that Cruse identifies, Jerry Watts says that Ellison was at best "an apolitical artist" (12). If we agree that Ellison was committed to making African American experience a visible part of American experience, though, then he could never leave off being "political" in his actions. As a black man in a racist society who was also being allowed to enter social spaces previously barred to blacks, he had always to be "political," in private and in public.

In 1965 Ellison told Warren, "My problem is not whether I will accept or reject American values. It is, rather, how I can get into a position where I can have the maximum influence on those values." Or, as he explained to Callahan concerning his relationship as a black artist operating within a tradition of American democracy that has not always included blacks, "It ain't the theory which bothers me, it's the practice: My problem is to affirm while resisting" (Morel 59, 225). This statement of principle is precisely the lesson that *Invisible Man*'s narrator had to confront through the example of his grandfather. The political problems and the strategies for confronting them that *Invisible Man* identifies in the late 1940s and early 1950s continued to preoccupy Ellison for the rest of his life. Lewis Morel suggests that because "Ellison saw little hope in black consciousness to produce true progress for blacks in American society," his problem was how to reframe American society so that being black meant being neither invisible nor a problem to be evaded (60).

Danielle Allen's incisive work on post-*Brown* American civic politics, *Talking to Strangers*, takes up this problem to explain the solution that Ellison found. Allen connects him not only to American political practice but also to the long tradition of political theory from Aristotle to Hobbes. She spells out the logic of Ellison's democratic theory and makes explicit how his work engaged the dramatic social changes being brought about by the Civil Rights movement. In so doing, she gives a living political context to Posnock's cosmopolitanism by asking what cosmopolitanism means as a political practice. Allen argues that the Civil Rights movement marked a decisive turning point in American history because it challenged the way the majority of United States citizens understood their own relationship to the civic ideals put forth in the Constitution. Answering the challenge posed in *Invisible Man*'s "Epilogue" or in essays such as "The Little Man at Chehaw Station" (*Collected*) Allen frames the progress of American political history as a series of interpretations—she calls them social reconstitutions—of the principles laid down in the Constitution and Declaration of Independence.

According to Allen and Ellison, the American "Constitution is more than paper; it is a plan for constituting political rights and organizing citizenship, for determining who has access to the powers of collective decision-making that are used to negotiate a community's economic and social relations" (Allen 6). Yet the Constitution itself cannot literally provide the answer to all the political dilemmas and social situations that arise within a democratic society. Citing the Magna Carta as an example, Allen observes that an effective constitution need not be written down. One must "look beyond the document" to a place where one finds not just state laws but "the customary habits of citizenship." From this perspective, the United States in fact "has had several foundings," and the most important one was the Civil War because it superseded the constitution of 1789 as "a refounding" by establishing universal white male suffrage, outlawing slavery, and granting (male) African Americans full citizenship and voting rights (6).

This Civil War reconstitution, Reconstruction, did not hold, however, and was overturned in 1877 by the Hayes-Tilden Agreement, which permitted federal troops to leave the South and a new war on freed blacks to begin. The withdrawal of federal troops confirmed the status quo of black-white social relations in the South that "the Civil War refounding" could not overturn with the 13th, 14th, and 15th Amendments. As Ellison notes in "Going to the Territory," after the "ambiguous victory of the North," freed slaves went from "participating as a group in political affairs" to "being forced to live under a system which was close to, and in some ways worse than, slavery." Thus, he writes, "within thirteen years Afro-Americans were swept from slavery to a brief period of freedom, to a condition of second-class citizenship" (*Collected* 600). In 1877, de facto slavery resurfaced in the sharecropper system and legalized Jim Crow laws that lasted until a combination of technological advances in farming and *Brown* did away with the agrarian lifestyle on which so much of the unequal relationship between whites and blacks in the South depended.

Although Allen identifies 1920 (when women were given universal suffrage) and 1971 (when the voting age was lowered from twenty-one to eighteen) as two other moments of reconstitution, she argues that the most decisive reconstitution since the Civil War occurred "between *Brown v. Board of Education* (1954) and the Civil Rights and Voting Rights Acts (1964–5)" (163). One reason that this reconstitution remains "epochal" and "still undigested" is that it confronted and is still confronting the foundational sin of American democracy: slavery and its aftermath. Even if "the U.S. Constitution devised institutions that went a long way toward solving the problem of radical distrust within a democratic citizenry," Allen argues, the fact that those institutions "could not solve the [slavery] problem once and for all is proved not only by the U.S. Civil War of 1861 but also by the small civil wars

of the 1960s" (xx). After *Brown* these "small civil wars," which were a continuation in a different time and through different media of earlier battles
for Gettysburg, Shiloh, and Richmond, were fought again in the 1950s and
1960s in such places as Selma, Birmingham, and Little Rock. Moreover,
because their climactic battles were staged on television, before a massive
audience that felt morally implicated by what they were witnessing, these
little civil wars had a decisive and galvanizing effect on American society.
According to Ellison, thoughtful Americans have always understood that,
despite slavery and the hard human boundary it seemed to establish between whites and blacks, the meaning of "being American" was bound up in
a collective knowledge that the moral dilemma posed by whites' treatment
of blacks lay at the heart of American self-knowing. Upon receiving the
National Book Award, Ellison said that American literature since Emerson
had acknowledged that "the Negro was the gauge of the human condition
as it waxed and waned in our democracy" (*Collected* 153).

Ellison could hardly have known when he gave that speech in 1953 that a
version of his argument about classic American literature would be enacted
publicly in less than five years as television cameras and magazine photographs documented Elizabeth Eckford's attempt to enroll at the previously
all-white Central High School in Little Rock, Arkansas. In his second
novel, as in *Invisible Man*, Ellison was portraying the Civil War as not yet
over and in a sense as a war that black Americans were losing every day. In
his notes to the novel, he observes of one character that what he "is trying
to say [is] that what the president views [as] peace is actually the Civil War
continued in the form of words and the manipulation of prejudices" (*Three*
978). The now iconic photograph of Eckford being refused admission and
turned away, while being cursed by a white woman, Hazel Bryan, is both
shocking and revealing, argues Allen, because it announces that the Confederacy has at last been defeated. The social roles demanded of blacks and
whites in Jim Crow society no longer applied, since Eckford, not Bryan, is
the "hero" of the picture. As Allen argues, "citizens enact what they are to
each other not only in assemblies, where they make decisions about their
mutually intertwined fates, but also when, as strangers, they speak to one
another, or don't, or otherwise respond to each other's presence" (10).

By trying to enroll at the segregated Central High, by risking visibility
as a black American, Eckford was violating her customary place in society
(as Ellison's "invisible man" did in his memoir), yet she was merely acting within the framework of her recently established legal rights as an
American citizen. The photo of Eckford and Bryan, like the televised mass

demonstrations staged between King and Sheriff Bull Connor in Selma, Alabama, symbolized the reconstitution of American social space. For the first time since the Civil War and the Hayes-Tilden compromise, the assumptions carried by the federal law would win out over long-established social custom. The visibility that Ellison's protagonist could risk only in a novel framed as a memoir was suddenly the province of all blacks in the world beyond the novel, which Ellison's writing sought to penetrate.

This transformation of society would not affect (and was not for) blacks only. As Allen and Ellison both suggest, it would entail a radical reconsideration of what it meant to be an American. Just as Frederick Douglass agitated after the Civil War to challenge Americans not to surrender the victory of the Civil War, so would Ralph Ellison in the wake of this second Civil War place himself before Americans to prepare them for the new roles that history was requiring of them. At the end of *Invisible Man*, his narrator remarks, "Our fate is to become one, yet many—This is not prophecy, but description" (568). These words referred to the fact (as the 1970 *Time* essay explains) that culturally and politically, whites and blacks were already mixed up in each other. But in another sense his words were a call for social revolution that became prophecy. In the years immediately following the publication of those words, the narrator's visionary statement was being made evident by the events of American history. Thus, Allen notes that since 1877 the phrase "become one" had meant in practice "white rule."

What *Invisible Man* demonstrated and the Civil Rights movement exposed (the 1957 picture at Little Rock memorializes this moment) is that the social contract between American whites and blacks required "dominance on the one hand and acquiescence on the other" (Allen 13). As long as whites were dominant and blacks acquiescent, a kind of social stability, enforced by the legalized violence of the courts and the penal system, could hold in American society. Blacks since 1876 had been asked to sacrifice their social mobility and legal rights to preserve the status quo of American society. Ellison in fact makes this point in "Extravagance of Laughter" when he characterizes himself as an "embodiment" and "symbol of the Civil War's sacrificial bloodshed" (*Collected* 624).

By Allen's terms, *Invisible Man*, as political treatise, explains and clears the way the way for the "reconstitution" that would soon take place through the Civil Rights movement. With the grandfather who had to give up his guns after Reconstruction or the narrator's account of his choice not to fight back fully when called an insulting name, *Invisible Man* documents and protests a society that rests on the unfair demand that its black members "acquiesce" to "domination" by its white members. Using *Invisible Man* as a reference point, Allen argues that all civil communities require at some point "a sacrifice" on the part of one or a group of their members in order to function without dangerous physical strife. For American blacks, however, the sacrifice required to make society work was unfair. *Invisible Man's* narrator identifies the nature of this sacrifice and refuses to subject himself to it any longer.

In *Three Days* Ellison explicitly portrays this sacrifice through the device of an eloquent, surreal talking Negro lawn jockey who shocks and upbraids an uncomprehending white character with a version of Allen's argument. The white character would dismiss this talking jockey as a mere *"iron monster,"* but the "monster" insists that *"mine is a human figure"* (185). *"I tell you no lies, I suffer immeasurably and unceasingly. And do you know why? I'll be pleased to inform you, baby; I carry the weight of society on my shoulders. You just think about that, baby; and you'll see that it's true. It's not you, not the President, not the political gang, and not the preachers, but yours truly. I carry the stinking weight"* (189). The jockey's words are not understood by his white listener; however, the combination of *Brown* and blacks' willingness to assert their legal rights was "reconstituting" American social space so that blacks no longer had to "carry the stinking weight" and thus conceal from whites' view their "human figures."

After *Brown*, Americans were unwilling to continue to structure society according the severe ratio of white dominance to black acquiescence that had pertained since 1877. Allen suggests that *Invisible Man*—the narrator says at the outset that he is responsible for all—dramatizes how African Americans have sacrificed themselves through their historic social invisibility, yet also seeks to challenge this tradition by rendering its narrator, and the people's story he represents, visible to society (14). Ellison's post–*Invisible Man* career constituted a heroic effort to enact and normalize the social revolution that his novel had called for. As I discuss in chapter 1, it may be that he sacrificed his career as a novelist to fill this role as extemporary political theorist and civic statesman. Certainly, he was offered up as a sacrifice by other black intellectuals intent on preserving the rhetoric of black anger. Ellison, however, chose to surrender this easy (if understandable) position of black anger, which had also driven him while writing *Invisible Man*. Thus, against the post-King mantra of "burn, baby, burn," Ellison argued, as Allen says, that democratic citizens should not understand themselves to be connected through their relationship to "one" static society but should think of "themselves part of an invisible whole" that "they cannot see" (17). The metaphor of "one" promotes "a desire for homogeneity"; to make a people "whole," however, promotes "an aspiration to the coherence and integrity of a consolidated but complex, intricate, and differentiated body" (17). Ellison did not ask other blacks to give up their blackness but asked all Americans to surrender the notion that in a diverse society one cultural identity could supersede the others.

In stressing "wholeness" over "oneness" as the ideal condition that citizens of a democracy should seek to attain, Allen clearly and intentionally echoes arguments that Ellison made in his essays. In "The Little Man at Chehaw Station," he argues that "Americans tend to focus on the diverse parts of their culture (with which they can more easily identify), rather than on its complex and pluralistic wholeness" (*Collected* 500). Here he does not mean the oneness (which can imagine no dissent from itself) of race pride, which his black and white critics often insisted upon, but the knowledge that "Americanness" necessarily "creates out of its incongruity an uneasiness within us" because this uneasiness is "a constant reminder that American democracy is not only a political collectivity of individuals, but culturally a collectivity of styles, tastes and traditions" (500). Ellison's crucial point, which a logic dedicated to perpetual oneness (be it "blackness" or "whiteness") can neither allow nor comprehend, is that "we Americans are, all of us—white or black, native-born or immigrant—members of minority groups." Such a condition may provoke "feelings of isolation" amid "the pluralistic turbulence of the democratic process" and cause Americans to "cling desperately to our familiar fragment of democratic rock."[21] Nonetheless, from this fragment, which we might also call the self, Americans can only "confront [their] fellow Americans in that combat of civility, piety and tradition which is the drama of American social hierarchy" (500).

Ellison, who once had suffered a beating for being black (in the aftermath of the Scottsboro Boys incident), knew well that such combat does risk "physical violence." Insofar as these multiple social energies "draw their power from the Declaration of Independence, the Constitution, and the Bill of Rights," however, Americans must accept that the "freewheeling fashion" of these sacred documents "prod us ceaselessly toward the refinement and perfection of those formulations of policy and configurations of social forms of which they are the signs and symbols" (*Collected* 501). Over and over, in journals, before countless college students, and in commencement addresses, Ellison used his fame as the author of *Invisible Man* to tell his fellow Americans that the principles laid out in the Constitution "interrogate us endlessly as to who and what we are; they demand that we

keep the democratic faith" (*Collected* 502). Such defiant hope was expressed
in opposition, as Allen says, to "the period from the Civil War to World
War II"—roughly the period that *Invisible Man* reflects on—when "the effort to make the people 'whole' was defined by an attempt to make it 'one,'"
(19). Ellison recognized that the years since the publication of *Invisible Man*
constituted a difficult period during which "practices of citizenship" were
evolving "so as to accommodate frankness about difference." As the reactions he elicited from Claghorn and his black critics attest, Ellison practiced
that frankness at great cost to his own reputation (19).

Allen suggests that Ellison remains a polarizing figure precisely because
even today "citizens in the United States have not yet fully come to grips
with what has changed since the 1950s" (8). Of particular interest to an understanding of Ellison's complicated legacy is Allen's observation that "the
seesawing back and forth of African American political ideology between
assimilation and separatism is itself a product of our failure to address more
directly the question: what modes of citizenship can make a citizenry whole
without covering up difference?" (19). On Allen's reading, none of the usual
critical questions raised about Ellison's legacy—is he a failed novelist? an
elitist political quietist? an inauthentic Negro?—can comprehend his legacy.
No doubt Ellison wished to write another novel, and no doubt he wanted
it to be a masterpiece, but the author of *Invisible Man* understood that a
second novel, from Ralph Ellison was not going to bring about the social
"reconstitution" that he desired. The career choices he made suggest that
he thought America needed the example of leaders and intellectuals ready
to jettison the Jim Crow principles that had defined American citizenship,
needed that example more than it needed the entertainment that novels
provide. All Americans, not just black Americans, would be asked on occasion to sacrifice themselves in the name of "wholeness," which means, as
Allen says, that the "discovery of the centrality of sacrifice leads to the realization that democratic citizenship consists primarily of reciprocity" (105).
A commitment to reciprocity, Ellison understood, would change what it
meant to be "white" or "black" and, finally, "American." This was Ellison's
message in *Invisible Man* in 1952, and it was his message to Mr. Claghorn
in 1970. Contrary to a legacy of silence, Ellison's work, for those who will
engage it, insists that (American) identities fixed to specific historical positions would evolve and become something else.

Ellison's career makes better sense when we decide that his drama was
less concerned with the relatively small matter of writing another novel
than with articulating the challenge confronted by all Americans: how each

American might achieve meaningful recognition, visibility, within American society. As a private citizen who aspired to be an artist, Ellison could never do more than he did in writing *Invisible Man*. As someone who subsequently understood himself to be a very public example of what others were either going through or hoped to go through, Ellison could enact in his work as a public intellectual what it would mean to live in an America where being born a Negro was not something one would have to explain as if it were a "problem." Pursuing this work, Ellison would, until his death, inhabit places in American society that Negroes had never really occupied before. Like that of his novel's narrator, Ellison's voice still calls to Americans asking us to be transformed into a new and ever evolving whole. *Ralph Ellison and the Genius of America* retells Ellison's story to help readers understand his true achievement as a black intellectual and an American visionary.

Chapter 1 takes its cue from Philip Roth's *Human Stain*, a novel that can be read as a portrayal of Ellison and as a sequel to *Invisible Man*. Roth explores Ellison's commitment to the belief that there are many and often changing ways to be an American and that Americans' multiple ethnic identities are always in flux. Whether one calls this stance "cultural pluralism," as Ellison did, or "cosmopolitanism," as Posnock does, Roth employs it to critique the ways in which a separate but equal multiculturalism has come to characterize American intellectual culture. Roth's narrative conceit—to tell as a Jew the story of a black man who passed as a Jew—answers Ellison's narrative conceit in *Invisible Man* that a nameless black narrator might speak for any reader of his story; it thus affirms the continuing vitality of Ellison's reflections concerning what he often called America's fluid "culture of cultures." In so doing, *The Human Stain* responds to a much longer historical dialogue about the connection between ethnic and American identity that is at the heart of Ellison's work.

Chapter 2 reclaims Ellison's status as a defiantly "black" intellectual by attempting to give *Invisible Man* a literary history it never has truly had. Greeted by white readers as an expression of "universal humanity," the novel was also an epic of "oppositional" Negro history intent on galvanizing black readers to political action. Recovering this *Invisible Man* involves a reexamination of Ellison's misunderstood friendship with Richard Wright and his crucial debt to Wright's documentary history, *12 Million Black Voices* (1941). In that book Wright created an epic story of defiant black experience out of what had been boxes of unsorted photographs. Ellison, deeply moved by the book, was challenged to answer Wright's achievement with his own epic of black experience. In this chapter, I hope to revise the view of Ellison and Wright as opposed writers by showing that they were parts of the same cultural-aesthetic whole.

Chapter 3 turns to the question of political leadership and to Ellison's own self-presentation as a Negro leader by examining his largely ignored friendships with Robert Penn Warren and Pulitzer Prize–winning Southern historian C. Vann Woodward. In 1955 Ellison remarked that *Invisible Man* was in part an attempt to define the limits and possibilities of Negro leadership in a society that seemed unable to accept any Negro who challenged the necessity of segregation. This chapter thus traces the separate journeys made by Warren, Woodward, and Ellison to arrive at the same point: a shared recognition that each of them, like other white Southerners and African Americans, had a share in creating the other's identity, a recognition that should form the basis of a new American racial and cultural politics. In important ways, Ellison's personal friendship with Warren and Woodward mirrored the political one between Martin Luther King Jr. and Lyndon Baines Johnson which succeeded in increasing the rights of blacks in American society. Not strictly personal, these friendships became for Ellison a lived enactment of his response to King's movement and embodied his arguments about how the prospects of a truly integrated society depended on the ability of leaders (such as himself) to inhabit positions in American society that Negroes had not occupied before.

Chapter 4, by demonstrating how intertwined his work was with its premises and aspirations, seeks to correct the persistent misperception that Ellison remained aloof from the Civil Rights movement. In a sense, *Invisible Man* was a playbook for the movement to come. The novel was a critique of black leadership during the Jim Crow era, but it suggested that there were black masses ready to follow the right leader. As it happens, King became the Negro leader that Ellison's narrative sought but could not quite imagine. Read this way, Ellison's novel is not just a Jim Crow artifact or "merely" an aesthetic masterpiece but a living text that helps us understand why King succeeded as a leader and how Ellison's anti–Jim Crow commitment to equality was the basis of what made the Civil Rights movement effective. Ellison then responded to the meaning of King not by writing a novel (the one he was writing imagined a black assassin of a white political figure, not the reverse) but by becoming arguably the American intellectual most committed to understanding the type of citizenship that King's example required of Americans.

Ralph Ellison and the Genius of America describes, in ways that were impossible while he was alive, the arc of Ellison's career and how that career radiated into so many areas of American possibility. As great and as important as *Invisible Man* was and is, that novel was part of a larger historical action in which both Ellison and significant black leaders like Martin Luther King Jr. were transforming the meaning and possibilities of race in American society. Ellison's early work predicted the Civil Rights movement, and his later (post-1953) work both imagined and tried to enact appropriate responses to the revolution in American life that the Civil Rights movement represented. Ellison's prophetic essays placed black experience at the heart of American identity. In a symbolic sense, his vision was confirmed by Barack Obama's election as president some fifty-six years after Ellison's invisible narrator had asked his readers if, on the lower frequencies, he did not speak for those who could listen and act on his words. Ellison is arguably the most important black intellectual after Du Bois, yet his achievement as a black intellectual is inseparable from his achievement as an American visionary. I hope to present a version of Ellison as he was but as we perhaps have not yet seen him: the essential figure of twentieth-century American letters. The most basic question of the American experiment, evident since the founding of the nation, has always concerned how the slaves and their experience could be incorporated into a democratic society. Ellison is the essential poet, historian, and, arguably, prophet of this fundamentally American drama.

1

Philip Roth's Invisible Man

I should like to conclude ... with the image of his hero that Ralph Ellison presents at the end of *Invisible Man*. For here too the hero is left with the simple stark fact of himself. He is as alone as a man can be. Not that he hasn't gone out into the world; he has gone out into it, and out into it, and out into it—but at the end he chooses to go underground, to live there and to wait. And it does not seem to him a cause for celebration either.

His intellectual position was virtually identical to mine, but he was presenting it as a black American, instructing through the examples drawn from *Invisible Man*.

PHILIP ROTH

W HEN RALPH ELLISON died in 1994, his passing was met with a mixture of acclaim and regret. Ellison's importance as a novelist and cultural critic was widely acknowledged, but amid this celebration of his achievement as one of the major figures of American literature there ran an undercurrent of doubt. Since at least the publication of *Shadow and Act* in 1964, Ellison's public appearances both in print and on the podium provoked his audience to wonder when he might produce his next novel. In 1951, a few months before *Invisible Man* was to be published, he was writing a friend, "So I'm trying to get going on my next book before this one is finished, then if it's a dud I'll be too busy to worry about it" (*Trading* 21). By 1963, Ellison admitted in print that he had been "remiss and vulnerable" to "demands" that he "publish more novels" (*Collected* 188). To his dying day, though, he assured questioners that he was working on one and hoped to be finished soon. With his death the obvious question emerged again with a sense of finality that threatened to overpower the work he did accomplish: why did Ellison, arguably the most gifted writer and critic of his generation, not publish another novel? Does his failure to produce another novel, despite his continual assurances that more fiction was under way and soon to be seen, brand *him* a failure? What in fact is Ellison's legacy?

In 2010, sixteen years after his death, and nearly sixty years after he began his second novel, his work-in-progress was published by his literary executors, John F. Callahan and Adam Bradley, as *Three Days before the Shooting*. This long, unfinished work amplifies on the tantalizing draft earlier published as *Juneteenth* and in many ways enriches our understanding of Ellison as a writer of genius. In places, the second novel reads as if Ellison were drafting versions of his essays that consistently argued for a pluralistic American culture. Yet at the heart of the book is the assassination of a racist "white" senator by his "black" son. This son, who is "light" like his father but who resents his "white" coloring, vows, "If I ever find the son of a bitch who gave me this color I'll *kill* him!" (*Three* 759). His attempted act of murder arguably repays the Senator for betraying the black community that had raised him. Whether this is an act of justice or of race madness is a question left open. This unfinished book, however, the longest unsolved mystery of American letters, reveals an Ellison passionately confronting the questions raised by the Civil Rights era. Had he published a version of it in his lifetime—say, by 1970, as he apparently thought of doing—his career might have been seen differently. He might have been less vulnerable to the charges made against him by some blacks who were angry that he was not more bluntly oppositional in his politics. Had he published a version of his second novel, his most prominent biographer could not have equated his failure to finish it with his seeming alienation from other black intellectuals (though readers would have been free to say it diminished the achievement of *Invisible Man*). Almost certainly, had he published his novel, he would not be the isolated figure of African American letters that he became. Certainly, he would not be known as the "classic" black American author who wrote "only" one novel. He also would not be Ralph Ellison.

Ellison's gifts as an intellectual and as an artist were such that the word "genius" seems appropriate to describe them. Nor was he afraid of whom he crossed when making his arguments—Irving Howe, Hannah Arendt, and the historian Stanley Elkins were all subject to Ellison's formidable analytical skills. He struck many as arrogant, yet, there is a kind of modesty to Ellison's career. He did not take advantage of the esteem in which he was held to publish lesser though workmanlike books. As Stanley Crouch remarks, he "betrayed the national ethos of money and self-obsession expressed through career ambitions" (1). His famous contemporaries and near-contemporaries—Saul Bellow, Philip Roth, Norman Mailer, John Updike—published numerous novels that were not up to the standard of their best work (more good or even fair novels than great ones), whereas

Ellison published one indisputably great novel and no others. If Ellison's career displayed arrogance, it resided in the claim (quoted in the Introduction) that he made to Mr. Claghorn. That is, he apparently chose to stake his reputation on *Invisible Man*—his only necessary work.

Although Ellison was not completely unknown when *Invisible Man* was published, he did not write it with the expectation that it would make him famous. Yet he did become famous, and he became famous in a literary culture that demanded the constant manufacture of more literary product. Ellison, who once ran with the Marxists, declined to manufacture more product. His fame—the fame that an intellectual experiences—persisted, and not because he did not publish more novels. Nor did it persist because his life made for a good American success story: the poor black kid born in Oklahoma, the hobo-train-riding college dropout in Alabama, the "low-mo hustler" in New York who reinvents himself as a novelist of genius. Rather, his fame persisted because his novel seemed to be more alive with each passing year and because he said things in his essays and speeches that many people found challenging and even threatening. All of which is to say that after *Invisible Man*, Ralph Ellison was never invisible—except as a second novelist.

Unfortunately, the height of his fame probably came during the late 1960s when he was famous for not being black enough, or for not being the "right black" for the times. In his second novel, a character remarks that "there are many ways of being black. There are the ways of the skin, and the ways of custom, and the way a man feels inside him" (*Three* 775). Ellison's critics, though, were less capacious in their understanding of identity than Ellison's remarkable character Love New, who represents a way of being black that seeks to leave off the hurt and rage left over from slavery. For Love New, racism is a tool of the "State" that afflicts blacks *and* whites with a kind of violent madness and is a dead end for everyone except those few who profit from it. Ellison's fiercest critics—Love New might label them "State Negroes"—were intent on attacking him through premises that were from the pre-*Brown* era. Thus, an iconic, though possibly apocryphal, story of how Ellison was framed by his angriest critics occurred in 1967 at Grinnell College when a young African American student called him an "Uncle Tom." According to some accounts, Ellison, though well versed in the dozens, broke down crying in response to the taunt.[1]

In Arnold Rampersad's biography, this story clinches his argument that Ellison's career is tragic because it failed of its promise, given his "alienation from other blacks" (4). Hortense Spillers tells a different story from this era, however, one that is more in keeping with the confident "stick to Mose" Ellison evident in the author's letters to Albert Murray. "I distinctly remember a student dinner, sponsored by black students at Brandeis University during the winter of 1969," Spillers recalls, "when Ellison, skewered by young radicals for an insufficient demonstration of 'blackness,' made the table eat those words" (10). On Spillers's account, Ellison's "blackness" was not so fragile as to put him perpetually on the edge of tears when his political position was challenged. This Ellison, Spillers notes, "needed no lectures—this prickly personality—from folk who had just discovered their 'beauty' that morning." Contrary to Howe or Rampersad, Spillers's recollection suggests that Ellison's sense of self-affirmation as a black intellectual derived from his belief "as his writings attest, that black culture was robust enough to be at home anywhere in the world, or, moreover, pliable and robust enough to bring the world to it" (11).

Where one story reveals a guilty, whimpering Ellison, the other story identifies a defiant black intellectual who in a sense was invisible despite being out in the open. The stark disparity between Spillers's 1969 Brandeis recollection and the 1967 anecdote underscores how difficult Ellison's story *as a black author* is to tell. Indeed, as his novel teaches, those most committed to understanding his story are also those most likely to project their own critical fears and prejudices on to him. Despite his published works and the many books written about him, Ellison's life remains mysterious, just as his achievement sometimes seems clouded by the mammoth novel that until recently almost no one had ever read. As the facts of his life recede, and the speculations about what his life meant proliferate, Ellison in death seems ever more a version of the fiction he created: a black man in disguise, invisible.

Perhaps even better than Ellison's biographers, Philip Roth's remarkable novel *The Human Stain* addresses the question of Ellison's complex legacy as a black American author. Contrary to Ellison's critical warning, Roth mixes up *Invisible Man* with it's author's life and in so doing subjects to critical interrogation the myths that have been constructed about his life and work. Roth's novel invokes *Invisible Man* as the origin of its own narrative act while it ingeniously reflects on Ellison's status as an "invisible" intellectual targeted because of his "color" and his "disappearance" as a novelist—as if he were a version of his famous protagonist. At the heart of Roth's extraordinary novel is the story of Coleman Silk, an African American who passes as Jewish American. Silk is neither quite Ellison nor quite a version of Ellison's nameless protagonist, but through Silk, Roth clearly and cogently reflects on a number of Ellisonian cultural dilemmas. Initial readers of Roth's novel saw in Silk a version of Anatole Broyard, the *New York Times Book Review* editor, who also passed as a Jew and who was "outed" as "black" by African American scholar Henry Louis Gates Jr. Certainly, Broyard's life resembles Silk's, and the novel does invite one to think of Broyard, who was, in fact, a friend of Ellison's and one of whose children, coincidence or not, shared the name of a central character from Ellison's unfinished novel: Bliss, who, coincidence or not, was of indeterminate racial identity.

Roth's novel, though, is more than a roman à clef. Even if one questions whether the book is "literally" about Ellison, the terms of its analysis and its telling do derive from *Invisible Man*. Moreover, in situating Ellison's legacy within a postmodern present dominated by a culture of cynically opportunistic identity politics, Roth's novel reflects upon the literary-historical period he shared with Ellison and points to their shared bond as American novelists. As Ross Posnock notes, what unites Ellison and Roth is that they rejected "the rhetoric of proprietary, essentialist notions of culture" because "such notions depend on the primacy of identity rather than action, an origin rather than an appropriation" (*Philip* 95). Roth's novel dramatizes the risk and costs of such a stance and is itself an elaboration of what Ellison often called the pluralist—but what Posnock has renamed as the cosmopolitan—vision of America's "culture of cultures," for which appropriation, not piety, is the animating force. Posnock asserts that the "real" Broyard "in passing, affirmed racial classifications," but Roth's portrayal of Coleman challenges racial classifications and does so along the lines explored by Ellison in *Invisible Man* and in his essays.

Posnock suggests that *The Human Stain* is not a conventional novel of passing because Silk rejects the self-purifying aim of passing and instead "embraces undefended immersion in the present moment and attunement to the precarious" (*Philip* 195). Certainly, Ellison's critical perspective, as distinguished from Silk's "attunement," was always a response to a long-standing historical situation. Speaking of Ellison's commitment to a black culture robust enough to be at home anywhere in the world, Spillers notes, "It is the latter possibility, I believe, that the latter-day revolutionaries missed, just as it is the subtle dimension of critique that the current schools of 'anti-essentialism' have not fathomed" (10–11). Spillers alludes to the unfairness with which Ellison has been treated by many black critics but also suggests that Ellison might question whether some instances of putative "cosmopolitanism" may only shield its adherents from the way racism continues to affect the possibilities of those born black in America. As Spillers suggests, the historical fact of racism in American history may make such "immersion" more precarious that Posnock's elegant formulation can acknowledge. This is to say not that either Roth or Ellison would oppose the cosmopolitan position that Posnock adduces but that the *The Human Stain* portrays the costs of such a position as well. In this respect, *The Human Stain* is a bookend to the historical period of Civil Rights initiated by Ellison's *Invisible Man*. It reflects on the era in which the statement "our fate is to become one, and yet many" seemed to become true as description, not as prophecy, and yet its truth nonetheless does not eradicate the pain of racial difference that many, though not all, Americans still suffer (*Invisible* 568).

Posnock is right to suggest that reading Silk and seeing Broyard may make it harder to see how Roth's novel unsettles familiar racial-cultural alignments. For if Broyard or Silk passed for white, then there is a sense in which the success of the novel depends on the premise that Roth (through the narrator Zuckerman) may pass for black. The revelation of Coleman's "true" identity is shocking only to the extent that the reader believes that Roth can imagine a plausible "black" character. Otherwise, the book reads like literate minstrelsy. The point here is to suggest not that the novel portrays Roth's own desire to be black but that Roth, like Ellison at the close of *Invisible Man*, insists that his reader must have the imaginative empathy to identify with a character who may be black or white or Jewish or none or all of the above. In aligning Zuckerman's Jewish American perspective with Coleman's African American perspective, Roth's narrative depends on the premise that the two are unknowable except *in relation* to each other. This logic exactly reflects Ellison's persistent cosmopolitan claim that "Negro" and "American" were mutually constitutive terms. Roth, like Ellison, questions whether cultural authenticity exists, and thus for him a novel about passing can never quite represent a sense of cultural betrayal. To Roth, you can't betray a culture, exactly, so much as you become part of a different one or change the meaning of the one that claims you.

Ellison never surrendered the self-designation of "Negro" even as he quoted his friend Albert Murray's observation that in America "all blacks are part white, and all whites are part black" (*Collected* 442). As readers of Roth's 1961 "Writing American Fiction" and *The Facts* (1988) will recognize, Ellison's novel and subsequent essays captured Roth's attention as the era's definitive exploration of the relationship between a communal ethnic identity and a more general American identity. The arguments about being a Negro American writer that Ellison makes in *Shadow and Act* voiced

Roth's own concurrent position in that era as a Jewish American novelist. *The Human Stain* resurrects Ellison as a kind of victim of identity politics in order to reposition Roth's own place in the recent American canon. As such, *The Human Stain* may be the most audacious literary act of Roth's audacious career, since it can be read as a sequel to Ellison's novel, as an investigation of Ellison's fate after the publication of *Invisible Man*, and as Roth's assessment of his own career as a Jewish American novelist. Again, Coleman Silk is neither Ralph Ellison nor Ralph Ellison's invisible man, just as Nathan Zuckerman is not Philip Roth. Yet in the context of the novel and Roth's career, Silk emerges as an identifiable amalgam of Ellison, Ellison's famous narrator, Zuckerman, and Roth himself. Roth gives his African American protagonist the comfortable, mostly stable academic life he himself might have enjoyed had he completed his PhD at the University of Chicago, a version in fact of the professorial life that Ellison chose to lead after publishing *Invisible Man*.

Ellison spent much of the second half of his life as a distinguished professor of literature, subject to attacks concerning his racial politics. *The Human Stain*'s "black" intellectual is a successful academic whose career ends ignominiously after a searing encounter with identity politics. Seeking revenge, Coleman Silk begins a book meant to reframe his personal loss as narrative triumph. Unable to finish it, Coleman asks Zuckerman to finish it for him. It is difficult to imagine Ellison requesting someone else to finish his own work, but there is the sense that Roth is writing the sequel to *Invisible Man* which Ellison could not finish. Zuckerman will not act on Coleman's request until after Coleman's death, just as Roth does not presume to assess Ellison's legacy until after Ellison's death. Once Coleman dies, though, the secret meaning of his life overwhelms Zuckerman. Standing over Coleman's grave, Zuckerman thinks he is being possessed by the dead man. "Not quite knowing what was happening, standing in the falling darkness beside the uneven earth mound roughly heaped over Coleman's coffin," Zuckerman confesses, "I was completely seized by his story, by its end and by its beginning, and, then and there, I began this book" (*Human* 337).

"Seized by" suggests that Zuckerman's identity is being usurped for Coleman's purposes. "Seized by" also conveys how Roth understood his relationship with Ellison, since to Roth much of his career could be seen as but an implication of Ellison's *Invisible Man*, even as *The Human Stain* allows Roth to imagine appropriating Ellison's work as if it were his own. Thus, when Roth has Zuckerman bury his novel's subject as a Jew and resurrect him as an African American, he is also claiming a kind of interpenetration between his Jewish American Zuckerman and Ellison's African American invisible man. Ultimately, Roth revises Ellison's story not so much to lay him to rest as to release the true meaning of his life to history.

Being Ethnic Together: Roth and Ellison

If Roth is said to follow any author, it is usually Saul Bellow, whom Roth addressed as his "other" reader in the dedication to *Reading Myself and Others* (1985). Roth has acknowledged his debt to Bellow many times, but such gestures may have more to do with Bellow's having been a mentor figure who furthered Roth's career when it was just beginning than with their shared aesthetic concerning questions of cultural identity. As Roth himself occasionally pointed out, any critical Roth-Bellow connection has often come from readers' own interest in the presumed ethnic continuity of the two writers, rather than from a careful analysis of their work (*Reading* 271–302). Bellow's representative Jewish characters—such as Tommy Wilhelm, Moses Herzog, and Artur Sammler—are struggling souls involved in avowedly spiritual quests for higher meaning; they take their "Jewishness" for granted. Roth's Jewish characters, by contrast, understand their Jewishness in secular terms and as a reflection of their unabashedly American selves. Bellow, rightly, has always been celebrated as a *Jewish* American author, whereas Roth has sometimes been reviled as one. It is telling, for instance, that although Irving Howe generally championed Bellow as a Jewish American link to previous generations of Jewish writers, going back to the East European *shtetl*, he attacked both Ellison and Roth for betraying what he took to be the traditions and concerns of their respective ethnic groups. Intuiting the relationship between Ellison and Roth, Howe virtually canonized them as *the* ethnic American writers whose importance consisted in their having abandoned their ethnic identities in the pursuit of "universal" American, literary selves ("Black"; "Philip").

Roth, a close reader of Ellison from the beginning of his career, recognized that he and Ellison, as American writers, were linked perhaps more closely than they could have been had they shared the same ethnicity. At different points in his career, Roth looked to Ellison to justify his own perspective as a Jewish American writer. In his essay "Writing about Jews," we find him implying that the writer he most resembles is Ellison. "Just as there are Jews who feel that my books do nothing for the Jewish cause," Roth notes, "so there are Negroes, I am told, who feel that Mr. Ellison's work had done little for the Negro cause" (*Reading* 222–23). When Howe, or similar-minded critics, castigated Ellison or Roth for exploiting their "authentic" cultural knowledge for the entertainment of (Roth) or accommodation to (Ellison) mainstream white culture, each writer responded by defending his own literary artistry, pointing out that portraying the complexity of American experience required formal ingenuity. More aggressively than any other literary American writers in the past fifty years that I can think of, Ellison and Roth each insisted that his fluid "Americanness," rather than his ethnicity, constituted a necessary component of his "true" aesthetic practice; moreover, each emphasized the supremacy of literary art over the issue of racial identity without ever surrendering the claim that literature affects society.[2] One can argue that both of their careers were defined by their continued refusal to be "pigeonholed" as ethnic writers, just as their work consistently prompted Howe and others to challenge them on the question of what is now called cultural authenticity—whether it is possible to be, as it were, authentically ethnic and American at the same time.[3] Roth thrived in the wake of such pigeonholing and went on to write many strong novels that examined his ethnic Jewish American conflict from virtually every conceivable angle; Ellison's fiction retreated to his study, where he worked for the rest of his life on a sequel to *Invisible Man* which he refused to publish, and thus his "literary" career became something of a mystery.

One can see how Roth's sense of himself as a writer was intimately linked with his understanding of Ellison in the way he positions Ellison's work against Bellow in his influential 1960 essay "Writing American Fiction" (*Reading*). The literary and intellectual encounters between Roth and Ellison from the 1960s are part of the background out of which Roth's *The Human Stain* emerges forty years later. After praising Bellow for meeting the difficult task of creating "a most remarkable thing," a self in literature, Roth identifies Ellison as having gone further by creating a self that is also politically engaged in his world. Here Roth speaks of his desire to create subjects not simply at odds with society, as he says is the case with Bellow's Eugene Henderson, but characters who would take responsibility for the "communal predicament," as Ellison's hero does. Few readers of Ellison have ever said anything as insightful or as essential about Ellison's work as Roth does here; he identifies with Ellison not for his alleged aestheticism (which is in fact why he moves away from Bellow) but because Ellison's *Invisible Man* presents a voice whose invention depends on the recognition that he is implicated within a "community [which] is both subject and audience" (*Reading* 190). That Roth calls on Ellison's example to clinch his argument underscores how Roth from the beginning of his career has regarded Ellison as a touchstone for understanding self, identity, and art with respect to the larger community. Tellingly, Roth structures the essay so that his survey of recent American writing concludes with *Invisible Man*, as if he need not complete his argument but merely introduce *Invisible Man* as its definitive expression.

His turn to Ellison at the end of this essay anticipates his use in *The Human Stain* of *Invisible Man* as a fiction through which to represent his defining interest in "the vision of self as inviolable, powerful and nervy, self-imagined as the only seemingly real thing in an unreal-seeming environment" (*Reading* 191). If Roth in *The Human Stain* politicizes Ellison's work, then what we see in "Writing American Fiction" is that that reading was from the beginning of Roth's career central to his interpretation of *Invisible Man* and that, more than any work by Bellow, Ellison's *Invisible Man* authorized Philip Roth's career.

This view is fitting, since the kinds of identity conflicts that drive the plot of most of Roth's novels are versions of the identity conflict that bedeviled Ellison as a public black intellectual. Where Ellison's responses to his critics became such brilliant essays as "The World and the Jug" or "The Little Man at Chehaw Station," Roth's responses more often found novel form in the Zuckerman books and *Operation Shylock* (1993). If Roth consistently reflected on the questions that provoked Ellison's most searching writings, then one must also acknowledge that virtually all of Roth's works each refers to, comments on, and is complicated by previous Roth works. Thus, I hope that I am reinforcing rather than straying from my argument when I observe that in order to see how Roth reflects on Ellison in *The Human Stain,* one must first review how in Roth's novels Roth is always reflecting on Roth. For if Roth is right to say that Ellison as a writer was concerned with a communal predicament, then Roth is more likely to use or create a communal predicament in order to ignite the self-reflections and self-dramatizations of his hero. In *The Ghost Writer,* for instance, the Holocaust's dramatic interest is that it is the setting for Nathan Zuckerman's antics and aspirations as a writer. Ellison, by contrast, invokes in his fiction the history of slavery as a communal predicament that is being confronted and individualized through the story of his various protagonists ("Invisible Man"; Hickman; Todd in "Flying Home"). From this perspective, Howe's criticism of Roth made more sense than his criticism of Ellison, whose fiction always expressed his community's predicament.

Upon publishing *The Human Stain* (2000)—the conclusion to a trilogy that began with *American Pastoral* (1997) and *I Married a Communist*

(1998)—Roth told Charles McGrath, "I think of it as a thematic trilogy, dealing with the historical moments in postwar American life that have had the greatest impact on my generation" (Interview). Conceiving the trilogy as a kind of critical account of what had happened since World War II, Roth was in effect writing a history of the lifetime of the America that created Ellison and Roth, which is also to say the America that Ellison and Roth endeavored to create. More important than Roth's evocation of World War II, the Communist hysteria of the 1950s, or the Vietnam War, though, is Roth's choice to filter these novels through the perspective of his complex authorial alter-ego, Nathan Zuckerman. In the initial trilogy of Zuckerman books (packaged in 1985 as *Zuckerman Bound* and including *The Ghost Writer*, *Zuckerman Unbound*, *The Anatomy Lesson*, along with the novella "The Prague Orgy"), the narratives focused on Zuckerman's career as a Jewish American author. The character's adventures echoed the adventures of his creator, who had written a series of fictions that outraged the communal sensibilities of Jewish elders. As Roth would show in *The Ghost Writer* (1979), stories such as "Eli the Fanatic" and "Defender of the Faith" earned him the enmity of Jewish religious leaders and community groups and marked him as a transgressive Jewish American intellectual—a "rude boy," as Posnock has named him. Each book in the first trilogy portrays a kind of escalating drama that emerges from the successive outrages that Zuckerman, or Roth, commits against "Jewishness" in America. Roth's ultimate outrage to this community was *Portnoy's Complaint* (1969), a work that reveled in its obscenity and its ability to flaunt, for the author's own aesthetic purposes, every cultural stereotype of Jewish American identity.

Ellison could have chosen to depict in novel form his own difficult position with other black intellectuals and quite possibly have had a completely different and, arguably, more "successful" literary career. One would like to see a novel version of Ellison's exchange with Howe—Roth, after all, put his into *The Anatomy Lesson* by turning Howe into a pornographer on the run from the law. Instead, Ellison toyed endlessly with a book that explored the communal costs for blacks should they choose to believe in the promises of white Americans. Ellison the private novelist was questioning the optimism of the Civil Rights movement, while the public Ellison was facing slings and arrows from those who said he was being too optimistic, too accommodating, as a black leader.

Roth's predicament, though, was never as severe as Ellison's. The weight on him as a "Jewish" author in America could not equal what Ellison had to carry as a "Negro" author. The history of being Jewish in American was just too different from the history of being black in America. Ironically, by the time of the second Zuckerman trilogy, many of the concerns that had driven the first trilogy had played out. During Roth's career, Jews had become cultural and political players and could no longer be associated with the *shtetl*, as in Roth's portrayal in "Eli the Fanatic." By the 1980s it was impossible to say that Jews had not achieved complete success as mainstream participants across a range of American cultural and political interests. Bellow won the Nobel Prize, and students of Jewish philosopher Allan Bloom (depicted by Bellow in *Ravelstein* [2000]), were neocons running United States foreign policy. In *The Counterlife* (1986), having seemingly exhausted Newark's potential for conflict, Roth moved his Zuckerman family drama to Israel and toyed with the idea of killing off Nathan Zuckerman altogether. Shortly thereafter, he dropped Zuckerman for a time and named his protagonist "Philip Roth," who, in *Operation Shylock*, ventured to Israel not so much to confront the meaning of Jewish American identity as to situate Roth's work in a world-Jewish literary context going all the way back to Shakespeare's *Merchant of Venice*. The cultural anxieties that Roth portrayed in his first Zuckerman novels no longer mattered: being a Jew was consistent with being a big shot in American culture and politics, and by then Roth was a big shot in American letters—becoming with Saul Bellow the only living novelists to have had their works included in the Library of America.

The second trilogy reflects this transformation. Zuckerman's adventures as a Jewish American author are no longer at the forefront of the narrative. Instead, he looks to the past and latches on to other characters' stories to create his narrative. Most startling for those who had followed Roth's career from the beginning was *American Pastoral* (1997), steeped in 1940s and 1950s nostalgia that seemed to revoke the point of view of the earlier Zuckerman novels. No longer siding with the Jewish son against the Jewish father, Zuckerman now tells a story of cultural loss and betrayal unimaginable to the pre-*Counterlife* Zuckerman. The protagonist, Swede Levov, is nearly destroyed by his commitment to the assimilationist ideals of the American dream. *American Pastoral* provoked the grateful response of longtime Roth critic, Norman Podhoretz, who declared that Roth had returned to the Jewish fold that had rejected him when he wrote *Portnoy* and stories like "Eli the Fanatic" ("Bellows"). Yet rather than suggesting that Roth in the second Zuckerman trilogy was apologizing to the Jewish fathers whom he had rejected in his earlier fiction, it is perhaps more accurate to say that Roth's late Zuckerman trilogy reflects upon the cultural transformations that had made conceivable his and Bellow's rise as major American authors.

If this second trilogy reveals Zuckerman to be an established and non-controversial Jewish author, then *The Human Stain* challenges Podhoretz's reading of *American Pastoral* because its protagonist cannot fit so easily within a framework that justifies such a thing as an "authentic" Jewishness. On Podhoretz's reading, Coleman Silk's story would have to be one of cultural betrayal along the lines some have suggested of Broyard or Poderetz of Swede Levov. Silk betrays his African American self by passing as a Jew, and his story therefore must be a "tragedy" because he was untrue to his people and thus to himself. Given that prior to *American Pastoral* a reading of Roth's entire career testifies to the aesthetic necessity of betraying others' sense of what constitutes cultural-group propriety, one may well ask whether Silk is any less an African American for pretending not to be one. If you are what you are, and what you are is a consequence of the cultural possibilities available to you during the historic coincidence that is your life, then how can you ever betray yourself or your "cultural identity"? Aren't you always and invariably but a local expression of your historic moment's possibilities?

Such questions Ellison asked again and again in his essays, and Roth explored possible answers in novel after novel. Whereas Roth seemed less vulnerable to such questions with each successive novel, Ellison, with no new novels to protect him, became more vulnerable as the perennial totemic target of black intellectuals dissatisfied with the place of blacks in American society. Yet in 1962, when Roth and Ellison appeared together at a Yeshiva symposium, "The Crisis of Conscience in Minority Writers in Fiction," Ellison seemed to be on top of the world in his position as a black writer, while Roth was on the defensive. In this moment, which Roth recounts in *The Facts* (1987), Ellison and Roth were united against a common antagonist group: cultural purity fanatics. Indeed, Roth confesses that his very identity as a creator was at stake as he nearly became the sacrificial victim of his Jewish readers' rage had it not been for the timely intervention of Ellison, who, in Roth's view, was a hero for having already triumphed over similar kinds of attackers. Roth names this episode his "Yeshiva Battle," and it reveals the enormous psychological relief that the young Roth took in just knowing that Ellison was an established voice on the American scene.

Recalling that night, Roth admits that he was thrilled to share the stage with a writer whom he viewed with "awe" (*Facts* 125). As Roth underscores, at this moment Ellison was at his peak as a cultural authority, while Roth was for his part a minor writer who, despite the National Book Award for his first book, was struggling to be known as a major American writer.

What stood in his way, or so it seemed to him, were the very Jews he was writing about. After the *New Yorker* published his controversial story "Defender of the Faith" in 1959, outraged Jewish readers wrote to suggest that Roth was more dangerous to Jews than organized anti-Semitic groups. One prominent rabbi asked the Anti-Defamation League, "What is being done to silence this man? Medieval Jews would have known what to do with him" (*Facts* 127). His presence at Yeshiva, Roth suggests, gave such readers a chance to see if they could indeed render him mute. After he finishes his short presentation, the moderator sets the tone for the question-and-answer period by asking: "Mr. Roth, would you write the same stories you've written if you lived in Nazi Germany?" (*Facts* 127).

Rather than observing that had he lived in Nazi Germany, he would likely now be dead, Roth tries to argue the finer points of the art of fiction. This time his usual strategy fails him. When he realizes that he is "not just opposed, but hated," Roth, amazingly, fades into a silence that seems to approach death.

> My combative instinct, which was not undeveloped, simply withered away and I had actually to suppress a desire to close my eyes and, in my chair at the panelists' table, with an open microphone only inches from my face, drift into unconsciousness. Ellison must have noticed my tenacity fading because all at once I heard him defending me with an eloquent authority I never could have hoped to muster from halfway out in oblivion. His intellectual position was virtually identical to mine, but he was presenting it as a black American, instructing through examples drawn from *Invisible Man* and the ambiguous relationship that novel had established with some vocal members of his own race. His remarks seemed to appear to the audience far more creditable than mine or perhaps situated the audience so far from its real mission as to deflect the inquisitorial pressure that I had envisioned mounting toward a finale that would find me either stoned to death or fast asleep. (*Facts* 128)

Although Roth did not provide a detailed account of Ellison's remarks, Ellison likely told the Yeshiva audience a version of what he had told an interviewer four years earlier when asked to define the relation of his minority group to the broader American culture:

> The American Negro people are North American in origin and have evolved under specifically American conditions: climatic, nutritional, historical, political and social. They take their character from the experience of American slavery and the struggle for, and the achievement of, emancipation; from the dynamics of American race and caste discrimination; and from living in a highly industrialized and highly mobile society possessing

a relatively high standard of living and an explicitly stated equalitarian concept of freedom. Its spiritual outlook is basically Protestant, its system of kinship is Western, its time and historical sense are American (Unites States), and its secular values are those professed, ideally at least, by all of the people of the United States. (*Collected* 292)

Ellison's argument is classically pluralist-cosmopolitan and striking in its insistence that any definition of Negro identity must be placed in contexts that are not specifically black. For Ellison, how one defines "American" is virtually identical to how one defines "Negro," and as a result this definition works both ways. Ellison understands slavery (along with its opposite ideal, equality) as an essential fact of both American and Negro American history. While being the descendant of slaves is a distinctive experience, the fact of slavery and its abolition is one that all Americans share and must live with—even immigrants who arrived years after the Civil War. Implicit is the claim that what Ellison says about Negroes applies to Jews insofar as both ethnic groups exist in relation to themselves and other Americans.

That night the Yeshiva audience likely consisted of second- and third-generation American Jews. Fresh in their minds was the experience of the Holocaust, a mass tragedy, like slavery, that seemed to mark them uniquely as an oppressed people. Ellison's point, however, was that Jews and Negroes relate to each other as Americans; the possibility of being Americans together should mitigate the painfulness of their distinctive ethnic histories without abolishing their claim to identities that cannot be characterized *solely* by the term "American." "Inevitably," Ellison wrote, competing ethnic histories and "forms came together; there is always an *integration* of artistic styles whether it is done out of admiration, out of need, or out of a motive of economic exploitation" (*Collected* 445; emphasis added). I emphasize the word "integration" because Ellison crucially transformed a term of social and political experience into the basis for what he saw as the highest form of literary practice. In 1969, five years after the Civil Rights Act, he told a gathering of African American scholars in his important but often overlooked "Haverford Statement" that "as a writer who tries to reduce the flux and flow of life to meaningful artistic forms, *I am stuck with integration*, because the very process of the imagination as it goes about bringing together a multiplicity of scenes, images, characters, and emotions and reducing them to significance is nothing if not integrative" (*Collected* 429–30; emphasis added).

Ellison often repeated the arguments that he made at Haverford. When asked to comment on artists of the militant Black Arts movement who had criticized Ellison's conservative stance, he generally responded that such movements (Communist writing being another) often failed to produce anything of aesthetic significance precisely because emphasis on cultural separatism prevented such artists from achieving the kind of imaginative suppleness, or integration, that makes great art possible.[4] For Ellison, cultural separatism made for bad art—not to mention providing excuses for the kinds of bad Americanism that kept Jim Crow alive well into the twentieth century. Thus, for Ellison as for Roth, integration was as much an aesthetic imperative as a social ideal. This understanding of integration is crucial to the Roth-Ellison definition of cosmopolitan American identity and also to the practice of literature. Better than Roth, Ellison explained to a skeptical audience that his peer was not attempting to exploit recent Jewish history so much as to render in artistic form how it was being transformed by a collective engagement with American experience.

In *Invisible Man* Ellison's act of aesthetic integration was conceived also as a profound gesture of social integration. Roth is one of countless readers who answered this gesture by reading his own story into that of Ellison's narrator. Yet because the novel ends with Ellison's hero hidden underground, writing to an unknown audience, with no clear plan for emerging except the hope that others will recognize their predicament in his and thus be inspired to social action, some readers questioned the novel's commitment to effecting social change. These readers tended to ask precisely what social action is implied by a hero who ends up talking to himself in a basement and hoping that someone is listening. To reframe this central question in literary terms, one might ask what possible sequel could emerge from this story.

As quoted in the Introduction, the political scientist Danielle Allen argues that Ellison's novel was part of a general reconstitution of American social life congruent with changing laws and the emerging Civil Rights movement. According to her, *Invisible Man* is the one American novel that imagines and prepares the way for the social revolution that *Brown v. Board of Education* would initiate. For Allen, Ellison best imagined "forms of citizenship that help break down distrust and generate trust" (xxi). Ellison recognized that "democracy puts its citizens under a strange form of psychological pressure by building them up as sovereigns and then regularly undermining each citizen's experience of sovereignty" (Allen 27). Ellison's protagonist experiences a version of this insight with every adventure, but not until the end of the novel (though also reflected in its Prologue) does he realize that what is required of democratic citizens is the risk of trust. Only if Americans open their channels of communication to all frequencies of Americanness, as it were, will the American democratic experiment thrive.

Antagonists such as Irving Howe or associates of the Black Arts movement did not accept that "Ellison explicated what it is like to be an individual in a democratic world of strangers, where large-scale events are supposed to arise out of one's consent but never really do" (Allen 27). Instead, his antagonists chose to make Ellison himself the sacrificial victim of the large-scale social event that no single novel, no matter its perspective, could simply by its publication usher into being. For his part, as the Civil Rights movement, the 1964 Civil Rights Act, and the 1965 Voting Rights Act transformed his novel into living social truth, Ellison became insistent about giving it an unambiguously positive ending. As the barriers to legal segregation shockingly fell, Ellison chose to explain how his narrator's insistence in 1952 that "our fate is to become one, and yet many—This is not prophecy, but description" was not reefer "buggyjiving" but had become the social reality Americans were obligated to face and accept as a national challenge (*Invisible* 568). Ellison's brilliant elaborations of *Invisible Man* as a living social document were given in lectures such as the one Roth witnessed and published as *Shadow and Act* and *Going to the Territory*. Instead of a second novel, these essays and talks became Ellison's sequel to *Invisible Man*. His identity gradually changed from practicing novelist working on a new book (a successor to *Invisible Man*) to a kind of demanding professor of literature who specialized in one work, *Invisible Man*, and its relationship to a pluralist American culture.

In essence—as he gave talks and wrote essays—Ellison's ultimate fate was to trade places with his famous narrator. Where his protagonist goes from being a speaker to being a writer (ranter to writer, in Ellison's famous formulation), Ellison goes from being a writer to being primarily a speaker (though never a ranter). He himself somewhat ruefully made this point in a 1974 television interview with Arlene Crewdson and Rita Thomson when he acknowledged the irony of having switched roles with his own creation: "because you notice that the [invisible] man moves from someone who talks all the time (the exact reversal of what has happened to me, I now talk all the time) but he started out as an orator in school, and he really ends up, though he doesn't say so, by writing a book" (*Conversations* 264). As grateful as Roth remained to Ellison for saving him at the Yeshiva Battle, *The Human Stain* suggests that Ellison paid a terrible price for his commitment to the social and political possibilities of literature. Roth seems to recognize that if his own identity as a writer was inextricably linked to the

Yeshiva Battle, this is what enabled him to create a shelf of fiction nearly as long as the one that Henry James left. Ellison, however, never vacated the Yeshiva Battle in the sense that he found himself forever explaining his own historical position—and its implied "communal predicament," in Roth's wonderful phrase—instead of writing fiction about it.[5] And Ellison's "silence" as a novelist, *The Human Stain* suggests, became a cross that he had to bear in exchange for seeing something approaching his egalitarian social vision come true in American life. In the end, Ellison's commitment to advancing the status of his group and thus helping to create an egalitarian America was greater than his commitment to having a successful career as a serial publishing novelist like Roth or Ellison's housemate, Saul Bellow.

On that night in 1962, Ellison was a hero who liberated Roth so that he could claim for himself his place as a Jewish American author. As *The Facts* documents, twenty-five years on, the Yeshiva Battle remained for Roth the symbolic origin of his career as a Jewish American writer. In depicting Ellison as a savior who rescued him from his fiercest critics, he also names Ellison as the one author who cleared the way for Roth to realize his true voice as a writer. At the Yeshiva Battle, with Ellison as witness and protector, Roth was, he says, "branded" as a "Jewish" writer, and thus his entire career from *Portnoy's Complaint* on was a response to and claiming of the symbolic "branding" he suffered that night (*The Facts* 125–30). In this episode, as with "Writing American Fiction," Ellison literally speaks for Roth. When in *The Human Stain* Roth reinvents Ellison, he is doing so as an inversion of what happened that evening when Roth let Ellison speak for him after Roth, uncharacteristically, had been unable to speak for himself. Roth's version of the Yeshiva Battle crystallizes the positions that the two men inherited as "minority" American writers and that anticipated the course their careers would take.

Roth's Invisible Man (Outside History)

The Human Stain's "invisible man," Coleman Silk, has had a conventionally successful life, but his true story and the meaning of his life are unknown. Roth signals Coleman's literary relationship to Ellison's protagonist by drawing on the language of *Invisible Man* to introduce his novel's narrative premise. The term "spook" sets off the central plot device of *The Human Stain* as an inversion and rewriting of the famous opening lines of *Invisible Man*: "I am an invisible man. No, I am not a spook like those who haunted Edgar Allan Poe; nor am I one of your Hollywood-movie ectoplasms. I am a man of substance, of flesh and bone, fiber and liquids—and I might even be said to possess a mind. I am invisible, understand, simply because people refuse to see me" (3). Through this bitter pun, Ellison's narrator identifies himself by invoking and then denying the same play of meanings that Coleman Silk, as it turns out, cannot quite evade. Refusing to accept himself as someone else's denigrating epithet, Ellison's narrator plays with and controls the reader's possible instinct to know him only as a racial epithet. In Roth's version, Coleman is not so fortuitous, nor can he contain the disparate meanings his use of the word "spooks" ignites. Expressing his irritation at two students who have not yet shown up for class six weeks into the semester, Coleman sarcastically asks if the chronically absent students are "spooks." The students are not ghosts (or CIA agents either), but they are African Americans, and "spooks" is taken by the class and the faculty to mean a denigrating racial epithet. Defending his language ("undone," as he sees it, "by the perfect word"), Coleman looks to undo the typology of invisibility that Ellison's narrator sets out: "How could I know they were black students, if I had never laid eyes on them. . . . What I did know, indisputably, was that they were *invisible* students—and the word for invisible, for a ghost, for a specter, is the word I used in its primary meaning" (*Human* 85). Roth's emphasis on the word "invisible" underlines that Ellison's concept of invisibility shadows Coleman's story. The "invisibility" of these black students is the narrative mechanism that triggers Zuckerman's exploration of Coleman's own "invisible" black self.

One may think that were Coleman to acknowledge his "true" identity, he would be excused, if not exonerated. Probably not, though. Were Coleman to conduct his own ritualistic ethnic cleansing, the charge of being a racist might become legitimate rather than opportunistic. He would be accused of exactly what Irving Howe accused Roth and Ellison of being: cultural self-haters. Revealing his racial identity would be not so much an act of acknowledgment as one of surrender to the very identity-logic his life rebelled against. Once his accusers replace Coleman's definition of "spook" with their definition, Coleman can do nothing to clear his name. The victim, in *Invisible Man*'s words, of these people's "inner eyes," Coleman discovers that the classic Ellisonian position of invisibility no longer protects him. Unlike Ellison's protagonist, Coleman cannot revenge himself through narrative because he cannot complete his memoir—titled (what else?) *Spooks*. Until the spooks incident, the secret of his success had been that he could control others' perceptions of him through his life: that is, his life, not any narrative he might write, was his art.

In the history of Coleman's secret, Roth's reader encounters Coleman through a version of himself that he has controlled by means of an artful repression. Coleman never quits being "black" or interpreting his life through the historical perspective that being born African American gives him. Rather, he does not let others' perceptions of what it means to be born black color his life. Defending his job by revealing his "authentic" identity would only deny the contingent and fully lived life he has made for himself. To his accusers Coleman might plausibly explain that his life should be appreciated for its aesthetic achievement and its concomitant refusal to accept the racial status quo as unchanging—the terms by which Ellison defended his novel to Howe. This would be a version of Posnock's "cosmopolitan" reading, but it would also be the Emersonian one that stresses the goal of self-invention as an inherent good. Ironically, Coleman defends himself by a different kind of race-based political correctness: clinging to his borrowed ethnic history, he insists that his fall is due to anti-Semitism. This argument is not convincing in a Roth novel, though, simply because such complaints have never stopped Roth's truly Jewish heroes from pursuing the possibilities of self-invention to the very limit of selfhood (which is what Coleman too has done).

For much of the novel, though, Roth gives his Ellisonian hero a place in society not available to Ellison's hero, whose triumph was fundamentally a narrative one. The reader perhaps could see him, but not the society of 1952 in which he was still legally unseen (separate and not equal). When Ellison's hero falls into his hole, in "a long drop that ended upon a load of coal," and is taunted as "a nigger in the coal pile," Ellison's joke is that out of the darkness will come the illumination that is his narrator's story (*Invisible* 556). When Roth's beleaguered and accused "Coal-man" refuses to reveal his black identity, it is not because he is afraid to be taunted as "a nigger in the coal pile" but rather because the structure of the story requires that Coleman's secret illuminate Zuckerman's narrative. Where Ellison's hero gets to tell his own story, Roth's hero's story is told by an "authentically" Jewish narrator, Zuckerman, who tacitly aligns his story with his hero's. Coleman never gets to tell his tale, and in this way Roth pretends to usurp Ellison's novel, if not its legacy.

What Roth does with Ellison's narrative is to tell a story of cultural fluidity that is threatened yet made possible by racial perceptions that are too stagnant to manage the social reality they would try to prescribe. Coleman surveys the possibilities of his life as a Negro and decides to take advantage of his light skin to play a role that resists the one scripted for him by a racist society. The fact of his success will undermine the assumptions of the racist society that provokes him to play the role, but no opportunity exists for the meaning of Coleman's role-playing to become evident except through Zuckerman's telling. At the end of *Invisible Man,* Ellison's hero cryptically admits that "the old fascination with playing a role returns, and I'm drawn upward again" (570). But what that role might be no one could say until history had changed—as it did with the Civil Rights movement. In this context, one cannot help wondering what Ellison would have made of *The Human Stain*'s enactment of his protagonist's role. Possibly, he would have taken a view similar to that of Coleman's sister, Ernestine, who underscores what Coleman lost by hiding his African American origins. Certainly, Ellison would be surprised to learn that his narrator had reappeared playing the role of a white Jewish man who has decided to pass in order to play his role in American society. Yet perhaps he would not have been, since Ellison knew that "playing a role" really means "choosing a role" and that in American society many roles are available to be played at any given instant by any given American. Moreover, his second novel hinged on a shape-shifter, Bliss, who could persuade as an improvising black preacher and as a race-baiting white senator—a range of transformation that makes Coleman's efforts modest by comparison.

In "The Little Man at Chehaw Station" (1977), Ellison noted that "in our intergroup familiarity there is a brooding strangeness, and in our underlying sense of alienation a poignant, although distrusted, sense of fraternity. Deep down, the American condition is a state of unease" (*Collected* 504). This state of "unease" is Coleman's as he is not quite at home among his family of either blacks or Jews. Yet the fact of American culture, Ellison says, consists of "many available tastes, traditions, ways of life, and values that . . . have been ceaselessly appropriated and made their own," and this process is enacted "by groups and individuals whose own backgrounds are historically alien" (510). Committed to accepting and exploring the idea of the basic fluidity of American being, Ellison invented the classic American shape-shifter, Bliss Proteus Rinehart, and even signed some of his own letters as Rinehart, or variations thereof. He also indicated that the character Bliss in the second novel is another one of Rinehart's permutations.[6] Coleman too might be seen as a version of one of Rinehart's ingenious impersonations or at least as someone intoxicated, as Ellison's hero was, with the freedom that becoming Rinehart seems to offer. Cosmopolitan cultural fluidity, Ellison and Roth suggest, is not just a matter of self-invention but also (sometimes unwitting) social collaboration. Thus, just as Ellison's character becomes Rinehart only when someone else recognizes him as Rinehart, Coleman becomes "white" because he sees that others see him that way.

His Aristotelian moment of identity recognition and reversal occurs when his Jewish boxing coach, Doc Chizner, advises Coleman to keep his "blackness" to himself: "If nothing comes up, you don't bring it up. You're neither one thing or the other. You're Silky Silk. That's enough" (*Human* 98). This silence becomes what Zuckerman calls Coleman's "secret": the key to his identity. Where Ellison's protagonist is invisible as the victim of others' inadequate vision of him, Coleman exploits others' assumptions as the basis for his own freedom. Given Rinehart's lesson that "freedom was not only the recognition of necessity, it was the recognition of possibility" (*Invisible* 491), then why should the color of Coleman's skin mark a fixed identity?

Roth portrays Coleman's Rinehartian freedom by rewriting what is probably the most well-known scene from *Invisible Man*: the Battle Royal. In Ellison's version, the hero is made to fight, blindfolded, among a group of other black boys for an amused and titillated white audience. Ellison's hero assumes that he has been invited to give his valedictorian speech, but he has really been invited to be humiliated, to learn his place in a segregated society. In this pivotal episode, Ellison suggests that blacks are positioned to fight one another in the cultural arena in ways that can only reinforce their own cultural impotence. Roth's hero, by contrast, with his blackness invisible to others, fights mostly white kids, never loses, gets paid, and uses the money to pay his tuition at an integrated college.

In one scene Coleman's white manager instructs him not to knock out his "nigger" opponent early in the fight but to "carry" him until the audience gets its money's worth. Coleman does not feel implicated in the man's casual racism. Instead, he is furious to have been asked not to do his absolute best, so he knocks out his opponent in the first round. Why? "Because I don't carry no nigger" (*Human* 117). In contrast to the "spooks" episode, Coleman's use of a racial slur here is intentionally ironic. It expresses his victory over the racial trap that Ellison's Battle Royal represented: Coleman recalls the blindfolded boxer, Tatlock, who spurned Ellison's hero's offer to "act out" the conclusion to their fight and promised to knock out the hero for his own pleasure rather than that of the white onlookers. But Coleman does not direct his rage at his black opponent (just another boxer) and refuses to gratify the white audience. By making his white manager complicit with an act the manager cannot comprehend, Coleman turns him into the unwitting dupe of his own unexamined racism.

One may argue that Coleman is in flight from an authentic black identity, but his triumph here does not clearly yield such a reading. Zuckerman suggests that to say that one has betrayed one's white or black identity is to say that one *has* a white or black identity to betray. It seems rather that Coleman is making the best of a complicated circumstance and is ingeniously and courageously pushing himself forward as best he can. Where Ellison's invisible man found himself the victim of others' "inner eyes," Roth's hero will not become the victim of "those of poor vision" (*Invisible* 3). Coleman may "pass" as white, but this is society's perceptual problem, not his. Coleman has simply "chosen to take the future into his own hands rather than leave it to an unenlightened society to determine his fate—a society in which, more than eighty years after the Emancipation Proclamation, bigots happened to play too large a role to suit him. . . . All he'd ever wanted, from earliest childhood on, was to be free: not black, not even white—just on his own and free" (*Human* 120).

Roth's wording here recalls the narrator's self-description at the outset of Ellison's story. Referring to the Emancipation Proclamation, Ellison's narrator says, "I was in the cards, other things having been equal (or unequal) eighty-five years ago" (*Invisible* 15). He lives in the aftermath of slavery and its severe social codes. Coleman, however, commits himself to the pursuit of "raw I," or the purest form of Rinehartian individualism, an ambition worthy of Rinehart, not to mention Benjamin Franklin or Frederick Douglass: "To become a new being. To bifurcate. The drama that underlies America's story, the high drama that is upping and leaving—and the energy and cruelty that rapturous drive demands" (*Human* 342). Roth's Coleman enjoys a unique story of purely individual triumph that Ellison's narrator sees only in terms of a future different from the past that bore him. But this is also because Coleman, unlike Ellison's hero, need not represent the communal predicament nor aspire to lead anyone to an enlightened vision of American society. A typical Roth hero, the game is his to name.

Zuckerman declines to portray any persistent misgivings Coleman may have had about his choice but makes it clear that Coleman cannot simply relinquish his "black" identity, since "being black" is ineradicably part of who he is. He is reminded of this fact when, like Roth at Yeshiva, he endures an ordeal of being "branded" black: serving in the U.S. Navy, Coleman is thrown out of "the famous white whorehouse called Oris's" because a white prostitute identifies him as an African American. Castigating himself for suffering the inevitable punishment of staging his "revolt of one against the Negro fate," Coleman comes as close as Zuckerman ever imagines to losing self-control over his invisibility (*Human* 183). He survives, though, and when the Shore Patrol finds him in the morning, Coleman has acquired a souvenir to mark that night, a U.S. Navy military tattoo. Zuckerman identifies this tattoo as "a true and total image of himself" because it marks an "ineradicable biography" (184). The U.S. tattoo marks Coleman as being born black, even if virtually no one but Coleman and his family can know this, and perhaps especially because Coleman cannot remember how he got it. It marks not exactly the *fact* of his race but the history he carries *because* of his "race," which includes the perception of race that others have. Like Roth at Yeshiva, Coleman comes away from the experience determined to confront his ethnic identity on his own terms. If his choice seems to eradicate the kinds of ethnic conflicts that Roth's fiction ordinarily thrives on, then Roth suggests that Coleman carries that conflict within as a form of self-mastery that is a version of Roth's reading of *Invisible Man* (conveyed in the epigraph to this chapter). For Roth, Coleman's choice not to be known as black is neither a refusal nor an evasion of his racial heritage; it gives him a life as complicated and as courageous as choosing to be known as black would have given him.

Coleman is postracial in a world still bound by race perception. The historical bind that Coleman must negotiate is suggested in his relationships with his two premarriage girlfriends, one white and one black. White Steena is (prior to Faunia) the love of Coleman's life. After he falls in love with her he decides he wants her to meet his family. Before the meeting, he tells neither his girlfriend nor his kin about the others' racial identity. Roth's portrayal of the encounter is deftly comic. No one acknowledges the peculiarity of the situation. On the surface, it is a typically awkward meeting between a potential daughter-in-law and her new family. The unsaid fact that she is white and Coleman is black (here he is not passing) nonetheless dominates the encounter. Coleman has constructed the meeting out of the cosmopolitan hope that one's human identity is prior to one's racial identity. His hope is insufficient to overcome the social expectations of that time, though, and the reader understands that his "secret" is his reaction to this failed encounter. As Steena explains to Coleman later in a letter, she is not a racist but she fears their partnership could not withstand the scrutiny of others' racism.

Prior to his love affair with Faunia, Coleman's one fear is that of being known—being visible. Besides Steena and Faunia, his secret is known to another significant love interest, Ellie, a light-skinned African American woman. Ellie allows Coleman to have it both ways—to pass as black and as white. Indeed, it is Ellie (whose name may contain a wry allusion to Ellison) who initiates Coleman into the complexity of identity brought on by his ambiguous skin color. Upon meeting Coleman, she identifies him immediately as someone who is passing: "What are you anyway?" Coleman gives the answer learned from his coach, Doc Chizner: "What am I? Play it anyway you like?" Ellie reveals to Coleman that he is not unique. She guides him around the Village and points out others who are passing for white. "See that one? The smoothie?" she asks. Coleman is dumfounded. "You're in Greenwich Village, Coleman Silk, the four freest square miles in America. There's one on every other block. You're so vain, you thought you'd dreamed it up yourself" (*Human* 134–35). Coleman learns not only that is he not special but that he has an identity that may be known by others. Ellie's knowledge makes him fear that he might lose the power of his secret. If he is going to play it either way, he is going to have to pass for white. And if he is going to be white, he can play his identity with others only one way, though the trade-off is the opportunity to move more widely in American society. Coleman does not sell out his black identity; insofar as he owns his self he can do anything he wants with it. As Bonnie Lyons shrewdly observes, "His one socially defiant act makes possible his acceptance of society's rules" (89). His unconventional freedom expresses itself in a conventional role: a university professor, a family man, an ordinary person but for his origins.

Invisible within History

Despite its protagonist's freedom, Roth's novel acknowledges the claim that Coleman's past has on him in the form of his family. Coleman detaches himself from his family, but Zuckerman situates Coleman's story within the family frame that Coleman repudiates. As the self-reliant American, Coleman heeds Emerson's advice in "Self Reliance" that one must be willing to "shun father and mother, and wife and brother, when my genius calls me. I would write on the lintels of the door-post, *Whim*. I hope it is somewhat better than whim at last, but we cannot spend the day in explanation" (*Essays* 262). Coleman's "whim" to pass becomes the expression of his genius. This same rapturous drive of Emersonian "Self-Reliance" prompts Coleman to abandon—to symbolically murder—his family. Knowing that his decision to pass for white means that his mother will never get to see her grandchildren, Coleman admits to himself that he is "murdering her on behalf of his exhilarating notion of freedom!" (*Human* 138). When he tells his mother of his decision, she says she should have seen this coming, since as a baby "you were seriously disinclined even to take the breast.... There was always something about our family, and I don't mean color—there was something about us that impeded you. You think like a prisoner. You do, Coleman Brutus. You're white as snow and you think like a slave" (139). Roth contrasts the language of Emerson with the language of African American history. Ellison's narrator says, "I am not ashamed to be descended from slaves. I am only ashamed that I was ashamed" (*Invisible* 15). The opposing positions occupied by Coleman and his mother do not contradict the insight contained in those words. Neither wants a life restricted by the legacy of slavery, but how does one leave that pernicious legacy behind when society still carries it? Is Coleman actually wrong to think that in choosing to become the self he envisions, he too is casting off the legacy of slavery, despite the justified disappointment his mother experiences? To Zuckerman, Coleman is at worst a traitor to his family, and this story is one that Zuckerman knows well, as its possibility has characterized most of his own self-explorations in the first Zuckerman trilogy.

Of course, the family is the site of ethnic identity. To embody "the raw I," Coleman must achieve what Zuckerman himself failed to accomplish: he must separate himself from the strictures of his family identity. (One can read Zuckerman's admiration of Coleman's rebellion as a projection of his own anxiety about having disrupted his family's communal solidarity and of his friendship with Coleman's sister as atonement.) Coleman's "secret" divides him from his family, but more fundamentally, it arguably separates him from the historical conditions and opportunities that made his choice meaningful in social terms.[7] Unlike Ellison or his narrator, Coleman is not trying to change history so much as to sidestep it. A crucial difference between Ellison's *Invisible Man* and Roth's "Invisible Man" is that Coleman's "role" is not a potential collaboration between hero and reader that might change society; Coleman's "future" is known, not a matter of speculation. When Ellison wrote *Invisible Man,* he did not know that *Brown* and Martin Luther King were around the corner; he only hoped that such events might soon take place. On the other hand, Roth, writing after the Civil Rights movement, acknowledges that Coleman does not quite dwell in a world of infinite possibilities but must act in light of where his choices have taken him. *Invisible Man* portrayed a version of history that it was also resisting as its narrative gesture. History made its protagonist invisible, but the protagonist had sought a way to use invisibility to his advantage. He mastered his own story and hoped to change history through its telling.

In *The Human Stain,* "history" is something that Coleman cannot quite control, since by the time he dies, his "secret" means something else than it did to him when he made his choice to pass. In the 1960s and '70s, recognizing that history was changing the way *Invisible Man* could be interpreted, Ellison emphasized that his novel portrayed an instance of American diversity and that it was possible for all Americans—all readers—to identify with its story. As discussed in chapter 2, Ellison had written the novel specifically from black American experience, but he did not want it to be known as an artifact of the Jim Crow era. He did not want this only because he wanted his novel to last but also because he wanted the Jim Crow era to end. As Harold Bloom suggests, "*Invisible Man* might be reduced to a period piece if it were primarily a vision of African-American dilemmas. The novel's permanence stems from its universality" (*Genius* 808). As Roth's "Invisible Man," Coleman embodies Ellison's desire for this universalist ethos, but his success is undercut by the fact that his choice to pass was in effect a concession to the logic of Jim Crow. From this perspective, one could argue that Roth demonstrates how *Invisible Man*'s universalist ethos necessarily downplays the costs that Coleman, and perhaps Ellison's narrator too, suffered in being denied the comfort of their families.

As a "Negro" writer, Ellison advanced notions of identity that encompassed "Negro" and "American" as overlapping, mutually constitutive terms. Yet because Ellison was born into a Jim Crow society, and because the assumptions of Jim Crow would take generations to efface, he could not always blur the line between Negro and American without encountering resentment from one side of the line or the other. As his exchange with Irving Howe confirms, the expectations placed on a "Negro" writer were not the same as those placed on other writers. Although Roth too was called out by Howe for violating ethnic assumptions, the fact was that Howe's criticism of Roth did not stick, because there was no Jewish community of readers sufficiently powerful or interested enough to hold Roth down. Roth's Jewish readers evolved with Roth. *Invisible Man* hoped to initiate the very future that engulfed it, and it may be that Ellison did not publish another novel because *Invisible Man* came as close as he could imagine to depicting American reality as he understood it. Thus, although Ellison in his essays and lectures addressed the changing times as capably as he could, his critics continued to attack him according to premises that were still consistent with Jim Crow.

Ellison made a version of this point in a 1973 tribute to Alain Locke, but Roth's novel can be interpreted to suggest how difficult Ellison's integrationist position remained—even in the age of integration. It is no coincidence, then, that Zuckerman highlights 1953, the year after the publication of *Invisible Man*, as the moment in which Coleman's self bifurcates. This was the year that Ellison won the National Book Award and was acclaimed the "universal" author of his own self. Zuckerman notes of Coleman's break with his family that "the act was committed in 1953 by an audacious young man in Greenwich village, by a specific person in a specific place at a specific time, but now he will be over on the other side forever" (*Human* 145). Coleman at this crucial moment leaves his family at the same time that Ellison, student of Tuskegee and former editor of *Negro Quarterly*, symbolically integrated American literature. Each enters a new world in which the roles of black people have not quite been scripted. Roth's Coleman suffers no obvious sense of loss, whereas Ellison's situation is perhaps more ambiguous. He apparently never looked back (except in his secret novel), but his position was an isolated one.

After *Invisible Man*, Ellison became the toast of American letters and a university professor to boot. His success as a novelist, his seemingly effortless eloquence as a speaker, and his status as an important black artist made him a desirable presence at university symposia, conferences, and intellectual gatherings of all kinds. Reading *Trading Twelves*, his published correspondence with Albert Murray from the 1950s, one can watch the startling process by which Ellison goes from being a relatively anonymous, aspiring writer, publishing essays and stories that take up "the Negro question," to becoming what Henry James might call a Figure. It is a remarkable and indeed amazing transformation to witness, even in retrospect. Ellison, like Coleman, leaves an all-black college without graduating, but unlike Coleman's, Ellison's intellectual development is in part nourished by the time he spends with prominent African American artists. According to his interviews and essays, Ellison "bums" around New York, even sleeping in Central Park, all the while making friends with his "culture heroes," as he terms them, such as Richard Wright and Langston Hughes.[8] By the end of the 1950s his cultural connections are such that he shares a house with Saul Bellow and is neighbors with Lionel Trilling, Gore Vidal, and Richard Rovere. In the 1960s, he becomes an adviser to a sitting U.S. president.

If Ellison suffered more "as a black intellectual" than Coleman seems to have suffered as a "disguised" black intellectual, I would suggest that the rage the "assimilated" Coleman experiences when he is accused of being a racist also reflects on Ellison's own conflicted relationship with his post–*Invisible Man* black audience. Ellison's argument for the universality of his novel sought to extend *Invisible Man*'s meaning beyond the moment of its writing. Ellison likely would have been gratified by historian Leon Litwack's assertion that *Invisible Man* is in fact the one indispensable history of the Jim Crow era, but perhaps more important, Ellison came to see that he wanted the book to be more than a record of the past. He wanted, improbably, to help make the future as well. The narrator, hovering on the edge of his hole, remains forever frozen on the verge of completing his act. In a sense, he is waiting for history (the future) to make his most egalitarian aspirations visible.

History emerged in the form of the Civil Rights movement, and Ellison— decades before Obama—took to the podium to encourage Americans to accept the diversity of their shared heritage. "You cannot have an American experience without a black experience," he said over and over, to the derision of many (*Collected* 442). In *The Human Stain* the fact of the Civil Rights movement is acknowledged through Coleman's sister, but a brilliant scene between Coleman and his daughter underscores the truth of Ellison's observation even as it points to Coleman's shortsightedness regarding the meaning of his choice. Coleman is visiting his daughter at the school where she teaches. When her students are made anxious by the intrusion of this stranger into their routine, she reassures them not to worry, "he's invisible. Invisible, you can't see him" (*Human* 158). The scene suggests that Coleman's secret is something that he cannot control, since it also belongs to the history he has denied. The irony, of course, is that so does the daughter. Here Coleman is not just an iteration of Ellison's invisible man: his invisibility conceals not strength but ignorance. The white daughter is ignorant of her black heritage. Her ignorance of this heritage critiques the dream of Coleman's secret. Even if the daughter remains dead to her grandmother, the grandmother may be resurrected, should the daughter ever have a child. Without access to the grandmother's story, Coleman's daughter may find herself one day in the position of Ellison's most benighted white reader, that is, a "white" person confronting a "black" person with no idea how to explain her true relationship to this stranger confronting her.

Ellison provided a mechanism for such understanding, but his point was never enough for his critics. Nor did Ellison ever indicate he was a black self-hater. In his exchange with Howe he said that segregation bothered him in part because it made seeing a movie more difficult, not because he necessarily wanted to see movies with whites. Although he told Howe that he was in the struggle for Negro equality for the duration of the struggle, he also said that "I am, after all, only a minor member, not the whole damned tribe; in fact, most Negroes have never heard of me" (*Collected* 185). The limits to his fame, however, did not prevent him from becoming a scapegoat for the societal ills his work identified and fought, and his exasperation with Howe can only hint at how painful it must have been for him to be labeled a white apologist by black critics. With Howe, Ellison could employ a modified stance of "black" rage and amusement. Roth allows Coleman one moment of "black" rage when he uses the term "lily-white" to express his anger toward an uncomprehending white interlocutor. Ironically, this is a phrase Coleman's brother had directed at him for choosing to be pass as white. The brother severs Coleman from his mother: "Don't you even *try* to see her. No contact. No calls. Nothing. Never. Hear me? *Never*. Don't you dare show your lily-white face around that house again" (*Human* 145). After Coleman loses his job and his dignity, he directs his anger at his lawyer, whom he informs that he is sick of his "lily-white face" (81).

I do not think, as many readers may, that Roth has Coleman say this to suggest that he has internalized his brother's words as a form of racial self-hatred. Rather, I think they slip out at this moment to suggest that Coleman never quit thinking of himself as "black" or identifying himself with an African American point of view. His use of the term also conveys the painful isolation that he experiences as someone who is "between" races. For his part, Ellison never ceased identifying as a Negro, though he advocated that Americans understand themselves to be in a state of collective cultural limbo or flux. But in moments of stress, Ellison too could imply that the line between black and white was not so permeable. In his reply to Howe, he acknowledged "passing" as a cultural phenomenon and clearly disdained it as an act of cultural cowardice:

> Negro American consciousness is not a product (as so often seems true of so many American groups) of a will to historical forgetfulness. It is a product of our memory, sustained and constantly reinforced by events, by our watchful waiting, and by our hopeful suspension of final judgment as to the meaning of our grievances. . . . [M]ost Negroes recognize themselves as themselves despite what others might believe them to be. Thus, although the sociologists tell us that thousands of light-skinned Negroes become white each year undetected, most Negroes can spot a paper-thin "white Negro" every time simply because those who masquerade missed what others were forced to pick up along the way: discipline—a discipline which these heavy thinkers would not undergo even if guaranteed that combined with their own heritage it would make of them the freest of spirits, the wisest of men and the most sublime of heroes. (*Collected* 171)

If Ellison's language seems unusually heated, one must remember that he is defending his own identification with other Negroes against Howe's charges of betrayal; nonetheless, his disdain here for those who pass is striking. So is his implied understanding that only a Negro knows what it means to be a Negro. Ellison clearly rejects Howe's claim (and Norman Mailer's too, given his reference to Mailer's "The White Negro") to be able to speak from the perspective of a Negro, even if Howe calls on Richard Wright as a witness. Here Ellison's remarks recall Coleman's brother's rejection of Coleman's stance.

In *The Human Stain,* Coleman's sister, Ernestine, spells out to Zuckerman what Coleman missed while living behind his "lily-white face." Her argument, one consistent with Ellison's remarks above, is that Coleman in effect missed enjoying the transformations of the Civil Rights movement because he could not "come out" without risking the life he had created. One suspects that Ernestine's perspective would be shared by Ellison as well, though he might point out that it was arguably the "discipline" that Coleman learned as a black person that enabled him to accomplish the extraordinary feat of self-control represented by his passing. One can likewise easily imagine Ellison reading Roth's novel as he did Howe's essay: as a misguided appropriation of Ellison's aesthetic achievement and his black identity. Possibly, Ellison would point out that Roth's arch-individualist is answering the creator's own personal aesthetic and cultural desire more than he is making an authentic response to African American history and culture. Ernestine tacitly presents this view, though her role is also to allow Roth to straddle both sides of the identity fence.

In reading Coleman as an evocation of Ellison's predicament, one inevitably misses the pride that Ellison continued to take in being a Negro. Roth's choice to make Coleman a boxer recalls Ellison's interest in boxing and especially in Jack Johnson, a figure who recurs often in his letters and in his second novel. In a 1956 letter to Albert Murray, Ellison fashions himself as the Jack Johnson of black intellectuals:

> So just as with writing I learned from Joe [Louis] and Sugar Ray [Robinson] (though that old dancing master, wit, and bull-balled stud, Jack Johnson is really *my* mentor, because he knew if you operated with skill and style you could rise above all that-being-a-credit-to-your-race-crap because he was a credit to the human race and because if he could make that much body and bone move with such precision to his command all other men had a chance to beat the laws of probability and anything else that stuck up its head . . .) here I'll also learn from your latest master legal strategists, the N.A.A.C.P. legal boys, because if those studs can dry-run

the Supreme Court of the U.S. and (leave it to some moses to pull that one) I dam [*sic*] sure can run skull practice on the critics. (*Trading* 132)

Whether Roth saw this letter matters less than that it underscores how distant Ellison-the-boxer is from the refined, integrationist Ellison one encounters in American, and African American, literary history. This Ellison recalls the one whom Spillers met in 1969 but who somehow remained invisible (except to Mr. Claghorn). Here Ellison identifies Jack Johnson—who got into trouble for flamboyantly dating white women—as "a credit to the human race" rather than simply to his own race, but the context in which he makes this remark complicates the universalist language in his published essays.

Throughout his letters to Murray, Ellison speaks in the African American vernacular—from one "Mose" to another. With Murray he is addressing someone who speaks "the idiom," the special language of African Americans that Coleman does not practice, and thus someone with whom he shares a special culture and language. Connecting his writing to the Civil Rights movement, Ellison conceives his stance as a black intellectual as defiantly oppositional. Making body and bone move: this is what Ellison in his literate, polished interviews and speeches meant to do. At times his response to his audiences was to want to make them over, and he wanted to knock them out with the irrefutable knowledge he had to bring: that whatever else the white American is, he or she is essentially black. They are black not because they share the intimate history Ellison shares with Murray since that history cannot be shared outside the group, nor are they black even because all Americans share the legacy of slavery. Rather, they are black because their story—the American story—can be reinvented and reclaimed by Ralph Ellison in *Invisible Man*. This is, I think, the message of *Invisible Man*, and it is the one to which Roth, Ellison's true heir, responded in his own work and especially in *The Human Stain*.

As Ellison fell out of favor with other African American intellectuals, he may have sometimes felt as if he were passing—not as a white man but as a Negro. A poignant 1959 letter to Murray describes how Ellison once found himself as a type of spy during an NAACP convention.

I went down to look at the delegates to the N.A.A.C.P. convention yesterday and I must say the mixture is as before—Only now the clothes are more expensive and there are more young people around. I don't know what I was doing exactly, but it was quite meaningful to simply stand there in the lobby and feel them moving and talking around me. Hell, I know what we want, I just like to hear the idiom. Fifteen minutes in a meeting with some of those studs and I'd want to start a fight, but just seeing them walk and pose and talk and flirt and woof—that's damn pleasant. (*Trading* 209)

Invisible to his peers, Ellison soaks up the idiom, reveling in the nuances of black speech and culture in an environment where being black matters more than being American, even if the speakers are meeting in order to more fully express themselves as Americans. Ellison does not need or want to hear their arguments; likely he would only want to argue with them, as he often did with black intellectuals not named Wright or Murray. Nonetheless, he conveys to his friend the evanescence of the language he goes there to hear, the fragile sense of a culture that is disappearing, and Ellison the unseen poet with it. He hears in their voices and language, sees in their gestures and style, a shared cultural creation that may even matter more than the "rights" they gather to fight for, since those freedoms, if achieved, will speed the disappearance of the idiom that Ellison here celebrates.

Unlike Coleman, Ellison clearly suffered from his sense that his style of "being Negro" was becoming invisible. Compare the NAACP letter, which depicts Ellison as invisible but at home, with one written the following year, which reveals Ellison to be hopelessly exiled among the white Americans he has chosen to educate. In this 1960 letter he tells Murray of a typical evening at Bard College, where he was then employed as a professor. "On Wednesday nights after I've taught all day, I sometimes go to a local bar to eat and have a few drinks and there I dance from time to time with the students. Once in a while it works up to a mild swing—jukebox—but man, it's a sad substitute for the real thing and a real whiff of downhome funk would explode the joint" (*Trading* 226). Again, Roth does not give Coleman such ambivalent feelings. The account movingly depicts Ellison lost from his group, separated from the cultural stream that allowed him to write *Invisible Man* in the first place. He tells Murray that as a kind of parting tribute for the class he had taught, his white students at Bard wrote on the blackboard "*YOU WERE RIGHT ABOUT THE DAMNED CIVIL WAR!*" (*Trading* 205). For Coleman, Homer's Trojan War, the great epic of rage, defined his identity. For Ellison, the Civil War defined not only Ellison but all Americans. Who knows, though, how affected his students were by his argument and at what cost Ellison taught them that lesson? And who knows too whether Ellison's second novel was itself an explosion of "downhome funk" directed at the U.S. Senate and the political body it represents?

Ellison's Secret

If Ellison had a "secret," it was the novel that he continued to write all his life while choosing to publish only a handful of selections from it. Roth's novel acknowledges this—it even pretends to write Coleman's story as if it were a sequel to *Invisible Man*. I doubt, though, that Roth knew the ways in which Coleman's story reflects upon the book Ellison did not quite finish, even if the mystery of Coleman's life tacitly alludes to the second novel's mysterious disappearance. Henry Louis Gates Jr. speculates that Anatole Broyard never wrote the novel whose promised appearance even Norman Mailer was said to fear, because he could not let go of his secret identity as a black man ("Passing" 188). And there is a sense in which this may be true of Ellison as well. Harold Bloom attributes Ellison's long silence as a novelist less to an "inability to finish a second novel that would meet his own high standards" than to "social pressures that could have been relieved only if he had abandoned his own very individual stance" (*Genius* 809). Bloom may be right. During the years that Ellison was defending his status as an American, he was working on a novel that was largely a celebration of black American culture unavailable to white Americans and, indeed, one that celebrated and sought to capture in literary form the virtually untranslatable cadences and rhythms of the vernacular black American life he knew. Ellison's "secret" novel was also about the "secret" experiences of blacks (as had been *Invisible Man*). Even if the existence of this novel was no secret, the fact that it espoused the point of view of a pre-integration Negro identity in order to comment on then contemporary American society (and the attempt by Southern senators to undo *Brown v. Board of Education*) would have surprised admirers of *Invisible Man*. Ellison's novel was a secret not in the sense that no one knew about it but rather in that its fictional premise about a separate Negro life put it at odds with his integrationist persona.[9] It depicts the pain of a "separate but equal society" but also portrays the security of keeping with your own kind if the others—the outsiders—will just leave you alone.

Like *Invisible Man*, *Three Days before the Shooting* was rooted in an epic expression of specifically African American experience, or what the author called "our kind of time" (323). At one point, Hickman, the novel's hero and central consciousness, thinks that "in spite of all the confusion it caused back in those bus-riding days our knowing exactly where the color lines were drawn made for a sense of security. We were young and adventurous, and having elected to perform in a land a-whirl with hostility there was nothing to do but to deal with the world as we found it. No need for anyone to tell us the rules or reasons, because there were always those FOR WHITES ONLY signs, their facial expressions, attitudes and quick-trigger violence. . . . So with our manhood challenged on all sides we blazed our own trails, musical, moral and social, and used our outlaw music as our sword and shield" (570). From within segregation came a vibrant, affirmative culture—in its way more sustaining than any "American" culture one might ascribe to white Americans as a whole.

"How do we know who we are, Daddy Hickman?" asks the "white" child Bliss at one point. Hickman's answer is, I think, Ellison's as well: "We know where we are by the way we walk. We know where we are by the way we talk. We know where we are by the way we sing. We know where we are by the way we dance. We know where we are by the way we praise the Lord on high. We know who we are because we hear a different tune in our minds and in our hearts. We know who we are because when we make the beat of our rhythm to shape our day the whole land says amen!" (*Three* 323). Such moments of ecstatic communal self-recognition occur frequently through-out the second novel. In terms of communal affirmation, Ellison wrote nothing in *Invisible Man* that surpasses these sections. I would say they are unsurpassed in African American literature. Well before Toni Mor-rison's *Beloved* (1987), Ellison was, in private, portraying a version of a black "Sweet Home" but without the stigma of slavery. The second novel is an ex-traordinary tribute to an idealized pre–Civil Rights movement that African American identity created out of the shared experience of slavery.

Some of this comes through in *Juneteenth*, but reading the whole manu-script enriches the experience immeasurably and complicates the enigma of Ralph Ellison considerably. In *Three Days*, Books I and II take place in Washington, D.C., which was, according to Ellison's notes, supposed to represent to Hickman "a place of power and mystery" containing "the past" but is "a continuation of the betrayal of Reconstruction" (973). The action of nearly half the pages of *Three Days*, though, occurs in Georgia and Oklahoma and consists of Hickman's journeys in search of Bliss and Severen, Bliss's son. Despite his efforts, Hickman never reaches the center of Washington or the power it represents, and thus the focus of the novel becomes the black sensibility of the pre-*Brown* era, cast somewhere beyond the channels of "official" power. Projected by Ellison to begin in "April 1953," the second novel was to delineate the moment before the cataclysmic change that was about to occur—rather like Robert Musil's unfinished *The Man without Qualities* (1930, 1942), which portrays the Austro-Hungarian empire on the eve of its destruction by World War I (*Three* 972). The book's "action takes place on the eve of the Rights movement," Ellison notes, "but it forecasts the chaos that would come later" (973).

The assassination of Bliss anticipates the Civil Rights movement, just as Hickman and his church members anticipate King and his marchers. But the atmosphere in which the novel is steeped was fading into the past as quickly as the gains of the Civil Rights movement were happening. In this sense the novel is less about plot than it is about a historical condition, and the book's drama lies in its expression. Through characters such as LeeWillie Minifees, who flamboyantly burns his Cadillac as a rite of bitter self-consumption, or Jesse Rockwater, who stages his own death to commemorate the end of his belief that Lincoln's death can be redeemed by American history, Ellison portrays, as he puts it, "a collapse of the walls which kept despair in bounds" (977). Wandering its vast landscape with Hickman as a companion, the reader palpably experiences the twinned sense of joy and loss that animates Ellison's writing, writing that for the most part he refused to share with anyone. He seems to have begun the novel out of despair that America would ever recognize blacks as "equal." Then, with history's sudden boomerang into "equality" for blacks, the book may have seemed to Ellison to be out of time with the times. Certainly it contradicts the optimism of *Invisible Man*'s concluding gesture and points to an Ellison "angrier" than the one who has been canonized as the optimistic integrationist.

The pivotal exchanges between "Daddy" Hickman and his adopted son, Bliss, which make up *Juneteenth* (what Ellison called book II) carry the poignancy of love scenes precisely because there cannot be betrayal or loss without first a feeling of intimacy. In these scenes, Hickman and Bliss recall a sense of shared identity that is both affirmative and secret, known only to those who have been initiated into its practices. Hickman is at Bliss's bedside because he had hoped (but failed because a racist social structure would not let him do it) to save Bliss from murder by his own son. As Bliss lay dying, the reader may wish that Hickman's presence would redeem his spiteful life: a death-bed resurrection for the racist "white" American. Such redemption seems possible when Bliss recalls having participated in the ceremony that celebrated Juneteenth. In those moments he and Hickman are carried "back to a bunch of old-fashioned Negroes celebrating an illusion of emancipation, and getting it mixed up with the Resurrection" (*Three* 314). Through their resurrection of the Juneteenth ceremony, Bliss and Hickman recreate and reenact the history of becoming and being African American.

Their shared rite, with Bliss on his death bed, is one of celebration and utter freedom.

For this moment, Bliss is no longer the racist "white" Senator Adam Sunraider but the "black" boy preacher that Hickman raised. In the hospital room the conversation takes the form of a classic call-and-response as they relive the glorious past (secret from the knowledge of whites). Yet their interaction is grounded in something more than speech: they find themselves "moving beyond words back to the undifferentiated cry," back to a time when there was no division among African Americans (314). In this episode, Ellison recreates this "undifferentiated cry" as a mysterious form of knowing that depends on an intense communal solidarity, a type of in-group expression not found in *Invisible Man* or in Ellison's public speeches. Though the second novel is not dressed in the raiment of the 1960s, it says that "black is beautiful" and arguably would have been acceptable within the context of the Black Arts movement.

If Ellison's essays speak to a moment when whites can embrace their shared heritage with blacks and blacks can be less skeptical concerning their interactions with whites, his second novel could not quite imagine such a union in the present of its narrative. The character Love New expresses what I take to be Ellison's ideal when he says that Americans must work to get beyond color "because if you accept the fact that you are neither black nor white, Gentile nor Jew, Rebel-bred nor Yankee-born, you have the freedom to be *truly* free" (*Three* 850). In the novel, however, the emblem of this freedom is Bliss (and perhaps Severen), the character who emerges from *Invisible Man*'s Rinehart. Bliss, despite Hickman's heroic interventions, is a lost cause. Hickman's parishioners try to tell him "what Hickman knows deep within his own mind but refuses to acknowledge: that the Senator is past saving, and the group knows this" (976). In the context of *Brown*, with "equality" winning the day in the courtrooms, in Congress, and on television sets, Ellison probably did not care to compromise the forward view of *Invisible Man* by publishing a novel that looked backward. As an artist and a spokesman, he refused nostalgia, and his estrangement from African American literature after *Invisible Man* was not simply a matter of jealousy that other black writers were getting attention. Rather, as a black artist and intellectual living through the Civil Rights era, he rejected the point of view that celebrated the past at the expense of the present.[10] Yet perhaps no other African American writer was so gifted in terms of talent, experience, and knowledge—to render the fading black past in fictional form. *Three Days* suggests how easily Ellison might have written something like Morrison's

Song of Solomon (1977), which looks back to a romanticized black past while invoking through the Seven Days black political anger and its frustration. Just as he chose not to write the kind of self-aggrandizing novels of cultural alienation that made Roth a major American author, however, so did he refuse "the look backwards" to the kind of vanished black community that Morrison invoked so effectively in *Song of Solomon, Beloved*, and *Jazz* (1992).

Ellison stranded himself from African American literature at the very moment that white and black readers were becoming interested in fictional-ized accounts of a romanticized black past. In an alternative literary history, his second novel might have become a cornerstone of post–*Invisible Man* African American literature. Instead of consigning himself to the "African American" shelves at the bookstore, though, Ellison held to the notion of himself as an American writer, and to *Invisible Man* as his definitive expression of that ambition. Thus as contemporary "African American" literature increasingly looked backward in time (though not as Proust did) to the Jim Crow era to define its aesthetic, Ellison was questioning the authenticity of any aesthetic or cultural point of view that was not "mixed" or "integrated." *The Human Stain* questions the "authenticity" of identity and in that respect is an affirmation of Ellison's post-*Brown* legacy. Yet if one considers Cole-man Silk as a meditation on Ellison, and one further reflects that Coleman is the failed author of a book that Zuckerman in a sense writes for him, how ironic to realize that the real Ellison, the supposed failed author of a never finished second novel, was in fact writing and not publishing a magnificent novel about the "uniqueness" of black American culture.

Moreover, Ellison's second novel is, arguably, more politically angry than any other well-known post–*Invisible Man* black novel. *Song of Solomon*—one of the strongest African American novels after *Invisible Man*—portrays blacks killing whites in return for whites killing blacks, but it ends with its protagonist, Milkman, dreaming of flight out of America and a return to Africa. The ending implies no solution to the "problem" of being black and perhaps even a wish for the abolition of African American identity—an interpretation that is reinforced by the fact that Milkman seems to be dying at the hands of a black friend he once saw as a brother. Ellison's unpublished novel, however, acknowledges, although with bitter irony, the cultural con-nectedness of all Americans at the same time as it celebrates the distinctive ingenuity of black culture. Through Bliss, it both suggests that this culture is available to all who would enter it and that whites, when the chips are down, will betray blacks for social advancement. At the center of the novel is not the murder of anonymous white persons by anonymous black persons, as in *Song of Solomon*, but the assassination of a "white" U.S. senator by an angry "black" son.

Perhaps Ellison would have been content to publish a book that "merely" dramatized "the way we walk" and "the way we talk" could he have figured out what to do with the "betrayal" at the center of the novel. "Bliss," Hickman at one point asks the unconscious senator, "how after knowing such times as those you could take off for where you went is too much for me to truly understand.... I mean the *communion*, the coming together" (*Three* 325). In his notes to himself about the novel, Ellison says that Hickman is "bringing up the child as a bridge between the old savage relationship which obtained between the races and his vision of a more human society" (973). But the bridge cannot hold; it seems to be the one Ellison could not cross. Thus, he notes that "Sunraider is not killed because he abandoned Severen's mother, nor because of his overt political acts, but because he betrayed his past and thus provided Severen the deepest intellectual-emotional motives for the murder" (976). Betraying the past is a political act, though, especially if one is a senator. Killing the Senator is also a political act, since the Senator's betrayal symbolizes white America's relationship to black Americans. This act is far more incendiary than Bigger's accidental murder and then desperate burning of the white girl in Wright's *Native Son*, and beyond what Morrison's *Song of Solomon* imagines as well.

In 1982 Ellison told John Hersey, somewhat cryptically, that the Kennedy assassination upset his progress on the novel, which also contained an assassination, because this coincidence caused him to worry that history was usurping his fiction ("Speaking" 290). Kennedy's murder began a season of 1960s assassinations. In light of the publication of *Three Days*, Ellison's remark indicates his recognition that the assassination in his novel carried potential meanings he was not sure he wanted to allow. Published during the 1960s, the book might have been read as a call to "alienated" blacks to murder white leaders. Until President Lyndon Johnson aligned himself with King, most white politicians could have been interpreted to be versions of Sunraider—by their actions if not by their origins. After Johnson ratified the Civil Rights movement with the Civil Rights Act and the Voting Rights Act, blacks had gained in a decade more than they had lost in the hundred years since the Civil War. Ellison wanted to weigh in on the side of progress. Nonetheless, his notes to the novel also suggest that he viewed the assassination as essential to the story he was trying to tell—to his aesthetic purpose. "Severen," Ellison tells himself, "remains the problem. Is the assassin to be left out of it? Impossible. It is he who puts the whole idea to crucial testing" (*Three* 976).

Then again, Bliss's presumed death can read another way. Perhaps Hickman's final intervention redeems Bliss. On this reading, their last communion together would return Bliss to the fold. His death would enact the sacrifice required to bring forth the transformed America that Ellison argued for in his essays. Whatever the case, Ellison did not portray Bliss's final moments. The conflict between black communal affirmation that Hickman embodies and the communal rage and despair the Severen enacts is never reconciled. Because he was writing a novel and not a history or even a prophecy, Ellison need not have solved the contradiction at the heart of the book. For him, though, politics, history, and aesthetic vision were inextricably linked. *Invisible Man* could be read as a bitter indictment of American history and contemporary American politics, but it did conclude with a gesture of hope. The second novel, arguably, underscores the "bitter" historical context of *Invisible Man*, but it has no gesture of hope that is not betrayed. As discussed in chapter 3, the novel's only white heroic figure is the martyred Lincoln, whose shadow covers all of the book's episodes as the white American willing to die for black progress. Perhaps at times Ellison envisioned Bliss as a tragic echo of Lincoln's role, but the book as he wrote it has Bliss betray the meaning of Lincoln's death. Or he could have left the ending open, as he did with *Invisible Man*—let history decide—but instead, he kept writing the book, revising the same scenes over and over and never composing the very few "transitions" that would have been made the novel more obviously complete. According to the editors, at the end of his life he returned to the earliest drafts of the novel and was revising them so that Hickman, not McIntyre (the white narrator of Book I), was more involved in the Georgia and Oklahoma sections. The editors suggest that this work proves Ellison's intent to publish the novel, but one can also argue that by that time in his life the book had become a refuge, a secret place to dwell that was close to the home he knew before he left Oklahoma and before he made his name and became known as the black intellectual who fell out of favor with his group. In the second novel, the only black who is separate from his group is Bliss, and he may have been white anyway.

John S. Wright compares the writing of Ellison's second novel to the process by which "creative musicians" "conjured up from the deep well of their semiconscious imaginings" and then "worked backwards" to create their aesthetic productions (236). Wright's "gestalt" reading of Ellison's creative process suggests that writing for him was something he practiced every day just as a musician stays sharp by playing his instrument regularly. The implication is that after *Invisible Man*, Ellison wrote fiction for himself. His friends, including John Wright, indicate that Ellison enjoyed reading aloud from his unfinished novel to very appreciative audiences. One can well imagine many of the sections of the second novel being performed aloud. But Ellison did not share his book with strangers. Consequently, his writing career became a mystery: he was the novelist who no longer published novels, the expert of American identity who remained avowedly Negro. In retrospect, it seems that Ellison was always holding something back. The posthumous *Three Days* testifies to his tendency to withhold, and one can only hope that his "secret" will finally be released to history so that his work may be more fully known and his reputation less misunderstood.

Dancing

Roth's Coleman Silk dies misunderstood by his own community but also with dignity, since his death occurs while he is living on his own terms. Whether Coleman is murdered by Les Farley or that murder is Zucker-man's invention (there is no way to know) matters less than Zuckerman's speculation that with Faunia, Coleman has at last been able to be fully himself. He need not complete *Spooks* because of the physical and spiri-tual consanguinity he enjoys with Faunia, a version of Steena who accepts him as he is. Zuckerman imagines that Faunia knows Coleman's secret and loves him anyway. Having shared his secret, Coleman dies as one who owns rather than denies his history. Where Ernestine sees Coleman as a victim of racial history, Faunia sees him as cursed simply because of his humanity: what marks him is not his hidden blackness but the universal burden of his "human stain." Zuckerman says that Coleman's suffering has "nothing to do with grace or salvation or redemption. It's in everyone. Indwelling. Inherent. Defining. The stain that is there before its mark" (*Human* 242). The moral here transcends race, yet Coleman is distinctive: the song he sings, so true to his own situation, is distinct from the song of the group and therefore like no other. Letting Coleman live and die on his own terms can be read as Roth's way of saying to Ellison that your way was, after all, magnificent and I could not imagine my work without you.

In the mid-1970s, when only Ellison knew whether he truly intended to publish another novel, he was frustrated that *Invisible Man* had initiated a tradition seemingly without heirs. Speaking at a 1973 Harvard conference held in memory of Alain Locke, Ellison voiced his disappointment with the current era of American writing: "I had hoped that by the 1960s people like you would be telling me who I am, and maybe you tell me sometimes, but what I have found is that during the decade these strains of continuity, these linkages between people on the basis of ideas and experience were automatically, arbitrarily thrown overboard. That is disastrous for writers; it is disastrous for any sort of human enterprise because we live one upon the other" (*Collected* 446). Roth's attempt to integrate his story with Ellison's story can be seen as an affirmation of the cosmopolitan-pluralist ideal each defended that night at Yeshiva nearly forty years earlier and again at Harvard in 1973. Roth told Stanley Crouch that readers would avoid discussing what Roth took to be the book's central achievement: "crossing over the ethnic fence" (Pinsker 472). It is not simply "crossing over the ethnic fence," however, that makes the book Ellisonian but the integration of "black-Jewish" perspectives into an American one.

When Ernestine instructs Zuckerman, the James Joyce of Newark, about prominent African Americans in the history of his city, or chides him for his ignorance of African American history, she sounds suspiciously like Ralph Ellison. She prompts Zuckerman to revise his view of his own cultural history. The black neighborhoods of Newark, which so repulsed Zuckerman in *The Anatomy Lesson* (1983) and seemed to him to mark the annihilation of his own being, become again through Ernestine's intervention a place where Zuckerman is welcome. Coleman cannot go home, but Zuckerman can. The novel ends with Zuckerman on his way to Newark to join the Silk's in their Sunday family gathering. He comes as a symbolic member of the family, a friend of Coleman and a version of the Jew that Coleman became. Zuckerman is not black and Ernestine is not Jewish, but through Coleman they share a common history. Their friendship fulfills the hope of Ellison's novel—his recognition that on the lower frequencies, Coleman's sense of self and Zuckerman's sense of self come together as fellow Americans.

On this reading, Zuckerman (and, by implication, Roth) becomes the one who completes the reader's gesture that Ellison's narrator had called for at the end of *Invisible Man*. To the extent that Roth cannot fully tell Ellison's story, or that he tells Ellison's story by making him into an imaginary Jew, we can say that Roth uses Ellison to explore his own Jewish identity and thus enacts the cosmopolitan ideal that characterizes both writers' work. One of the book's indelible moments occurs when Coleman and Zuckerman hold one another while dancing to the 1940s swing that Ellison and Roth both loved. In this scene, it seems to me that Roth reaches out to the memory of the artist who inspired his own career: "On we danced. There was nothing overty carnal in it, but because Coleman was wearing only his denim shorts and my hand rested easily on his warm back . . . it wasn't entirely a mocking act. There was a semi-serious sincerity in his guiding me about the stone floor, not to mention a thoughtless delight in just being alive, accidentally and clownishly and for no reason alive—the kind of delight you take as a child when you first learn to play a tune with a comb and toilet paper" (*Human* 26).

Two old men dancing, the follower and the leader, sharing a song that neither can end.

2

Richard Wright's Apprentice

It is not for me to judge Wright's courage, but I must ask just why it was possible for me to write as I write "only" because Wright released his anger. Can't I be allowed to release my own?

RALPH ELLISON to Irving Howe (1964)

After reading your history—I knew it all already, all in my blood, bones flesh, deepest memories, and thoughts; those which are sacred and those which bring the bitterest agonies and most poignant memories and regrets. Part of my life, Dick, has been a lacerating experience and I have my share of bitterness. But I have learned to keep the bitterness submerged so that my vision might be kept clear; so that those passions which would so easily be criminal might be socially useful. I know those emotions which tear the insides to be free and memories which must be kept underground, caged by rigid discipline lest they destroy . . .

RALPH ELLISON to Richard Wright,
upon reading *12 Million Black Voices* (1941)

RALPH ELLISON did not write *Invisible Man* because he wanted to be the first black writer in the American literary canon. He already understood writers such as Frederick Douglass, W. E. B. Du Bois, and Langston Hughes to be important American writers. Ellison did not write *Invisible Man* because he wanted to "transcend" his blackness by becoming the toast of the white literary world. He knew himself to be a Negro, and he would not surrender that identity to join any club. Ellison wrote *Invisible Man* for two obvious reasons and one essential one. He wrote to express a view of American life as rendered by a sensitive, intelligent *black* narrative consciousness, and he wrote to test his skill as a novelist against other great novelists. The other reason for writing was deeper than the two just mentioned can suggest. He wrote because Richard Wright had written.

A remarkable letter of February 1, 1948, from Ellison to Wright (RWEP LC) articulates Ellison's ambitions for *Invisible Man* and hints at his relationship with Wright's work. Beginning his own critical reception history as a novelist, the letter summarizes some responses to his recently published Battle Royal chapter: "I'm getting some of the same reactions produced by *Native Son*," he declares. He tells Wright that Roi Ottley is "dismissing me as simply 'a disciple of Dick Wright's'—which doesn't bother me, feeling as I do about your work." He mentions William Attaway's joke that once Ellison had finished his novel, other black novelists were going to have to find a different line of work. Despite the "undertone of reservation" he hears, Ellison intends to pursue his own vision. "You would think that by now they would have learned that no one but themselves can write their stories," he marvels, "and that writing is not a game of competition—unless with the great writers who came before us—and certainly I'm not interested in writing *better* than anyone, only in writing as well as *I* can with my own talent and my own intelligence." Ellison then defines the task of the novelist committed to a political vision of art: "If a writer is serious about his politics and its relationship to man, then he should at least attempt to master the ideas (artistic, technical, philosophical, metaphysical, etc.) which that political position embodies. . . . [F]or the work of the novelist only begins here, his task is that of giving shape to the *implicit* which radiate about any philosophical position."

Through the concept of "invisibility," Ellison would "radiate" the political and philosophical implications of being black in America and in the process transform the history of American literature. Although he is careful not to criticize the person he addresses, Ellison is subtly staking out a territory not yet explored by any American author, black or white—though his notion that art that "radiates" diverse intellectual areas recalls the prefaces of Henry James that he and Wright had discussed together. His assertion—years before *Invisible Man* was published—that his work was attracting the same reaction as *Native Son*, however, may jar some Ellison readers. Despite Ottley's sense that Ellison was a Wright disciple, literary history for the most part has defined Ellison and Wright as writers with opposing visions. Wright is the "angry" black writer who portrays the squalid circumstances of black life; Ellison is the "optimistic" black writer who portrays the ingenuity of blacks and the potential for "transcending" social inequality. Irving Howe—with considerable help from Ellison—canonized this point of view, but Howe was wrong—and so was Ellison to accentuate Howe's critical error.

In fact, Wright and Ellison, though different kinds of writers, were very close, and the manner in which they have been opposed has been one of the great misconceptions—perhaps I should say prejudices—of American literary history. Wright and Ellison came together like brothers and, in ways that are as important as they are difficult to specify, decisively influenced each other's work.[1] Wright commissioned Ellison's first piece of writing; Ellison was one of Wright's first readers for *Native Son* (1940), *12 Million Black Voices* (1941), and *Black Boy* (1945). As a black writer, Ellison understood politics and art as one, and he made this discovery through Wright. Ellison's apprentice efforts—essays and stories—were written with Wright as his intended reader. During the seven years that Ellison was writing *Invisible Man*, Wright was continually asking him "Are you finished yet?" When Wright wrote to praise *Invisible Man* because with it Ellison had entered the ranks of literature, Ellison may have felt that his fifteen-year apprenticeship as a novelist was finally over. He had begun publishing about Wright in 1941, and the last book published in his lifetime contained an essay on Wright. He apparently never stopped thinking of Wright as the single person to whom he owed his career. It may be more than a coincidence that Ellison never published another novel after Wright's death in 1961.

Ellison's 1948 letter is perhaps the earliest account we have of his coming to terms with his own literary reputation, and this reaction is mediated through his relationship with Wright. Ellison knew before he published his novel that for many readers his work would be linked to Wright's, and with good reason. In this same letter where he notes initial reactions to his book, Ellison suggests that Chester Himes's work is undeveloped because Himes has insufficiently learned from Wright's example. If Himes were "not such a mixed up guy," Ellison says, "he could have taken your *Atlantic* pieces along with *Black Boy* and learned enough to have written a compellingly serious novel." A few lines later he states that Himes's criticisms of Wright are "missing completely the self-struggle with which you earned the right to publish those pieces." Wright's self-struggle was not something Ellison missed; that struggle and the writing Wright produced provided essential building blocks for Ellison's own achievement. In later years Ellison would point out that he had many literary ancestors other than Wright, but he also would say that Wright incited him to become a writer and thus to create the kinships with Faulkner, James, Twain, Melville, Eliot, Joyce, Malraux, and everyone else out of whom he made himself into the writer he became.

Ellison met Wright through the agency of Langston Hughes. When Ellison arrived in New York in 1936, he had told Hughes that he admired Wright's poetry. Hughes wrote Wright, who was in Chicago, about Ellison, and Wright sent Ellison a postcard that read, "Langston Hughes tells me that you're interested in meeting me" (Rampersad 96). Soon thereafter, Wright came to New York, and the two became fast friends, spending time together at the offices of the *Daily Worker*, where Wright served as the chief reporter on black issues. In so many ways, their meeting seems fated. Six weeks before first encountering Ellison, Wright had drafted his manifesto "A Blueprint for Negro Writing" as if he were summoning the future author of *Invisible Man* to emerge from the obscurity where he had been waiting. In that essay, Wright had insisted that black writers were "being called upon to furnish moral sanctions for action, to give a meaning to blighted lives, and to supply motives for mass millions of people" (Webb 144). These sentiments characterized Wright's thinking about his own work, and they would be a blueprint for Ellison's initiation into being a "Negro writer." Ellison was attracted to Wright's call for a nationalist black literature and to his insistence that this new literature should have political consequences. In that same essay, Wright said that black writers "must accept a concept of nationalism" because they were "being called upon to do no less than create values by which their race [was] to struggle, live and die" (Webb 144). In *Invisible Man* Ellison's invisible narrator would put a Joycean twist to this sentiment in the passage where "creating the uncreated conscience of his race" requires "creating *the uncreated features of his face*" (*Invisible* 347), but the inspiration for that passage came from Wright and the powerful initial impression that Wright had made on Ellison.

Within a year of meeting Wright, Ellison would attend Kenneth Burke's lecture "The Rhetoric of Hitler's Battle," in which Burke interpreted *Mein Kampf* in terms of the political acts it implied and thereby predicted the historical nightmare that was on the verge of being enacted.[2] As a reader of Emerson, Ellison understood the claim in "The Poet" that "we are symbols, and inhabit symbols; workman, work and tools, words and things, birth and death, are all emblems" (456). That is, symbols, or words, always enact specific types of action. Through the example of Wright, Ellison saw first-hand one who was practicing the implications of the Emersonian-Burkean belief that the careful arrangement of words could have an impact on the world beyond the text. Before meeting Wright, Ellison had not considered becoming a writer, but through Wright's influence he realized that his ambition to make a difference as a Negro in American society could be served by writing.

What matters most about Ellison and Wright is not that their artistic sensibilities were different—that is true of almost all distinctive writers—but that as Negro American writers they started from the same place and shared the same premises. Constance Webb details how, according to Wright, Ellison was "terribly curious about art, the meaning of experience, and Negro experience especially" (145). Wright, recognizing that Ellison's yearning for art was inextricable from his yearning to represent black experience, suggested that he try his hand at writing and, according to Webb, approved of Ellison's initial efforts. A one point, though, he thought something Ellison was writing was too similar to his own work. "Ralph," Wright said, "this is my story, my style. You have copied my ideas, my words, and my structure! You must find your own symbols—you must tap the content of your own unconscious and use it! You must dig it out of yourself and not duplicate someone else!" (146).

This story captures with the power of myth Ellison's origins as a writer: his career begins under Wright's instruction; his letters to Wright are reports on his progress; his stunning success with *Invisible Man* confirms Wright's instruction. As a student of music and sculpture, Ellison had already been trained to learn as an apprentice to the appropriate master. According to Webb, Wright's outburst was provoked because Ellison had said to him, "You are the master—I want to know if it is any good" (146). Wright may have been dismayed and even frightened by his apprentice's obvious gifts. Ellison, though, accepted Wright's criticism as perfectly valid, and his career took shape in response to these lessons. The remarks above concerning Himes's misuse of Wright indicate that Ellison took it for granted that Wright's example was powerful and worth absorbing as part of the process of becoming his own writer. Yet Ellison's conception of himself as a writer never eradicated Wright's influence. Well after *Invisible Man,* he was writing essays in which he defined his work through Wright's example, and although he did make himself into a truly original writer, he never quit reflecting upon Wright's example and advice.[3]

In one of the most insightful essays ever written on Ellison, Larry Neal encapsulates the distinctions that later readers would discern between Wright's work and Ellison's work. Neal identifies the "definite sense of cultural nationalism" inflected in Ellison's early, Marxist-tinged essays for *New Masses* and in his work as an editor for *Negro Quarterly*. Neal further suggests that those in the 1960s and '70s seeking to articulate "a black aesthetic" should look to Ellison, rather than castigate him, since "if anyone has been concerned with a 'black aesthetic' it has certainly got to be Ralph Ellison" (46). John S. Wright suggests that Neal is making the case that it was Ellison, rather than Richard Wright, who enacted the logic of Wright's "Blueprint for Negro Writing" and thus provided the cultural-aesthetic model that literary radicals of the 1960s should have followed (19–21). From this perspective, Ellison was perhaps the first to recognize the political possibilities embedded in black cultural styles. Accordingly, his work stressed an aesthetic of black endurance and transcendence against Wright's aesthetic of psychological depression and cultural anomie. Neal does not say so, but by this logic Ellison's aesthetic better explains the success of the Civil Rights movement than Wright's fiction does.

In his 1948 response to being linked to Wright, Ellison betrays none of the frustration that he exhibits in 1963 when Irving Howe compares his work to Wright's. Ellison responded to Howe with perhaps his best known and most discussed essay, "The World and the Jug" (*Shadow*). Howe set Ellison off because he compared the two of them as *black* writers and he suggested that between the two, Wright was the more authentic "black" writer. In making this claim, Howe also in effect said that there existed aesthetic choices not available to black writers, since their sense of political urgency as blacks should overwhelm their desire as artists to convey ambiguity or complexity. For Ellison (and Wright too), one may be black before one becomes a writer, and being black may even be a part of what motivates one to write, but once one becomes a writer, being black is not a legitimate aesthetic criterion. Ellison dismissed Howe's argument because it depended on an impoverished sense of literature. Moreover, he objected to Howe's comparison of his work with Wright's by the same logic that he had earlier dismissed Ottleys' comparison. In that letter, Ellison had suggested that Himes's work suffered both because he was a poor reader of Wright and because Himes had failed to incorporate the influence of other writers (André Malraux, Arthur Koestler, and Ignacio Silone) who had been expanding the possibilities of the type of novel Himes was writing. Thus, just as Ellison told Wright in 1948 that he was in competition only with "the greats who came before us," he told Howe in 1963 that his work must be judged as an aesthetic achievement not bound by the color of the writer, rather than as a sociological treatise about blackness.

Ellison also tacitly criticizes Howe's simplification of Wright's work, but readers have taken Ellison's caricature of Howe's point of view as an expression of Ellison's own reading of Wright. Ellison stresses that Wright is "a personal hero," but he wanted readers to see a clear distinction between Wright's achievement and his own (*Collected* 164). In fact, Ellison claims for himself the role he assigned to Wright nineteen years earlier in "Richard Wright's Blues": "The writer's real way of sharing the experience of his group is to convert its mutual suffering into lasting value" (*Collected* 184).

Rather than consolidating his status as black spokesman, though, Ellison's response helped to canonize him as the black author above the fray of politics. Instead of being seen simply as a defense of the black writer's right to create, it was misread as a defense of Ralph Ellison's right to create better fiction than Richard Wright created. Ironically, Ellison's argument was a version of a view that had brought Wright and Ellison together in the first place. Each had insisted that to be "free" as artists, black writers must master all manner of form and aesthetic possibility, and both men looked to both white and black writers to create their work. To demand the freedom to write as one chooses, to insist that the black novelist can write or not write about black life from any perspective he sees fit, as Ellison did, was itself a political blow against the logic of segregation.

Ellison would have been better served had he written this declaration of artistic independence so that Wright received credit for it as well. Obviously, he was sensitive that his achievement be distinguished from Wright's, and there may have been no graceful way for him to insist on that distinction. Still, he need not have walked into Howe's Battle Royal. Had Howe only wanted to critique the representations of blacks in fiction, he might have looked elsewhere—to Faulkner or Margaret Mitchell—but instead he critiqued how black writers portray black characters—hence Ellison's defense of the black writer's freedom to create as he pleases. As Michel Fabre suggests, though, by classifying Ellison and Wright as representatives of authentic or inauthentic *Negro* positions, Howe fatally distorted the true relationship between them ("From" 199). In fact, Howe's logic is backward. Ellison and Wright occupied complementary positions because they were black artists responding to the same historical situation through their shared assumptions about politics, society, and art. Their novels were equally acts of protest against the Jim Crow status quo. Where they differed was in their aesthetic gifts and choices—questions involving form and language. Hence, Ellison called Wright a relative, not an ancestor.

The continuing appeal of Howe's attack is evident in Henry Louis Gates Jr.'s 1990s assertion that during the 1960s, "Ellison was shut out, and Richard Wright was elected godfather of the Black Arts Movement of the nineteen-sixties because Wright's hero in *Native Son*, Bigger Thomas, cuts off a white girl's head and stuffs her in a furnace" (Remnick, 398). If Howe makes Wright, who was no separatist, into a dummy for his own type of political ventriloquism, Gates's remark sensationalizes Wright as if he were the forerunner of Black Panthers. Lost in all this empty politicizing is Ellison's actual response to *Native Son* upon reading it in 1940: "Would that *all* Negroes were psychologically as free as Bigger and capable of positive action" (Fabre, "From" 201). But Ellison made this remark during legalized segregation when he and Wright were frustrated by a political situation in which blacks lacked meaningful political agency.

By 1963 the political situation had altered, and Ellison's reply to Howe reflected that change. Instead of accommodating himself to a white critic's view of his work (Wright revised *Native Son* and *Black Boy* so they could be Book-of-the-Month Club selections), Ellison, as a black writer, attacked the white critic's simplistic understanding. Unfortunately, "The World and the Jug" hurt Ellison and Wright more than it did Howe. For most readers, Howe's simplistic comparison held up.

Howe's attack and Ellison's reply did his reputation immeasurable harm because it worked to separate Ellison's work from the mainstream of its source: black experience and the example of Richard Wright. In "Richard Wright's Blues," Ellison had already written a beautiful tribute that expressed his solidarity, as a Negro and as an artist, with Wright's work. "The World and the Jug" does not efface that essay (Ellison included both of them in *Shadow and Act*), but its effect was to help accomplish what black readers such as Ottley would never have believed in 1948: it separated the apprentice from the master by suggesting that their views of black life were politically opposed. From this extraordinary misperception, others would follow that distorted the legacy of both writers. Wright's reputation was compromised by the belief that Ellison's success had surpassed (rather than enhanced) his achievement. It was further diminished by the cartoonish notion—suggested in Howe's essay and Gates's remark above—that Wright's "politics" was analogous to Bigger's panicked and unpremeditated incineration of a white girl. For Ellison, the misperceptions were more pernicious. Critics lost touch with his political origins as a black writer protesting segregation and its consequences. They also lost touch with Ellison's animating desire to reach black readers in the Jim Crow era even more than he wanted to reach white readers. Having lost touch with Ellison's essential and animating connection to the situation of blacks in American life, many readers deluded themselves into believing that Ellison could somehow be either above or removed from the Civil Rights movement simply because he was not making ill-considered "militant" pronouncements and justifying them through Bigger's example. After *Brown,* armed black political revolt no longer made sense even as a novelist's fantasy.

The lasting irony of "The World and the Jug" is that in the same moment Ellison became, in Rampersad's words, "probably for the first time in modern American history, a black intellectual had fought a public duel against a white intellectual and had won," he also seemed to sanction the critical move by which he would become the black artist who had transcended his black origins (*Shadow* 402). Ironically, by 1963 Howe's "authenticity" argument should have been seen as dated. What Ellison might have said—and this is not far from what Howe says—was that *Native Son* was necessary in 1940 and that it was essential to Ellison's career and also to the development of American literature. Although black anger is still a fact of American life, Ellison might have continued, the rules of American society have changed dramatically since 1940, and so has the political and social context of black anger. In their exchange, Howe writes as if the Civil Rights movement were not happening, but not so Ellison. Nonetheless, Wright became the "authentic" voice of black life when he was dead and unable to respond to the rapidly changing political context. Meanwhile, though Ellison's stance was consistent with King's, his "authenticity" was compromised because he claimed the right to be a "black artist," and for many that phrase was an oxymoron.

A black artist, though, is what Ellison was, and never was he above politics. In 1955 he said that "too many books by Negro writers are addressed to a white audience" (*Collected* 213). He was not thinking of *Invisible Man*; a year before publishing his novel, Ellison had said his desire was to reach black readers. Referring to a review he had recently published, Ellison thanked Murray for sharing it with students at Tuskegee: "Thanks very much for seeing to it that a few Negroes read my reviews; I get the feeling that most times the stuff is seen only by whites and that, I'm afraid, doesn't mean much in the long run" (*Trading* 7). After *Invisible Man* had been given the National Book Award, Ellison shared with Murray an especially perceptive critical response he received from one whom he identifies only as "ole Eubanks," a friend, Tuskegee graduate, and manager of the food service at the Harlem YMCA where Ellison had stayed when he first came to New York in 1936. "I'm not lying," Ellison gushes, "I swear. Eubanks says to me, 'Ellison, you know you're a hell of a nigguh? This goddamn stuff is History, man. It's *history*! You read this shit one time and you get to thinking about it and you go back and damn if you don't find something else. You got to dig that stuff man, 'cause it's loaded!'" (*Trading* 40).

Among Ellison's many hopes for *Invisible Man*, one of them was that he wanted his work to influence black readers as he thought *Native Son* had done. Eubanks's Ellison—a version of Ellison's ideal black reader—looks back to the secret history that blacks created in the face of brutal social oppression. Shortly after *Invisible Man* was published to wide acclaim from influential white readers, Ellison asserted that "somehow despite all the fine reviews and other acts of recognition, it was seeing my name among those honored by the *Chicago Defender* that gave me a most real sense of accomplishment" (Morel 83, n.65). More than fifty years after the publication of *Invisible Man* and more than fifteen years after Ellison's death, the sense of pride that Ellison experienced after having been singled out for praise by the *Defender* (a black paper that played an important role in preparing the way for the Civil Rights movement) is no longer a prominent part of his story. This Ellison—Eubanks's Ellison, Wright's Ellison, the *Defender*'s Ellison—is essential to understanding the true scope of his career.

In the wake of "The World and the Jug," Ellison, the consummate black intellectual, became known, in a classic American joke, as the white person's black intellectual. By 1968 the irony of his position was on full display at the annual meeting of the Southern Historical Association. This appearance is not part of the usual Ellison story, but it symbolizes his unlikely path as a black intellectual whose career began under the eye of Richard Wright and was later authorized by Robert Penn Warren, the novelist and Confederate historian. In New Orleans at the invitation of the historian C. Vann Woodward, Ellison sat on the stage with Woodward, Warren, and William Styron. What was Ellison doing there among the elite of Southern white intellectual aristocracy? The short answer is that they were friends of his, but that answer evades the question. He was there to make sure the complexity of "history" was not lost on anyone—to explain to all who would listen that you cannot understand "Southern" history without understanding that blacks as much as whites are "Southerners."

The audience in New Orleans was "mixed." In fact, the blacks present were there not only to hear the thoughts of Ellison but also to confront William Styron, whose *The Confessions of Nat Turner* (1967) had struck many black readers as a poorly conceived portrait of a revolutionary black hero (see Henrik). The question of how to represent the African American past had become especially pressing in light of the Civil Rights movement and the assassinations of Malcolm X and King. Pitted against angry black readers, Styron was on the defensive. He could offer no defense for his Nat Turner other than the familiar one of the novelist's freedom to imagine as he saw fit. For skeptical readers, however, Styron's imagination was precisely the problem. They wondered if his version of Turner emasculated a black revolutionary, and was this not a version of what the U.S. government was always doing to true black leaders? Their concern was that Styron's novel erased any historical line that might be drawn to connect what was happening in the 1960s to a spirit of revolt that had existed during slavery. At stake for these readers was not the novelist's right to construct fiction as he pleased but a view of black American history itself.

Invisible Man had drawn a line from the past to the present through the committed example of resistance carried on by the narrator's grandfather and in the figure of Frederick Douglass, who looms so powerfully over the narrative.[4] *Invisible Man* conveyed the pain that African Americans had experienced as a consequence of being brutalized as the cost of trying to maintain their humanity. In one of the novel's crucial passages, Ellison's narrator speaks of a dream in which *"they came forward with a knife, holding me; and I felt the bright red pain and they took the two bloody blobs and cast them over the bridge, and out of my anguish I saw them curve up and catch beneath the apex of the curving arch of the bridge, to hang there, dripping down through the sunlight into the dark red water"* (560). The sense of black history as a collective emasculation—as something that was being killed before it could be born—was an important component of the experience of "invisibility" that Ellison's novel hoped to convey and fight.

Styron's book had no similar objective, and his exposure to angry black readers might have struck Ellison with the force of a Burkean perspective by incongruity, since by 1968 Ellison too was being questioned by angry black readers (though not in New Orleans). *Invisible Man* was not commonly understood, despite Ellison's persistent explanations, as an attempt to reflect on African American history and strategize the next move African Americans needed to make in order to get a bigger slice of the American equality pie. No matter how many times Ellison said that he worked out "the concept of *Invisible Man*" in response to the fact that "*my people* were involved in a terrific quarrel with the federal government" over the question of equal rights, some black readers were going to remark, "I couldn't understand what he was saying. He wasn't talking to *us*" (*Collected* 524, 355; emphasis added). James Alan McPherson describes Ellison's visit to Oberlin a year later where African American students bluntly told Ellison, "You don't have anything to tell us" because, the student said, "you're shooting down Ras the Destroyer, a rebel leader of black people" (*Collected* 359). Ellison refused to "make any apologies" for what was "just one man's view of what he saw," but was told by one student, "That just proves you're an Uncle Tom" (*Collected* 359).

Arguably, the only person present who might have saved Styron from his attackers was Ellison—as he had saved Philip Roth at Yeshiva University a few years earlier. When Styron, however, faced questions that asked him to justify his authority to speak for Turner, Ellison declined to save his friend from ridicule. He would not vouch for Styron's fictionalized view of African American history; he would only say, ambiguously, that "I haven't read the book and [Bill] knows that—well, maybe he doesn't" (*Conversations* 159). *Well, maybe he doesn't.* This evasive, and seemingly improvised phrase, has all of the canniness of his novel's grandfather, since he knew from Woodward's invitation that Styron would be present. Ellison, though, chose to distance himself from Styron. One questioner tells Styron that he is "very sorry that Mr. Ellison did not read your book" because "intellectually you would have had a little bit more trouble with Ellison" (*Conversations* 168). Anyone familiar with Ellison's performances at similar symposia knows how characteristic it would have been for him, whether he had read the novel or not, to intervene with a point of view that might defuse the situation. Instead, he acknowledged that fiction is not history and thus requires freedom of imagination, but cautioned that "Negroes have a high sensitivity to the ironies of historical writing" and thus "a profound skepticism concerning the validity of most reports on what the past was like" (*Conversations* 154). In other words, Ellison emboldened Styron's black critics.

It is easy to imagine that Ellison had in fact read the book and also to think of him attacking Styron's overly Freudian and historically implausible account of Turner's rebellion. But he did not need to do so, because the black readers present were doing an excellent job of critiquing Styron's book on their own. When his own work was attacked by black readers, though, Ellison had a different answer: he took one for the team. Using the Booker T. Washington "'crabs-in-a basket' metaphor," Ellison elsewhere notes how often when "a Negro threatens to succeed in a field outside the usual areas of" accepted black competence, the "others feel challenged" (*Conversations* 127); he says this is a "protective reaction" on the part of the group and "a heritage of slavery," when to stand out from the group meant to risk death. Thus, as a black writer he must "endure the agony imposed by this group pessimism" (126). Styron, though, is a not a Negro, and he is talking out of school. That Ellison did not provide a rationale for his friend suggests that he had no answer that could defend Styron's vision of black identity against the charges issued by the self-proclaimed heirs to Nat Turner's crushed rebellion. In this instance, he let the team speak for him.

Ellison's loud silence regarding the meaning of Styron's novel strikes me as almost unbearably eloquent because it speaks to the contradictory position he was made to occupy in American letters. On the one hand, he was the great black novelist articulating the rage of being born black into a country predicated, as Stephen Douglas told Abraham Lincoln in the 1858 debates, on "the white basis." On the other hand, he had also written the definitive twentieth-century answer to the works of Emerson and Thoreau, which called for an American literature true to the Founders' ideals of equality and democracy. He spoke for the group, but he also threatened the group's identity by venturing into regions previously unoccupied by blacks in American life. Thus, Ellison could be praised as either the Jim Crow poet of the Negro people in America or the prophet of their acculturation into this "other" American society that had defined itself by denying the Negro people their humanity. It was an impossible role for him—or anyone else—to play, made more difficult by having to play it in the midst of the turbulent American 1960s.

Ellison was silent, but he had to be thinking something. Perhaps it is not too fanciful to suggest that, savoring the privileged perspective he was allowed upon this ironical scene, he had a moment to recall the events of thirty years earlier when his most prominent literary friend had been Wright. Thirty years earlier Wright and Ellison had plotted a revolutionary assault—from a Negro perspective—on the body of American literature. By the time Ellison was sharing a stage with the cream of white Southern intellectuals, Wright had been dead for seven years, and he and Ellison had not been close since before *Invisible Man* was published in 1952. The fact of Ellison's presence spoke to the surprising influence of his work, though, just as it verified Wright's sense that a blueprint for Negro culture, properly executed, could change the context of American literature. *Native Son* and *Black Boy* had shocked readers upon their publication, yet they played a role in helping to create a cultural context in which Styron's work could be challenged. Indeed, Styron surely wrote the book in part as a response to Wright, Ellison, and the cultural changes their work anticipated. In this respect, Ellison's presence at the 1968 gathering of the predominantly white Southern Historical Association was an unlikely triumph of his friendship with Wright.

In New Orleans, Ellison's ethos throughout is composed and even magisterial. He betrays nothing of what he had felt in 1941 upon reading Wright's *12 Million Black Voices*, a short history of black experience in America. Then, Ellison's statement to Wright was "We [blacks] are not the numbed, but the seething" (Jackson, *Ralph*, 187). Indeed, it was the "seething" Ralph Ellison who began *Invisible Man*, and this work, no less than *Native Son* or *Black Boy*, emerged from the same historic "black" anger that provoked Styron's questioner to attack Styron's *Nat Turner*. Ellison worked hard to master the seething origins of *Invisible Man*, but its expression and control were essential components of what made him such a great artist. In this battle with himself and his people's history, he sought Wright as his guide, a sort of Virgil to his Dante.

Richard Wright's work spoke to Ellison and demanded that he write his own vision. Wright inspired Ellison to write, and when Ellison did write, it was to add to the story Wright had told. Without Wright, there would be no *Invisible Man,* and in that sense no Ralph Ellison either.[5] What follows here is an account of Ellison's friendship with Wright which provides a view of Ellison before *Invisible Man, Brown v. Board of Education,* the Civil Rights movement, affirmative action, and Barack Obama. This Ellison absorbed, word by word, not just *Native Son* and *Black Boy* but Wright's underappreciated *12 Million Black Voices* (1941). His immediate reaction, cited at the beginning of this chapter, suggests that no other "black" literary work affected him as deeply: that book was both a call to black arms and a précis for the novel that Ellison would write.

What we find when we recover the Ellison that Wright knew is a deeply talented, mostly anonymous black man who sees his life as a version and extension of other black lives that have preceded his own. His struggle to write *Invisible Man* was a struggle to represent those lives. His silence before Styron was yet another version of that struggle.

Because Wright Wrote

Richard Wright's presence is evident throughout *Invisible Man*. Ellison used aspects of Wright's experience in the Communist Party in his account of the narrator's drama with the Brotherhood. The grandfather's advice that hovers over the narrator's actions in *Invisible Man* may be a revision of the moment in *Black Boy* where Wright is punished for not understanding his grandfather's assurance that his death would secure him a place in heaven. Where Wright rejects his grandfather's advice, Ellison's protagonist engages his grandfather's words in his quest to overturn a racist society. Further, *Black Boy* begins with Wright hiding in a hole underneath his burning house—a scene that Ellison may have been thinking of when he put his own narrator into a hole in order to begin his story. Many other examples could be adduced, and most of them demonstrate that Ellison transformed Wright's example into something else. But which is more important—that Ellison revised Wright to find his own vision, or that Wright was the essential point of origin for Ellison's discovery of *his* vision?

Criticism of Wright and Ellison has been quite adept in following Ellison's lead to explore how he distinguished himself from Wright. I do not think that Wright was the authorial father figure Ellison had to replace; that role was more properly Faulkner's, as Ellison acknowledged when he called himself Faulkner's bastard child (Skerret). If one must resort to family metaphors, Wright was the patient older brother encouraging the talented and willful younger brother. His letters in the 1940s consistently praise Ellison's efforts—his essays and his stories. He told Ellison that "Richard Wright's Blues" was the best essay he had ever read by a Negro. Wright's generosity to Ellison is evident throughout their letters, as is Ellison's need to impress Wright. This need expresses itself not so much in his intellectual labors as in the studious care with which he oversees Wright's reputation and personal affairs in Harlem while Wright is in Mexico City, Quebec, and Paris. In his reply to "Richard Wright's Blues," Wright recognized that Ellison was on a different path from his own. Wright frankly tells Ellison that his discussion of the blues in the context of his work makes little sense to him. Ellison replies by saying that blues are essential to his conception of himself as an artist. In other words, both parties understood well before *Invisible Man* that their work expressed different visions, but their closeness was nonetheless a vital part of what made that book possible (Wright to Ellison, 25 July, and Ellison to Wright, 5 Aug. 1945, RWEP LC).

The most insightful analyses of the two writers have shown how Ellison broadened Wright's narrative frame. Alan Nadel's nuanced analysis of Ellison's debt to Wright is typical in that it explains how Ellison effected "a corrective enhancement" of Wright (*Invisible* 160). With the Battle Royal, Nadel shows how Ellison employs a Joycean strategy to recast Wright's early work so that it takes on a mythic significance. Thus, the brutal but singular fights that Wright endured as a young man are given a broader symbolic scope that takes in the entire Jim Crow South. The individuality of Wright's story becomes the collective experience of an entire people struggling for group self-actualization. Although Ellison mythologizes Wright, the phrase "corrective enhancement" may be misleading, since it implies that Ellison bettered Wright, whereas what he truly did was to transform the same situation and lead it to a different end by explicitly connecting Wright's "individual" vision to a cultural history.

Whether telling Bigger's story or his own, Wright's treatment of the individual anxiety experienced by black men inspired Ellison to see the narrative possibilities of group affirmation. Wright was not unaware of this interpretation. He had called Bigger "a native son" to emphasize that he was an American creation even though he might be construed as "a Negro nationalist in a vague sense because he was not allowed to live as an American" (*Early* 870). He also said that he was writing for the present: "I wanted the reader to feel that Bigger's story was happening *now*" (878). Wright wrote with a sense of personal and political urgency that Ellison, like his narrator's grandfather, understood as a long-standing historical condition evident since the end of Reconstruction and going back into slavery. In "How Bigger Was Born," Wright said that he wanted "to show what oppression had done to Bigger's relationships with other people, how it split him off from them, how it baffled him" (*Later* 872). Ellison began with this premise but sought resolution through his narrator's complicity with his audience. Wright wrote from a sense of angry hurt, and he wrote to expose his wound to the reader's horror and revulsion. Ellison too wrote from a sense of hurt, and ironically, he may have received less personal satisfaction from his writing than Wright did. Because Ellison more obviously than Wright wrote from a sense of being a member of a group, he also sought the restoration of the group through his writing. That ambition defined Ellison's political urgency.

When Ellison told Murray he wanted to write for Negroes, he likely meant that he wanted to write a book that did not reinforce the inferior social position of Negroes but would articulate a vision of resilience and hope unavailable to Wright's protagonists. In "Remembering Richard Wright" Ellison explains that for Wright Bigger embodied and was the logical consequence of the suffering inflicted on blacks "after the Civil War by the terror of the Ku Klux Klan, which swept the newly freed Negro through arson, pillage, and death out of the United States Senate, the House of Representatives, the many state legislatures, and out of the public, social, and economic life of the South" (*Collected* 857). Without political representation or social sanction, Negroes could only employ a "thousand ruses and stratagems of struggle." Negroes "got religion, felt that Jesus would redeem the void of living," or "projected their hurts and longings into more naïve and mundane forms—blues, jazz, swing—without intellectual guidance" (859). To Ellison, these "mundane forms" provided blacks with both the consolation of philosophy and the means for preserving a heritage that enabled them to imagine a better future. Through these forms Negroes were contributing to the creation of American culture, and that evident cultural power would translate, Ellison hoped, into political power and ultimately a new, visible place within American society. Ellison translated these "mundane forms" into *Invisible Man* and in the process conveyed the full power of the collective Negro aspiration that had been gathering in the decades after the Civil War.

Ellison's response to Howe obscured his debt to Wright and seemed to attack Wright as well. Critics are right to notice that Ellison assimilated Wright's personal story to a larger black folk tradition that Wright did not represent in his fiction, but they are wrong to see this difference as a tendency that made Ellison and Wright opposed figures. Ellison's novel is a reading of Wright's work written by a cultural historian with a gift for modernist narrative. Through the novel form, Ellison historicizes Wright's works. If *Black Boy* is the story of how one determined person triumphs over intense social adversity, then, Ellison suggests, his book proves that "Wright is no exception" to a larger historical context in which "blasting pressures" over a "scant eight years have sent the Negro people hurtling, without a clearly defined trajectory, from slavery to emancipation, from log cabin to city tenement, from the white folks' fields and kitchens to factory assembly lines, and which, between two wars, have shattered the whole of its folk consciousness into a thousand writhing pieces" (*Collected* 131). Ellison here predicted the trajectory his own novel would pursue, but only because he perceived that the protagonists of *Native Son*, *Black Boy*, and "The Man Who Lived Underground" were living, fully rendered portraits of this shattering. Ellison's imagination, unlike Wright's, compelled him to want to imagine a folk process—a literary version of the political process that brought forth Martin Luther King—which would heal this shattering.

As Robert Reid-Pharr suggests, for many readers it was Ralph Ellison-the-critic who successfully presented Ellison-the-novelist as having "trumped" Wright by "immersing himself within the folk culture that his erstwhile mentor held at bay" (77). As Ellison recalls in "Remembering Richard Wright," though, in 1937 he had been "seeking out" Wright as "a personal quest" because he was looking for "Afro-American writers" who "recognized a relationship between modern poetry and jazz music" (*Collected* 660). Wright was part of Ellison's quest as a writer to link vernacular black expression to modernist advances in narrative art. In other words, Ellison sought out Wright for his narrative sophistication, not his primitivism, and also because Ellison was keen to see what another black writer could make out of a collision of black history with experimental narrative techniques. In letters to Wright, Ellison was explicit regarding their shared ambition to change the possibilities of fiction written by blacks. Upon reading *12 Million Black Voices*, Ellison confessed, "We have begun to embrace the experience [of Negro suffering] and master it. And we shall make of it a weapon more subtle than a machine-gun, more effective than a fighter-plane. It is like Joe Louis knocking their best men silly in his precise, impassive, alert Negro way. I think it is significant that I can feel pride in a Negro *book*." Ellison hopes to carry into his own writing the pride that Wright makes him feel as a Negro: "It gives me something to build upon, my work is made easier, my audience brought a bit closer. I'm a better man for having read it" (3 Nov. 1941, RWEP LC).

In his last essay about Wright, Ellison admitted that he had never intended to become a writer. It was an accident of his personal history. Ellison knew other writers before he met Wright, but it was Wright's personal experience and complexity that ignited Ellison's talent in a way that probably no other person could have. "I had never met anyone who, lacking the fanfare of public recognition, could move me with the unpublished works of his fictional imagination," recalled Ellison nearly forty years after their first meeting (*Collected* 663). Watching Wright compose his works was different from reading Eliot or Hemingway in the Tuskegee library. It allowed Ellison to realize something about himself that he otherwise might never have learned: if Wright could write a novel, then he could write one too. Just as important, Wright inspired Ellison's passion. In his November 1941 response to *12 Million Black Voices*, Ellison tells Wright: "When experience such as ours is organized as you have done, there is nothing left to do but fight." Indeed, for Ellison it "makes you want to write and write, or murder." Wright represented the perfect storm for Ellison's birth as a black artist because Wright wrote out of a highly developed sense of his own artistry and his desire to express what it meant to have been born black in America.

"If I had a heaven of my own" is a wish that appears in countless blues songs and in a sense names the historical and aesthetic context that *Invisible Man* seeks. No such wish exists in Wright's fiction. *Invisible Man* promises at once to find and to be that heaven for readers alive to the secret story it tells. Although the book does not exclude white readers from its vision (and, in fact, often casts a cold eye on its white readers), there is a dimension that can speak only to and for black readers. In his novel Ellison would reinvent, or reclaim, the history of the United States by telling the story of American blacks after the Civil War. The blues line might also be heard as "*if we had a heaven of our own.*" *Invisible Man* was an expression of this wish and the search for its fulfillment. Before Ellison could tell this story, he had to accept that in some essential way Wright had already spoken for him, and that speaking meant everything, yet also was not enough. In other words,

Wright had told his part of the Negro story, and Ellison in return would complete the history that Wright began.

Train I Ride

Lawrence Jackson says that Wright and Ellison "were close in the way that Hemingway and Fitzgerald were close; in the way that Robert Penn Warren and Allan Tate were close; and in the way that Eliot and Pound were close" ("Ralph Ellison's Invented" 25). Ellison's literary career began to take flight in 1941 with two essays about Wright ("Recent"; "Richard"). Three years later he published the classic essay "Richard Wright's Blues." Nearly twenty years later, and roughly ten years after *Invisible Man* came "The World and the Jug." Wright appeared as a subject in Ellison's essays whenever his own literary identity as a black writer was at stake. In "Remembering Richard Wright" Ellison acknowledges explicitly that Wright prompted him to become a writer—an extraordinary and generous admission, one that he did not make to Howe.[6] In this essay, Ellison—better than the biographers—stresses that their intellectual interests complemented one another and explains the sense in which they were ideal audiences for each other's work. At the most critical stage of his artistic and personal development, Ellison discussed with Wright everything he was reading and everything he was thinking or writing. Their peers included not only Hughes and Du Bois but also John Steinbeck, Ernest Hemingway, André Malraux, and Thomas Mann. "I could discuss such matters with Richard Wright," Ellison says. "Since Wright had assured me that I possessed a certain talent, I decided that writing was the direction I would take" (*Collected* 666).

In this, his last essay about Wright, Ellison portrays their friendship as one between colleagues, but the sentence above suggests a debt to Wright that Ellison could not repay except by writing something of his own. As was invariably the case when he wrote about Wright, he could not desist from describing his friend's achievement as a version of his own. Thus, Wright "set out to come into a conscious possession of his experience as Negro, as political revolutionary, as writer, and as a citizen of Chicago" (*Collected* 668). Substitute Harlem for Chicago and that description would apply to Ellison as a beginning writer as well. Ellison says that Wright wanted "to drive home to Americans, black and white, something of the complexity and cost in human terms . . . of growing up in a society which operated on one side of its mind by the principle of equality while qualifying that principle severely according to the dictates of racism" (672). Ellison admires Wright for a "personality [that] would not allow him to shun a battle," and thus he made of his life something that society said was impossible (669). Ellison remembers Wright as "a boy who grew up and achieved and accepted his own individual responsibility for seeing to it that America became conscious of itself. He insisted that this country recognize the interconnections between its places and its personalities, its acts and its ideals. This was the burden of Richard Wright and, as I see it, the driving passion of Richard Wright" (674). He pays Wright what is for Ellison the ultimate compliment: that Wright, as "a Negro American writer," was "as randy, as courageous and as irrepressible as Jack Johnson" (674). We know from his letters what Johnson meant to Ellison, and here he underlines the comparison: "If you don't know who Jack Johnson was, I'll tell you that when I was a little boy this early heavyweight boxing champion was one of the most admired underground heroes" (674). In comparing Wright to Johnson, the figure he told Murray was his own role model for the kind of writer he wanted to be, Ellison's sense of identification with Wright could not be stronger.

Both Jackson and Rowley suggest that Ellison and Wright were like brothers, and there is an important and unnoticed sense in which Wright reinforced ambitions that Ellison had received from his parents: long before he met Wright, they had conveyed to him that he could become something extraordinary. Ellison's father had given him the challenge of his name, Ralph Waldo Ellison, while his mother raised him to be what his famous narrator also aspired to become: a Negro leader. Yet it was Wright who incited Ellison to express this sense of destiny by becoming a writer. "But I've never even tried to write a story," Ellison protested when Wright suggested he take up writing. "Look," Wright said, "you talk about these things, you've read a lot, and you've been around. Just put these things down and let me see it" (*Collected* 663)." Ellison had seen things, many things, and he had seen them through the eyes of his parents. Ellison tells Wright that reading *12 Million Black Voices* inspired him to recall and claim the words of his mother: "As my mother used to say when life pressed her closely, I felt like yelling 'Lord, I'm filled up! I'm full!'" (3 Nov. 1941). Unlike Wright, whose vision was a function of escaping his family, Ellison sought to integrate his family's story into a tribal history. Despite the weight of the name his father had given him, Ellison looked to his mother when he began to answer Wright's charge.

An example of what Wright's friendship drove Ellison to rediscover about himself is evident in his early story "Boy on a Train" (*Flying*). In this story Ellison draws on the memory of his mother to recall a trip north that he took with his brother and mother after the death of his father. The mother's presence is crucial to the story and so is the pain that the eleven-year-old protagonist experiences in coming to terms with having been born into a society that discounts the humanity of his family because they have black skin. His recognition of the pain of their shared history as blacks in America is in a sense a version of the narrative consciousness that Ellison is trying to represent through his protagonist's difficult awakening: he narrates a birth into grief that is also a test of courage and resolve. Written about fifteen years before *Invisible Man* was published, "Boy on a Train" begins to formulate a version of the monumental question that *Invisible Man* would explore and that Ellison would discern in Wright's *Black Boy*: how to represent the resilience of Negro American life without being consumed by the soul-killing racism endemic to American society. One of Ellison's least discussed yet most autobiographically revealing works, this apprentice story reveals something precious of Ellison's formative vision as a writer, pointing ever so delicately to what Wright's example had wrought in him.

The reader encounters James, the "Boy on a Train," riding in a Jim Crow car as his mother tries to distract him from the somberness of the journey. She directs his attention to the fall colors of the passing trees and tells him that Jack Frost "made the pretty leaves" and that "he paints the leaves all the pretty colors" (*Flying* 12). This sense of wonder shared by mother and child contrasts sharply with the anger James witnessed from his mother when "a butcher had tried to touch her breasts" (13). Her response is defiant: "She had spat in his face and told him to keep his dirty hands where they belonged" (13–14). Traveling in a segregated car, becoming aware that the treatment his mother receives is partly the consequence of others' perceptions of their skin color, the boy begins to see how his life is affected by living in a racist society. The distance between the controlling narrative voice and what the boy protagonist sees is uncertain, in part because the narrator is seeking a way to transform the boy's initial perception of his relationship to society into a way to redeem the pain he suffers as a "black boy" in a racist society. Moreover, this pain that the protagonist comes to know is something that he recognizes through his mother: both a birthright and an initiation that he shares with and suffers through her.

The story captures James's consciousness when he realizes that the history that his mother carries as a Negro will likewise structure his understanding of the world. She tells her son that they had moved to Oklahoma from the South "because we had heard that colored people have a chance out here"

(*Flying* 17). The mother impresses upon the son the symbolic importance of the trip they are taking together: "Son, I want you to remember this trip," she says. "You understand, son. I *want* you to remember. You *must*, you've *got* to understand" (17–18). The mother asks the boy to understand not only that the trip has a symbolic meaning but also that he is responsible for carrying that meaning into the future. The boy's initial response to this heavy charge mirrors his mother's response to the butcher. He senses a nameless enemy upon whom he will exact revenge. "'I'll kill it when I get big,' he thought. 'I'll make it cry just like it's making Mama cry!'" (20). His love for his mother is so great and his will to protect her so strong that he extends his pledge to include the source of the world that has born him: "'I'll kill God and not be sorry!'" (20). The bitter comedy of his rebellion against God betrays his recognition that the love he and his mother share is bounded by the hatred that the white world (and its God) directs at them. A question the story raises but cannot resolve is whether the boy's love for his mother can overcome the anger that the world's hatred instills in him.

In just a few words, the story also conveys the unusual closeness between the mother and son. It memorializes the moment, already gestating in the son, when the mother's perspective and thus her own history become the basis for the child's perspective of his place in the world. "Boy on a Train" reveals not only the lasting influence his own mother's life had on Ellison but how difficult it was for blacks of his era to outgrow the angry moment of self-recognition that the boy experiences on the train. As Jackson's biography documents, Ellison would always be striving to live up to his mother's ambition for him. For his fifth birthday she gave him a toy typewriter and a facsimile rolltop desk, with a chair to match. Near his fortieth birthday, eight years after her death, Ellison affixed her name, Ida, to the dedication page of *Invisible Man*. Ellison had learned from his mother that he was born into a group history and that it was his role to advance that group toward a better future. He would recall how often she told him that "the hope of our group depended not on older Negroes, but upon the young, upon me" (Jackson, *Ralph* 12). Thinking of his friendship with Lyndon B. Johnson and the success of the Civil Rights movement, Ellison wrote his brother "that Mama would feel some of her sacrifices for us were paying off" (Rampersad 448–49). One of the proudest moments of Ellison's life came when Oklahoma City renamed one its libraries the "Ralph Ellison Branch Library." A buoyant Ellison told his audience: "You affirm my sense of life. You are testimonies to the faith of your fathers and mothers—especially your mothers" (503).

The protagonist of *Invisible Man* is advised to "be your own father," perhaps because its author did not know his. "Boy on a Train," Ellison's tribute to his mother and the ambition she instilled in him, suggests that he thought of himself as a Negro son trying to make the dreams of his mother's generation come true. The story suggests that Ellison understood his mother to have demanded of her son that he be a witness to and spokesman for the pain their family experienced as a consequence of belonging to a group that Ellison would later in one of his manuscripts refer to as "That Vanished Tribe into Which I Was Born: The American Negroes."[7] This task required Ellison to bring a degree of visibility to the Negro's place in American society and to do so, as the mother does in the story, through one's every public action—including putting a lecherous white man in his place. Ida Ellison's son must show a commitment to earning a distinguished place in American life, and this would mean not surrendering it once it was achieved. "Boy on a Train" intimates that Ellison's career, more than the succession of awards and positions he acquired after writing *Invisible Man*, was enacted as part of a long historical struggle going back at least to the Civil War and probably all the way to the nation's founding. The anger that James experiences and resolves to master is the historical dilemma into which he and his mother were both born. The boy's commitment to remembering what has happened is part of a collective historical will that that was seeking higher ground for blacks in American history—the same will that produced King and Malcolm X.

Learning to master the contradictory emotions that James and, presumably, every black child of that era suffered was for Ellison what constituted the tradition of the blues. In "Richard Wright's Blues," Wright is an embodiment of the blues tradition, but Ellison, as this story suggests, had been aware of such examples his whole life. Indeed, his formative years as an artist were a period of long preparation to write the communal history that is *Invisible Man*. In the forty years thereafter he repeatedly directed his readers to the heroic examples of the pre-*Brown* era who had also inspired him: Louis Armstrong, Charlie Christian, Duke Ellington, Mahalia Jackson, Jimmy Rushing, and the bass-playing genius Walter Page.[8] Less well-known examples—people who touched Ellison personally—such as Rocso Dunjee, Inman Page, William Dawson, and Hazel Harrison live on through Ellison's writing. These reminiscences were more important to him than his second novel, I would hazard, because he allowed them to be published and because he knew that the achievement of such people made his possible. Long before he wrote the many essays that recall the exploits of these legends of black vernacular expression, Ellison had worked for the WPA interviewing Negroes born into slavery and their near descendants. From them he heard countless folktales that expressed the guile, the wisdom, and the will to endure that would eventually make otherwise inexplicable examples such as Ellison, Martin Luther King, and Rosa Parks inevitable figures of American and Negro possibility. For Ellison, each of these instances of black folk tradition, created by "heroic" black figures, also met, named, and transformed the historical condition that "Boy on a Train" names.

To move from Wright's "psychology of oppression" to Ellison's "psychology of survival and transcendence," as John Wright puts it (20), Ellison arguably had to undergo a similar transformation within himself. If "Boy on a Train" shows Ellison's working through a version of the process by which "oppression" becomes "transcendence," then it is surely significant that Richard Wright was the figure who provoked him into risking the self-analysis that the story reveals. If the Ellison who was provoked by Wright to write "Boy on a Train" has been concealed from us, it is perhaps because this earlier Ellison became hidden by the magisterial figure who penned *Invisible Man*. Yet, the narrator of *Invisible Man* is "invisible" in part because he does not know what to do with the feeling of hurt that James experiences in this early story. This feeling of a hurt that is seeking redemption is what drove Bigger in *Native Son* and Wright in *Black Boy*; it also drove Ellison to try to embody in his writing the love he felt for his mother and Wright and other blacks who had survived history by asserting their dignity as humans.

Despite "A Blueprint for Negro Writing," Ellison knew that Wright was generally skeptical of black culture's folk forms because Wright felt himself to be outside them. Ellison also knew that although Wright's representative black figure, Bigger Thomas, was destroyed, Wright himself, whose origins were more harrowing than Bigger's, survived to create Bigger. *Invisible Man* demonstrated how such a conundrum was possible and how it expressed the history of blacks in America. Leon Litwack's *Trouble in Mind* can help clarify this conundrum and suggest further what "ole Eubanks" saw in Ellison and what young Ellison saw in Wright.

Litwack's Historical *Invisible Man*

"Nowhere is the paradox of black life in the U.S. more graphically revealed," Litwack contends at the outset of his history (subtitled *Black Southerners in the Age of Jim Crow*) "than in Ralph Ellison's portrayal of the black odyssey in *Invisible Man*" (xi). Using Ellison's novel to frame his history, Litwack reveals the extent to which Ellison's gifts as a novelist were inseparable from his gifts as a historian. Litwack documents—page by page, incident after incident, story after story—just how successful Ellison was in recording forms of experience that had existed outside the range of what he refers to in *Invisible Man* as "history's recorder." Wright's work, especially *Black Boy*, also figures prominently in Litwack's work because it provides several instances of the historical pattern of black disenfranchisement that Ellison's novel more self-consciously mythologizes. Litwack does not pit Ellison against Wright but regards them as part of the same story. He treats Wright's *Black Boy* as Ellison did in *Invisible Man*: he transforms its individual perspective into a broader historical frame of reference.

Trouble in Mind is named after a blues refrain—one that likely goes back to slavery days and is still performed today—which alludes simultaneously to the singer's present suffering and the hope for a better future. *Trouble in Mind* is the oral history that *Invisible Man* is not, and it details in nonmodernist language the oppressive, terrorizing social conditions that characterized black life from the Civil War until, roughly, *Brown v. Board of Education* (1954). Litwack's rhetorical strategy is not to speak for his subjects, or to presume to have mastered their story, but instead to let his subjects tell their own stories. Ellison's hero speaks for himself, but Litwack's work provides the context that shows what a difficult and unlikely act his speaking truly was. Litwack's work also names Ellison as the authoritative voice of the Negro past.

When Delmore Schwartz proclaimed *Invisible Man* a classic, he said it did not matter that its hero was black. In fact, it mattered very much that Ellison's narrator was black and especially so in 1952. In his 1955 *Paris Review* interview, Ellison highlighted his novel's relationship to black folklore to emphasize its cultural context. As Litwack acknowledges, Ellison's surrealistic novel gave him the lens through which to see a history that was otherwise invisible. Litwack's work is compelling not because it identifies and connects black folk sources to Ellison's novel but because it reveals what black folklore achieved as a living, collective social practice. Rereading Ellison through Litwack clarifies what Ellison meant when he told Murray that his novel was for black readers. Literary critics such as Henry Louis Gates Jr., Houston Baker Jr., and Hazel Carby have explained how writers such as Ellison and Wright adapted folk forms to engage a certain historical condition and reflect an ongoing group-historical consciousness. Litwack's work, though, makes concrete what these other critics have tended to "theorize," and better shows how ingeniously Ellison mixed history with myth.[9]

Reading Ellison through Litwack takes away *Invisible Man*'s retrospective, post–Civil Rights optimism and returns it to the bleaker—invisible—historical moment which it commemorated and within which he and Wright found their artistic voices. As Litwack observes, the journey of Ellison's hero requires him at "every step" to "perform the rituals expected of him and play the roles defined by whites, all of them equally dehumanizing, equally degrading, equally unrewarding. For thousands and thousands of Southern black men and women, this odyssey summed up the entirety of their lives" (xiii). Litwack's speakers reveal a version of Negro history rooted in brutal social oppression and the stubborn, often guileful, endurance that blacks managed to employ in order to survive prior to *Brown v. Board of Education* and the Civil Rights movement.

The guiding premise of Litwack's study comes from the language of *Invisible Man*'s grandfather: "Son, after I'm gone I want you to keep up the good fight. I never told you, but our life is a war and I have been a traitor all my born days, a spy in the enemy's country ever since I give up my gun back in the Reconstruction. Live with your head in the lion's mouth. I want you to overcome 'em with yeses, undermine 'em with grins, agree 'em to death and destruction, let 'em swoller you till they vomit or bust wide open" (16). Although Ellison's narrator does not understand the meaning of his grandfather's words, he is being given a code for survival during the Jim Crow era. He is also being challenged to confront heroically the social forces that oppress him and other blacks. The grandfather's surrender of his gun refers to the revolution of 1876, when the Northern troops left the former Confederacy in exchange for naming Rutherford B. Hayes as president over Tilden. The Hayes-Tilden compromise set in motion the rise of the legally segregated South and with it the eventual apotheosis of the Ku Klux Klan. Any pretense that the Civil War was going to make possible the transformation of American society through the enfranchisement of the Negro was abandoned, as was the promise of "forty acres and a mule" for every freed slave family.[10] Negroes were left to fend for themselves in a region dedicated to extracting from them every ounce of material wealth without acknowledging their basic humanity.

In order to survive the devastation that United States history has brought to bear on him, the grandfather has had to pretend to cooperate with a white power structure that he still resolves to see destroyed. His collaboration is actually a form of guerrilla warfare, and the narrative that makes up

Invisible Man represents another strategy for continuing the grandfather's subterranean war. Read as a type of prophecy, *Invisible Man* announced the end to the grandfather's war and the beginning of the new and different kind of fight that King would lead. No longer quite invisible, and no longer telling a story that is restricted to the hearing of other blacks, Ellison's narrator predicts the fully visible Negro's emergence out into the open of the American scene. Read as a history, as Litwack reads it, the novel's meaning is grim and suggests that the Negro's situation remains precarious and subject to the brutal whims of the white power structure.

Litwack's history details the plight of people who could not know that the future heralded by *Invisible Man* would ever arrive. "What the white South lost on the battlefields of the Civil War and during Reconstruction," Litwack notes, "it would largely retake in the late nineteenth and early twentieth century" (xiv). C. Vann Woodward's *The Strange Career of Jim Crow* (1955) portrays how white Southerners restaged and won the Civil War through an evolving progression of legal stratagems, court decisions, and tacit Northern complicity (see chapter 3). Litwack's history, by contrast, reveals the brutal social oppression that blacks experienced and the wary, double-voiced perspective that that experience enforced upon them. Although Woodward insists that Jim Crow did not have to happen the way it did and even suggests that Jim Crow violated the intimacy between white and black that existed prior to the Civil War, Litwack's *Trouble in Mind* suggests that surviving Jim Crow was a miraculous achievement, continuing a war that had never ceased to be fought.

If Litwack employs the voice of *Invisible Man*'s grandfather to frame the body of his narrative, then the grandfather that he presents speaks a language that is neither inspiring nor cagey. Litwack's grandfather story centers on Charlie Holcombe's recollection of his grandfather. Holcombe recalls how as a child he helped his grandfather with the chores, and during that time his grandfather initiated Charlie into the mysteries of being born black in the South. Once he finished the chores, Grandfather would sit down to "do a heap o' thinkin'" (3). Although he could neither read nor write, Grandfather Holcombe had devoted considerable thought to his situation and that of his family. He conveyed his wisdom to his grandson with a folksy metaphor: "Son, a catfish is a lot like a nigger. As long as he in his mudhole he is all right, but when he gets out he is in for a passel of trouble. You 'member that, and you won't have no trouble wid folks when you grows up" (4). In his younger years, Charlie Holcombe had tried to make a go of his own farm. The white laws had outwitted him, though, and the dream of his farm ended when he hit a white man who had cheated him. In exchange for the brief satisfaction of striking back at the system that enslaved him, Holcombe went to jail for a year. Later he had a son whom he sent to school and who graduated high in his class. The son's seeming success "was when the trouble started," says Holcombe (5).

Like his father before him, the son transacts business with white men and soon finds himself cheated with no recourse to justice. Eventually, Holcombe finds his son in the road facedown, beaten to death, and the perpetrators of the crime safe elsewhere. In that moment he recognizes the truth of the existential condition that years before his grandfather had tried to name for him: "Right den I knowed dey wasn't no use to ax for no he'p and dat I was jist a pore nigger in trouble" (6). Afterward, he would visit his son's grave and, like his grandfather, "do a lot of thinkin'" (7). Holcombe now understands that his grandfather's advice concerning the mudhole had correctly marked the limits of his own world. "If I'd kept here on the farm," he says, his son "woulda been alright. Niggers has got to l'arn dat dey ain't like white folks, and never will be, and no amount of eddycation can make'em be, and dat when dey gits outen dere place dere is gonna be trouble" (6).

From this story, Litwack presents his book's central theme: "what came to be impressed on several generations of black Southerners—the first born in freedom and coming to maturity in the 1890s and the early twentieth century—was the material, political, and military superiority of white people, the extraordinary power white men and women wielded over black lives and prospects in virtually all phases of daily life" (29). Charlie Holcombe's harrowing story stands in for thousands of others suffered by people who did not get to tell them so that they would be recorded into history. During this historical period, "tales of black ambition ended in disaster" for no other reason than that the ambitious one was born black (29, 30). Witness after witness to the Jim Crow era notes that one's survival usually depended on one's ability to remain invisible. "My motto was when I was a boy," says one, "Don't Meet Nobody. When I seen somebody coming or heard a horse, I'd step out of the road and they'd pass on by" (10). In *Invisible Man* Ellison's narrator gets into trouble for crossing the "white line" and leading a white man, Mr. Norton, to a part of black life no white person was supposed to see. His transgression is to violate the black community's self-enforced code of invisibility and thus to put the community at risk.

As Litwack shows, Negro Invisibility provides the form that makes any social encounter between white and black possible. Litwack quotes Benjamin Mays, who says that it is always the "Negro's responsibility to

find ways and means to get along with white people" even—especially—
if doing so means performing a kind of playacting.[11] Litwack also quotes
James Robinson who, with his brother, dropped their cloak of invisibility
and responded to some white boys' taunts with punches. The boys' father
wanted to whip his sons for risking their lives, but their mother defended
them. "They're black and they'll be black until they die," which means that
they will be "hated, scorned, cheated, and persecuted. At least they can have
the satisfaction of acting like men." Robinson survives that confrontation,
but that night the fear of surviving haunts him. "Would it be like this all my
life?" he wants to know. "Was there no escape from the tyranny of a Negro's
existence? I had no answer: I was sure there was none" (Litwack 40).

The answer, Grandfather Holcombe says, is to stay in your mudhole.
Ellison's narrator adopts this strategy and chooses to address his audience
from what amounts to a mudhole. Careful not to offend an audience that
may contain some whites, the protagonist prudently remains invisible while
he elliptically narrates the tyranny of the Negro's existence as he has known
it. Whether the narrator will remain invisible, as the speaker above advises,
is left ambiguous. *Invisible Man* portrays survival as a form of historical
advancement but also asks, what history is being advanced while one is
surviving? Except for the last one, each chapter ends with some form of
the message to "keep this nigger boy running." At his most optimistic, the
narrator portrays invisibility as a choice he has made and one that he can
manipulate to his advantage. But the book never quite answers the question
whether his "running" is the only possible end to the narrator's perpetual
beginnings. That answer is left to the reader.

In the opening paragraphs Ellison's hero dramatizes the historical double
bind that defines his invisibility. The book opens with a risky venture beyond his mudhole when the hero confronts a white man who has insulted
him. He contemplates killing the man but then decides against it. As if he
had learned the lesson that Charlie Holcombe could not, he sees that seeking revenge against the white man for calling him an insulting name may
not improve his situation. In fact, understanding that he cannot exact revenge commensurate with his own understanding of his historical predicament—that he cannot make the white man understand that he has violated
the hero's humanity—only reinforces for him the absurdity of his desire for
physical revenge. His situation is what Danielle Allen would call a failure
of reciprocity. Ellison's hero must sacrifice himself and relinquish his anger
to preserve a fragile social order. Instead of risking revolt, he makes a joke.
Laughing, he remarks that "something in this man's head had sprung out

and beaten him within an inch of his life" (4). Ellison's episode conveys as a matter of metaphysics the futility that Litwack's speakers experience when they know that striking back at one's tormentors is not enough to change one's place or salvage one's dignity.

The episode frames the reader's entry into the narrator's surreal account of what for him is a daily, even mundane condition. The narrative he offers is the product of his own "heap o' thinking," which represents his attempt to come to terms with the fact of his existence as a Negro. Like Charlie Holcombe, he finds the root of what he knows in the parable of skeptical resistance which his grandfather told him. While Ellison's narrator does not have the death of a son on his conscience, neither does he mention what became of his father, his grandfather's son, who may well have suffered a fate similar to Holcombe's son. The narrator's choice at the end of the narrative, to defer emerging from his hole until a later time, may reflect his understanding that to do so would return him (and thus his group) to the "passel of trouble" his story has already brought him. If so, then his narrative is both the act of undermining what his grandfather advised him to do and a concession to the folk wisdom Charlie Holcombe received from his grandfather.

Litwack notes that the pressure of feeling "that there is no escape from the tyranny of a Negro's existence" forced blacks to find "alternative" ways "to impart" their history. Often, this took the form of hearing family stories about what happened in slavery times—"how dey couldn' never do nothin' . . . but what the white folks say dey do" (43). Children forced to be invisible during the day learned at night that Nat Turner and Denmark Vesey risked visibility (and death) to lead slave insurrections—acts in keeping with the spirit of defiance that *Invisible Man's* grandfather claimed. On the other hand, sometimes "when former slaves shared their life histories with children and grandchildren, the telling itself might prove to be—for the narrator as for the young audience—a traumatic and unforgettable experience" (44). Hence, the narrator's casual allusion to slavery at the opening when he says that he is "not ashamed of my grandparents for having been slaves. I am only ashamed of myself for having at one time been ashamed (*Invisible* 15). The recognition that history produces shame and then more shame about being ashamed reveals an existential agony that can be named but not remedied by a pithy sentence.

The historical context that Litwack recovers should make it clear how difficult and even how traumatic it likely was for Ellison to write *Invisible Man*—how difficult it was for any Negro born before the Civil Rights era to tell his or her story to strangers. Litwack also helps readers understand how daring the conclusion to *Invisible Man* was, since speaking openly to a white person was the boldest and most dangerous act a black person could risk. Holocaust studies help to account for the trauma of telling the terror of the millions slain, but I am not sure that students of American history have figured out how to talk about the legacy of slavery for blacks, especially those of Wright and Ellison's generation. The historical nightmare that Litwack methodically documents is the context from which *Invisible Man* speaks to the reader. In Litwack's account, those who asserted their identities risked death. *Invisible Man* was an agonized version of the trauma that Litwack details, and Ellison may also have experienced it as the book's author.

Invisible Man attempted to pass on a story that seemed impossible to pass on. Perhaps predictably, Ellison was punished by some black intellectuals for speaking a history and point of view that had been kept secret from whites and rarely expressed in public by blacks except as a matter of music or song. In the novel, Ellison's hero, *simply by telling his story*, risks a visibility that could kill him. By taking responsibility for his story, as he says he does at the outset, Ellison's narrator is true to the spirit that allows all the black characters in the novel—except perhaps for Clifton but including even Bledsoe, Trueblood, Ras, the slave-mother of the Prologue's dream, and, especially, Mary Rambo—to go on and enact their history as living testament. By risking visibility, Ellison's narrator also predicts the courage of King and the Civil Rights movement when people's visibility meant they were offering their lives in exchange for the chance to be seen and heard.

In telling the story of the "daily struggles by black men and women to wrest some meaning and value out of their working lives," Litwack stresses how difficult it is for those who do not have a place within Negro history "to assimilate" it or its meaning (xv). Even after Douglass and Du Bois, blacks remained "behind the veil" of official history. They remained "invisible," Litwack suggests, mostly because no whites wanted to know their story, since it likely reflected so poorly on their own. Without imagining that his narrator was speaking to a sympathetic Negro audience—someone like Eubanks—Ellison might not have been able to risk the book's publication. And of course he was writing in response to Wright, and Wright's example gave him courage to risk the opprobrium that publishing his novel would bring. He had seen firsthand the controversies that Wright had endured after publishing *Native Son*, and he was prepared, as he told Wright, to face the punishment that some readers would bring upon him. He would accept this price in return for committing to literary form living proof that voices such as those that *Trouble in Mind* documents did not expire with their bodies and that the future might be changed from what the dead knew it to be.

Twelve Million Black Voices plus Two

Wright's influence on Ellison was never such that Ellison wanted to write the same kind of fiction—even if he could. Though they shared a cosmopolitan taste in literature that ran from the Russian masters to the modernists, their aesthetic sensibilities were too different to imagine that Ellison required some other outside literary influence to break from Wright's style. It was not until "The World and the Jug," however, that Ellison felt compelled to distinguish his work sharply from Wright's. According to Fabre, "Richard Wright's Blues" was Ellison's attempt to defend Wright against other critics, particularly W. E. B. Du Bois. "Bravely," Fabre says, "Ellison rhetorically countered the charge to which Wright was most open," the charge that he conceived of Negro life as unbearably bleak. Ironically, this is the very charge that ultimately vindicated Wright as a Negro intellectual to Howe and later black intellectuals. Fabre recognizes that Ellison used Wright to affirm his own critical concerns: specifically, that culture is determined by acts, not race, and that the Negro is "Western" rather than "African" ("From" 209). Yet Ellison's deference to Wright in 1945 is unambiguous. As he was publishing this essay, he was also telling Wright that others were looking to him for leadership, and "the wonderful thing is, I feel, that this will be because you dared to be simply what you are, an *artist*." Again, Ellison saw in Wright's example the same "courageous expression he also saw in the black folk tradition," because it "announced the Negro's willingness to trust his own experience, his own sensibilities as to the definition of reality, rather than allow his masters to define these crucial matters for him" (*Collected* 214).

Ellison looked to Wright rather than Langston Hughes or others of the Harlem Renaissance because he understood Wright to be doing the most to establish the groundwork for the future of Negro writing. In "Recent Negro Fiction," published three years before "Richard Wright's Blues," Ellison names Wright as the architect drawing the blueprint for that future. The young Ellison condemns the middle-class fiction of the Harlem Renaissance writers for standing aloof from the voice of the black masses. As Neal and others have recognized, Ellison's argument in 1941 predicts his subsequent, more developed point of view that Negroes have constituted a kind of distinct cultural group within America, a group whose consciousness is expressed most clearly through folk forms such as the blues and jazz.

In a gesture of autobiographical displacement, Ellison struggles to present Wright as the fulfillment and the promise of the future that the writers he surveys only hint at. I say that Ellison struggles because his presentation of Wright's triumph is mitigated by his sense that Wright's work suffers from the same sense of cultural deprivation that he says afflicts the novels of the Harlem Renaissance. Ellison thus suggests that the urbanization of Negro experience further entrenched this divide between a kind of folk consciousness and the doubtful hope for middle-class comfort. Wright's work represents the apotheosis of this trend: his Bigger Thomas, cut off from a sense of communal identity, drowns in his simulated freedom. On one hand, Wright's novel, when compared with previous Negro fiction, represented the integration of Negro life into American literature; on the other hand, it was symptomatic of how black culture was becoming isolated from its folk roots. Although Ellison questioned whether an industrial society would destroy the black folk consciousness that had been created as a mechanism to survive slavery and Reconstruction, he came to believe that only concerted political action by blacks pulling together as a group could change society. Ellison rejected not Wright's aesthetic but what that aesthetic implied about future social conditions for blacks.

Wright composed one work that answered Ellison's call in "Recent Negro Fiction," and that work likely played a decisive role in the creative process that culminated in *Invisible Man*. So many texts went into the making of *Invisible Man* that it is unnecessary to point to only one as critical, but *12 Million Black Voices* remains one of the most influential and also one of the least discussed. Though not a novel but a short, extraordinary history, *12 Million Black Voices* is a capstone to Wright's career and to twentieth-century African American writing. If Litwack's work reveals the history that Ellison's novel voiced, then Wright's work points to the hidden process that freed Ellison to assume *Invisible Man*'s narrative voice and achieve his mother's ambition. Readers of Wright often suggest, as Robin Lucy does, that "for Wright, folk culture is an element of an unusable past that cannot be translated into modernity" (263). But a careful reading of *12 Million Black Voices* suggests otherwise. In this intense, lyrical work, Wright articulated an explicitly Negro way of seeing that resonated with Ellison's own experience as a Negro and his ambitions as a Negro artist. It marked the destination and the point of departure for the journey that Ellison imagines in "Boy on a Train."

The work that became *12 Million Black Voices* began when WPA photographer Edwin Rosskam convinced Wright to compose a narrative to accompany an archive of pictures resting in the Farm Security Administration's files in Washington DC According to Rowley, Wright had long wanted to write about the Great Migration, and the project became for him "a labor of love" (237). Along with the vast research he undertook to prepare for the project, he also visited strictly segregated Washington to see the photographs. Confronting again the dehumanizing laws and customs that in effect denied blacks the rights of citizenship during the Jim Crow era, Wright saw these pictures of Negro suffering and joy through the prism of one whose "freedom" as an American was often illusory. As Rowley argues, this work "was driven by a passionate desire to bring about change" in the condition of blacks in American society (250). To further this aim, Wright converted sociology into prose poetry.

Before writing the text, Wright consulted his friend Horace Cayton, who had been working with a white sociologist, Lloyd Warner, on a study of juvenile delinquency on Chicago's South Side. Cayton's files gave Wright an inside view of the trials that confronted blacks from the Great Migration in the Northern cities. While visiting Cayton, Wright met Dr. Robert Park, a sociologist who had been tied to Booker T. Washington and to Tuskegee. Upon seeing Wright, the seventy-seven-year-old Park, ill and requiring a cane, insisted upon rising from his seat to meet the author of *Native Son*. "How in the hell did you happen?" Park asked. As a student at Tuskegee, Ellison had bristled at Park's description of the Negro as the "flower of the races," and when Ellison in his essays ridiculed the work of sociologists, it was often Park's work that he had in mind. Thus, it is appropriate to recall that Wright, Ellison's model for what a black writer might aspire to achieve, rebuked Park's point of view first as a successful black artist and then, more explicitly, in his "sociological" *12 Million Black Voices*.

Like *Trouble in Mind*, Wright's history expresses the perspective of the anonymous, invisible blacks since their arrival from Africa. Wright was also telling his own story, but this time through the voice of the Negro people. Yet where *Black Boy* and *Native Son* are full of anger, *12 Million Black Voices* tempers its outrage about social conditions with a lyricism uncommon in the rest of Wright's work. Ellison was stunned by the book. In his letter of 3 November 1941, he told Wright that reading it made him see "my blood, bones, flesh, deepest memories, and thoughts; those which are sacred and those which bring the bitterest agonies and most poignant memories and regrets." Ellison is struck by how different this book is from Wright's other work: whereas in *Native Son* "you sliced deep and twisted the knife to open up the psychic wound, *12 Million Black Voices* seizes hold to epochs to open up a continent and clears them of fog." The vista Ellison sees is his future work. "I felt so intensely the fire of our common experience when *reading 12 Millions Black Voices* that I felt the solder of my discipline melt and found myself opened up and crying over the remembered pattern of painful things" (Rowley 260).

Here is a passage typical of what Ellison encountered in *12 Million Black Voices*:

> We millions of black folk who live in this land were born into Western civilization of a weird and paradoxical birth. The lean, tall, blonde men of England, Holland, and Denmark, the dark, short, nervous men of France, Spain, and Portugal, men whose blue and gray and brown eyes glinted with light of the future, denied our human personalities, tore us from our native soil, weighted our legs with chains, stacked us like cord-wood in the foul holes of clipper ships, dragged us across thousands of miles of ocean, and hurled us into another land, strange and hostile, where for a second time we felt the slow, painful process of the new birth amid conditions harsh and raw. (*12 Million* 12)

The book's force inheres within Wright's deft use of the "we" construction. His "we" identifies a collective vision, a way of seeing that the book's heroes, the twelve million, all share. The narrative's rhetoric has the seeming simplicity of a children's story, but its truths are learned only through generations of experience. As Rowley suggests, in this work "Wright's empathy for his own people is more evident than in any of his fiction" (237). Sentence after sentence, Wright builds the powerful narrative of a people stolen for material exploitation, brought together by love, and living on through sheer courage. "Like the mystic whose ability it is to controll [*sic*] his mystic states," Ellison ecstatically tells Wright, "I am overjoyed to now be able to hold my life in my hands, turn 152 pages and see the course of it, my past and the outline of my future, flow past before me."

If the Negro people collectively are the narrative's hero, then the antagonists are the "Lords of the Land" and the "Bosses of the Buildings," the descendants of the Europeans who enslave the Negroes as the Pharaohs enslaved Moses's people. The Lords of the Land are the Southern landowners, often allied with Northern interests, who after the Civil War succeeded in replacing slavery with the sharecropping system. As Wright describes that period, the reader sees that sharecropping was in many ways a more effective and devastating way of controlling black labor than slavery had been.

Wright describes the process—described also by countless other historians but none so effectively as Wright—by which freedmen are obligated to commit to contracts that effectively make what they produce the property of whites. "If we black folk had only to work to feed the Lords of the Land," as they did in slavery times, then "our degradation upon the plantations would not have been the harshest form of servitude the world had ever known. But we had to raise cotton to clothe the world" (*12 Million* 38–39). When the crops do not bring in as much as the whites expect or demand, then the assigned debt is made part of the next year's crop estimate. The Negroes of course do not own any of the basic industries, so they are subject to the white man's law: "If we should escape to the city to avoid paying our mounting debts, white policeman track us down and ship us back to the plantation" (38).

When Negroes do manage to migrate to the North, they encounter a different form of oppression, one not unlike the bureaucratic hell that Kafka described in *The Trial* and *The Castle*. This is the realm of the Bosses of the Buildings, and their reign marks the Negro's passage from agrarian oppression to urban blight. With a remarkable economy of language, Wright explains how laws meant to ensure that American citizens have a safe, decent place to live are manipulated so that Negroes have to pay more than whites do for living spaces that are but hovels. When Negroes move into areas occupied by whites, the whites move to suburbs being built to maintain a racially segregated society. The dwellings the Negroes occupy are subdivided and converted into smaller quarters called "kitchenettes," where characters such as Wright's Bigger Thomas freeze and boil. "Kitchenettes" are what remain of a seven-room apartment after it has been stripped and cut up into seven small apartments. Where whites rented the seven rooms for fifty dollars a month, Negroes are required to pay six dollars a *week* for each kitchenette, so the landlords make an enormous profit. "A war sets up in our emotions," Wright says, between "our feelings" that tell us "that it is good to be in the city," where "we no longer need bow and dodge at the sight of the Lords of the Land," and the "part of our feelings [that] tells us that, in terms of worry and strain, the cost of living in the kitchenettes is too high" (105). For the truth is that "the kitchenette is our prison, our death sentence without a trial, the new form of mob violence that assaults not only the lone individual, but all of us, in its ceaseless attacks" (106). And so the group solidarity impressed upon Negroes among the Lords of the Land is reinforced by the Bosses of the Buildings.

In *12 Million Black Voices*, unlike *Invisible Man*, the usual markers of American history are not relevant. Neither the Declaration of Independence nor the Emancipation Proclamation marks a significant moment in the story Wright tells. Famous episodes such as the Revolutionary War, the Civil War, and World War I do not represent a victory for liberty, or the principle of self-government, but the process by which Europeans and their descendants seize control of the machinery that makes possible enormous profits built largely through the uncompensated labor of the slaves and their descendants. In the world Wright describes, not even the Freed Slave Act ever mattered, and neither, really, did the Civil War. Who cares if Kansans fought for the right not to have slaves brought to their territory, or that Emerson condemned Daniel Webster for refusing to defend the slave's right to run away, or indeed that the Civil War was fought, since following 1865 nearly all Southern blacks lack the right to possess their own livelihoods? In the world Wright describes, Negroes act with the knowledge that "we cannot fight back; we have no arms; we cannot vote; and the law is white. There are no black policemen, black justices of the peace, black judges, black juries, black jailers, black mayors, or black men anywhere in the government of the South" (43). For the Lords of the Land "life is a continuous victory; for us it is simply trouble in the land" (46).

To a point, a Marxist perspective influences the way Wright structures his narrative. But whites do not share the same position as blacks, and thus the narrative represents the Negro's historical situation as an evolving yet consistent collective class consciousness just as Ellison's 1941 essay "Recent Negro Fiction" did. This rhetorical formulation is typical: "When we were first brought here from our innumerable African tribes each of us spoke the language of our tribe. But the Lords of the Land decreed we must be distributed upon the plantations so that no two of us who spoke a common tongue would be thrown together, lest we plot rebellion" (*12 Million* 40). The Marxist dialectic that structures the plot cannot be separated from the ever emerging group-Negro consciousness that makes the work something other than a short history of labor exploitation on the North American continent. Speaking from within the collective "we" is what gives the narrative its extraordinary power (xviii). Wright uses a Marxist perspective to underscore that the Negroes' historical situation is largely a consequence of their material exploitation by whites. Wright's understated Marxism works because it denies the Lords of the Land and the Bosses of the Buildings their seeming mythic power. It accounts for how racism was materially beneficial for most white people but not reflective of some kind of God-ordained social order. Thus, Negroes are oppressed but not conquered. Their history is shaped by what the Lords and Bosses do to them, but the history they recount, whatever its trials, belongs to Wright's "we," and not to their oppressors.

Ellison saw the effectiveness of Wright's "Marxist" history of "America and the Negro," but it was Wright's affirmation of a Negro way of seeing and being that spoke to the apprentice black artist. In his letter he tells Wright, "Here is their statistics given personality: here, I believe, is the essence of what they must work with: all Marx and Engles, Lenin and Stalin wont [sic] help them unless they understand this part of the theoretical word made flesh." As *Invisible Man* attests, what endures in this world where blacks are denied by whites any form of social power—of social visibility—is the voice that sees and records the world as Negroes have known it. In a famous scene, Ellison's hero asks about those who are "too silent for the most sensitive recorders of sound; of natures too ambiguous for the most ambiguous words; and too distant from centers of historical decision to sign or even applaud the signers of historical documents. We who write no novels, histories or other books? What about us, I thought" (*Invisible* 432). He sees an answer to this question in the form of three young men moving on the train platform with "swinging shoulders in their well-pressed, too-hot-for-summer suits, their collars high and tight about their necks, their identical hats of black cheap felt set upon the crowns of their heads with a severe formality above their hard conked hair." These three men "clash with the crowd in their very immobility; standing noisy in their very silence; harsh as a cry of terror in their quietness" (433). These "transitory birds of passage" with their severe sense of form project a point of view, regardless of who might or might not be able to interpret it correctly. They need no authorization of their point of view other than their own experience and their ability to shape it according to their own vision of what is both possible and yet also required of them: to be square with the world that they know.

This is the lesson Ellison learned from Wright but also the lesson embedded in the Negro folk tradition that Ellison came to champion. In "Remembering Richard Wright," he recalls how in his state of Oklahoma, "our people fought back" and he connects this courage to the music being made by the great jazz artists (*Collected* 688). Here, in 1971, Ellison suggests that Wright's work was not quite attuned to this ritualistic aspect of Negro life, and this may be true in *Black Boy* or *Native Son*. But *12 Million Black Voices* expresses very powerfully what Ellison heard when Jimmy Rushing sang or what his narrator intuited from those "wild jacks-in-the-box" on the train platform (*Invisible* 432). Consider Wright's account of a Sunday worship meetings where the joy of Saturday night is transformed into a ritual of communal celebration:

> And the preacher's voice is sweet to us, caressing and lashing, conveying to us a heightening of consciousness that the Lords of the Land would rather keep from us, filling us with a sense of hope that is treasonable to the rule of Queen Cotton. As the sermon progresses, the preacher's voice increases in emotional intensity, and we, in tune and sympathy with his sweeping story, sway in our seats until we have lost all notion of time and have begun to float on a tide of passion. The preacher begins to punctuate his words with sharp rhythms, and we are lifted far beyond the boundaries of our daily lives, upward and outward, until, drunk with our enchanted vision, our senses lift to the burning skies, we do not know who we are, what we are, or where we are. (*12 Million* 73)

But those gathered do know who they are. Wright memorializes this moment for those who know all of this together, not quite for those who eavesdrop as sympathetic listeners, and certainly not for those who help make the history continuous by excluding its initiates from the society that would transform the basic meaning of their rituals. They have not lost themselves, but discovered the possibility of being other than who they are made to be by their bosses. This is precisely the sort of group community that Ellison would portray in his second novel.

In *Invisible Man*, Ellison also portrays a version of this church ritual when the hero, speaking at Clifton's funeral, finds himself borrowing the cadences he learned from preachers. Faced with the impossible but common task of speaking to the Negro community regarding the sacrifice of one of their favorite sons, the speaker must rely, as he has done in other speeches, on the rituals he knows from church. In this case, the speaker's audience is both white and black, but the scene invokes the archetypal one that Wright describes in the foregoing passage. His challenge is to find a ritual that will transform Clifton's otherwise meaningless death into something valuable for the community. Although he succeeds in getting his audience worked up in the way that Wright describes, the ritual invoked does not serve the same function as it does in that church. Their grief regarding their untenable situation, represented by Clifton's grotesque death, transmutes into anger and sparks the riot.

Once this ritual of communal self-affirmation leaves the sacred site of its enactment, the black church, its adherents become subject to the clubs and guns of those whose power they protest. The riot is their form of protest against a society that marginalizes them while profiting from their labor. Ellison's choice to situate this failed ritual among outsiders, nonblacks, reflects his political desire to extend the power of the black church (as King would do) beyond its normal context, and through its power to transform American society into one that respects its law as something that applies to all citizens. *Invisible Man* expresses that desire, as it expresses the invisible history of African Americans, but its hope must remain unanswered, if not unexpressed, at novel's end.

Wright's *12 Million Black Voices* shows what happens when Negroes are visible to each other and comfortably invisible to white society. In other passages, Wright describes the communal benefit that accrues from remaining distant—invisible—from the whites' malevolent gaze. He identifies the origins of this Sunday ritual when he relates how the slaves, placed in a subordinate position, stripped of the remembered communion of recollected folkways, had to invent themselves through a process of continual cultural renewal:

> We stole words from the grudging lips of the Lords of the Land, who did not want us to know too many of them or their meaning. And we charged this meager horde of stolen sounds with all the emotions and longings we had; we proceeded to build our language in inflections of voice, through tonal variety, by hurried speech, in honeyed drawls, by rolling our eyes, by flourishing our hands, by assigning to common simple words new meanings, meanings which enabled us to speak of revolt in the actual presence of the Lords of the Land without their being aware! Our secret language extended our understanding of what slavery meant and gave us freedom to speak to our brothers in captivity; we polished our new words, caressed them, gave them new shape and color, a new order and tempo, until, though they were the words of the Lords of the Land, they became *our* words, *our* language. (*12 Million* 40)

Here Wright achieves a lyricism at odds with most of his fiction. *Our words, our language.* One gets from it the joy of being Negro and the awe with which even the narrator regards the hard-to-define accomplishments that surviving in America has required. Wright also portrays "our bewilderment and despair in a world whose meaning eludes us" (128). Nor does Wright shy away from specifying the Negro's dismal status as an American material asset: "We black men and women in America today, as we look upon scenes of rapine, sacrifice and death, seem to be children of a devilish aberration, descendants of an interval of nightmare in history, fledglings of a period of amnesia on the part of men who once dreamed a great dream and forgot" (27). Still, as Ellison saw, the overall effect of Wright's narrative was to bind the Negro people into one story: a collective, continuous form of communal knowing that belies the critical attacks both he and Ellison suffered from other black readers. And if, through the despair, the communal voice can still express joy, then this joyousness testifies to the moment of victory the group achieves in its daily struggle against material oppression by the Lords of the Land and the Bosses of the Buildings.

Ellison experienced a version of this mixture of joy and anger when he first read *12 Million Black Voices*. So much of his future career is implied in what he tells Wright that a portion of it deserves to be identified and remembered as one of the most revealing, essential things Ellison ever wrote about himself. Try to recall Ellison eleven years before he published *Invisible Man*, a struggling apprentice writer not yet thirty years old, far from his future friendship with the white Southern intellectual elite represented by Warren and Woodward. This Ellison, seeking his voice, is under the spell of Wright's entrancing example when he reads *12 Million Black Voices* and sees his own story, the one the boy on the train had intuited, the one his mother had given him when she explained how his family fled the South to come to the territorial freedom of Oklahoma. He is four years from beginning *Invisible Man* and from writing the essay that identifies Wright as the black writer who has come closest to bringing the Negro experience to contemporary literature. Here, writing only to Wright in November 1941, Ellison's subject is his emergent "Negro Consciousness":

> After reading your history—I knew it all already, all in my blood, bones flesh, deepest memories, and thoughts; those which are sacred and those which bring the bitterest agonies and most poignant memories and regrets. Part of my life, Dick, has been a lacerating experience and I have my share of bitterness. But I have learned to keep the bitterness submerged so that my vision might be kept clear; so that those passions which would so easily be criminal might be socially useful. I know those emotions which tear the insides to be free and memories which must be kept underground, caged by rigid discipline lest they destroy. . . . Usually we Negroes refuse to talk of these things; the fact that I mention them now is an indication of the effect which your book has had upon me. You write of the numbness which our experience has produced in most of us, and I must say that while I was never completely numbed myself, I have had to rigidly control my thawing, allowing the liquid emotion to escape drop by drop through the trap doors of the things I write, lest I lose control; lest I be rendered incapable of warming our frozen brother.

In this moment of recognition and discovery, Ellison could not be any more direct in declaring that Wright's *12 Million Black Voices* speaks to and for him. Along with the love he feels for Wright, one can see the stifled rage he experiences as a Negro, a rage that he would ultimately transform into *Invisible Man.* The desire to warm "our frozen brother" signals his ambition to write for other Negroes. His admission that he has had to struggle to learn to control his anger anticipates the opening to *Invisible Man* (discussed earlier) and suggests how that book was born and helped him master his anger. More important, this rare, direct expression of the personal pain that Ellison knew as a Negro, so different from the image of himself that he portrayed for Howe, is elicited by Wright's text, in which the silent rage that Litwack documents is given full expression.

Here we see an Ellison utterly open to Wright and the story he tells. In this same letter Ellison says that "of this, however, I am sure now more than ever: That you and I are brothers, Dick." He names Wright as the necessary voice that has warmed and will warm him, Wright's frozen-hot brother struggling to find his own artistic voice. He perceives in a flashing illumination how *12 Million Black Voices* invokes and then brings together those voices, speaking as one body, chanting a song of the defiant lyrical beauty that is the history of the Negro in America. Ellison will work to contribute his own chorus.

When Ellison wrote his answer to Wright's *12 Million Black Voices*, he chose the perspective of a single anonymous hero who understood that "all dreamers and sleepers must pay the price" and that "even the invisible victim is responsible for the fate of all" (*Invisible* 14). In different ways, Wright and Ellison paid the price for the communal burden they carried. Wright died in exile with many of his completed books unpublished. The Ellison who could see his own story so powerfully expressed in Wright's saga of the Negro people mostly disappeared and became a version of Roth's Coleman Silk from *The Human Stain.* In 1941, *12 Million Black Voices* inspired Ellison to tell Wright in his letter, "I believe we [Negroes] need to enter a period of public testimony in which our essential oneness might be confessed and our brotherhood acknowledged and accepted." Much later, in 1970, Ellison declared, "I have always written out of a sense of the group experience as filtered through my individual experiences, talent, and vision." He added, "I think that now a very articulate group of young writers doesn't quite know what to make of me. I'm standing up there—speaking in terms of metaphor now—like a black militant leader with his bodyguard. I don't have a bodyguard but there's nothing like that to compel people to see if they can knock you off. I think that since I have not embraced some of their literary theories, they feel that I'm the enemy" (*Collected* 394).

In a 1945 diary entry, Wright noted that Ellison wrote to express his condition as a Negro, and that articulating such a perspective would constitute the meaning of Ellison's work: "Pending Ralph's visit, I keep thinking of him and of the fact that almost every act of a Negro is partly or wholly conditioned by his being a Negro. Ralph did not want to join the army because it is a Jim Crow army and he went into the merchant marine. He writes because he is a Negro; he really wanted to be a sculpture [*sic*], but he found he could not say what was hotly in him to say with stone and marble. Now again he [is] making decisions based solely on his racial identity. He has no choice" (Jackson, "Ellison's Invented" 27). Wright probably knew Ellison better than anyone. Here his astute analysis suggests that his friend's writing was at its core a response to his condition as a black American and not, as his readers have understandably assumed, a quest for a conventional literary career built on numerous novels and stories. One cannot help wondering what Wright would have made of the attacks that Ellison faced and whether Wright's presence on the scene might have made a critical difference in the way Ellison was later received by angry black intellectuals.

When *Invisible Man* was published, Wright wrote Ellison, "you can be proud of what you turned in, Ralph. You entered the ranks of world literature with your book, and there is no doubt about it" (Jackson, *Ralph* 441). Wright's entry into the ranks of world literature had won him international acclaim, but his literary celebrity in exile was nothing like the reaction that Ellison's rise would bring in the 1960s and '70s. During the most intense period of their friendship, neither man could have imagined the startling political transformations that would soon largely eradicate the Jim Crow world that together they had fought. Nor could they have imagined a black writer's receiving the acclaim that Ellison was given. Because Ellison lived a long life and achieved a degree of social success unimaginable when considered from the perspective of the world he knew with Wright, his story is easily assimilated to what might be called the "prospective" reading of *Invisible Man*. In this reading, the narrator looks forward rather backward. He imagines a society where the social action his narrative inspires miraculously transforms American society into one committed to "equality" for all. This is the world that Ellison came to know and is the subject of the next chapter. This was not the world that Ellison and Wright knew together when Wright's *12 Million Black Voices* moved Ellison to hot tears, eleven years before he finished *Invisible Man* and earned distinction from the *Chicago Defender*.

3

Ellison, Warren, and Woodward
The Other Side of *Invisible Man*

"She saw the books and the furniture and the paintings, so she knew you were some kind of white man," Albert Murray cracked to Ellison, but "what she didn't stop to notice was that you're a Southern white man."

There's no Southerner who hasn't been touched by the presence of Negroes. There's no Negro who hasn't been touched by the presence of white Southerners.

RALPH ELLISON to Robert Penn Warren, 1965

THE DRAMA OF *Invisible Man* does not end with the protagonist being happily absorbed into the American society, because such an ending was impossible when Ellison wrote the book. When he told Wright that *12 Million Black Voices* spoke for him, he was responding to his sense that Negroes had helped to make America possible but had not been allowed the opportunity either to take credit for or reap the rewards of their struggle. Once *Invisible Man* was being celebrated as a work of American genius, the novel's very success appeared to render the truth of a work like *12 Million Black Voices* "merely" history. This is not to say that being born black in America had suddenly become the same thing as being born white in America (this is not true today), but with *Brown v. Board of Education* (1954) it was clear that the conditions of being born an American, black or white, were changing radically. Recognizing that a historical transformation was suddenly occurring, Ellison became one of the new history's vanguard figures.

After *Invisible Man* Ellison occupied a status unprecedented in the history of American literature: an accomplished black writer whose achievement suggested that race, or racism, did not have to be a constitutive part of American experience. Ellison chose to use his podium to argue for the essential relationship between black experience and American identity. In his first speech as a prominent writer, Ellison commemorated his sudden visibility by asking his new admirers to confront the legacy of racism in American history as it was reflected in American literature. "Brave Words for a Startling Occasion" (1953) defined the American literary tradition in terms of its commitment to democracy insofar as that commitment was expressed in protesting the legacy of slavery. Rather than stressing his debt to Negro intellectuals such as W. E. B. Du Bois, Alain Locke, or Richard Wright, as he might have done, Ellison challenged his audience's assumptions by asserting that "except for the work of William Faulkner something vital had gone out of American prose after Mark Twain" (*Collected* 152). "Brave Words" along with contemporaneous essays such as "Twentieth-Century Fiction and the Black Mask of Humanity," "Change the Joke and Slip the Yoke," and "Society, Morality and the Novel" explicitly identify Ellison's work as being within a tradition established by Emerson, Twain, and Faulkner. In a sense, he was just carrying on the conversations he and Wright had when they discussed their work in the context of a broad literary tradition. Yet in articulating his work's connection to that of these earlier, white American authors, Ellison was also aligning their tradition—the so-called American tradition—within Negro American experience.

Before giving his speech, Ellison had already made this point to his most obvious white American precursor, William Faulkner, when he told the sole proprietor of Yoknapatawpha County that meeting him "really completes the day for me," since "you know, you have children all around now. You won't be proud of all of them, just the same they're around" (*Trading* 44–45). One can hardly underscore how much Ellison must have relished the meeting, and his remark tells us something about how he would occupy his new position as acclaimed Negro American intellectual. His deference to Faulkner had an edge to it: he was the bastard child demanding recognition. The joke acknowledges and conceals his nearly twenty-year odyssey as an aspiring black intellectual in the wilderness, but it also suggests that he knows that his presence may change how others see themselves more than it changes his sense of what he has done. Ellison was pointedly meeting Faulkner as an equal and as a relative.

Faulkner once said that he wanted to abolish the biography of the man that he had been and instead allow only the artist to survive through his works. Ellison, suddenly thrust into the spotlight as the nation's most acclaimed Negro artist, decided that he could not cultivate such a charming aesthetic fantasy regarding his status as a famous writer. He was part of and prophet to a changing history and was ready to announce this fact to people who might not yet be ready to hear it. His narrator had remarked that vision was a form of action and Ellison practiced that Emersonian insight to a remarkable and *still unacknowledged* degree. After receiving the National Book Award for *Invisible Man*, he was, as Rampersad affirms, "now speaking with unprecedented authority for a black American" (275). Rather than separate the meaning of his art and his artistic achievement from the world that had made it, as the modernists he admired might have had him do, Ellison chose to enact the political position implied by his art. For the rest of his life, he confronted the world beyond his novel with the vision of history that his novel enacted.

In that National Book Award address, Ellison remarked that "as a Negro," he was "attracted" to the works of Twain and Faulkner because they projected "the conflicts within the human heart that arose when the sacred principles of the Constitution and Bill of Rights clashed with the practical exigencies of human greed and fear, hate and love" (*Collected* 153). His point is not only that blacks and whites are both human but also that they are citizens whose relationship to each other is, or should be, mediated through their shared commitment to the Constitution and the Bill of Rights. In other words, a year before *Brown*, Ellison, with an uncanny sense of prophecy, was giving America's leading literary lights a preview of the landmark Warren Court decision that would forever change social relations in American culture. In giving his audience the word that blacks were no longer willing to settle for a position of social invisibility, Ellison signaled that his ambition was to address and begin to heal the wounds that American history had opened. In invoking the "sins against those principles that we all hold sacred," Ellison's quest as an artist, intellectual, and representative Negro American was to find what he called "home," by which he meant that place where Americans of all colors could live as equals. "The way home we seek," he said to initiate his career as the acclaimed author of *Invisible Man*, "is that condition of man's being at home in the world, which is called love, and which we term democracy" (154). Ellison's remark combined the aesthetic with the political. His literary criticism, like his fiction and indeed all of his work as an intellectual, was a form of social criticism and political action.

One of the aspects of democracy that *Invisible Man* explores, notes political theorist Danielle Allen, is how "democracy puts its citizens under a strange form of psychological pressure" that derives from being "an individual in a democratic world of strangers, where large-scale events are supposed to arise out of one's consent and yet never really do" (27). In retrospect, one can see that "Brave Words for a Startling Occasion," with its no less startling title, announced Ellison's arrival not just as a novelist but as a public intellectual committed to bringing his idea of democracy to the widest audience he could reach. That is, once Ellison arrived with *Invisible Man*, it became his role to enact a political-historical vision committed to an ideal of *polis* for all American citizens.[1] The political understanding of democracy that Allen says *Invisible Man* explores was flexible enough to address why blacks were frustrated to be invisible within American society and why white Americans might feel anxious after *Brown* to see their social order being changed so quickly.

Unfortunately, this crucial aspect of Ellison's career has been either trivialized or insufficiently understood. After *Invisible Man*, Ellison did not understand his role as a black intellectual to be to nourish his "blackness" but to work to integrate black experience with American experience. Given American history, though, such a position was virtually unprecedented, since, as Du Bois had pointed out in *The Souls of Black Folk*, being black and being American seemed like an anomalous, and even contradictory, set of realities. Understandings of Ellison's career veer between the two poles of thought that Harold Cruse identified in his classic, *The Crisis of the Negro Intellectual*. For Cruse, the black intellectual and political tradition in America has been divided between the integrationists, who go from Frederick Douglass through the early W. E. B. Du Bois to Martin Luther King, and the nationalists, who go from Martin Delany to Malcolm X. Cruse says the integrationists believe in the "Great American Ideal" (6), or "the living expression of that body of concepts sanctified in the American Constitution" (7). Critics who attack Ellison for being apolitical are usually attacking him for not being more of a black nationalist. Critics who celebrate his artistry or his intellectual brilliance may be tacitly praising his seeming capacity for assimilation.

Although belief in the "Great American Ideal" does seem to characterize the post–*Invisible Man* Ellison, I would still argue, following Allen, that he was neither an assimilationist nor a black nationalist. Allen suggests that "the seesawing back and forth of African American political ideology between assimilation and separatism is itself a product of our failure to address directly the question: what modes of citizenship can make a citizenry whole without covering up difference?" (19). Ellison's work raises this question as well, since, as he understood, the assimilationist/separatist dichotomy was a trap for "minority" Americans. Once defined by such a dichotomy, one either betrays one's group or risks being spurned by the majority. Moreover, as Allen reminds, Ellison did not expect racism in America to end anytime soon, so the vital issue that democracy raised in the post-*Brown* era was how to lessen its danger and still have a productive society in which more citizens could play active roles. Ellison embodied a form of citizenship that moved beyond the separatist/assimiliationist dichotomy.

Invisible Man was composed precisely on the dividing line between separatist and assimilationist. It marked the fulfillment of a black intellectual tradition begun by W. E. B. Du Bois in *The Souls of Black Folk* and carried through the work of Richard Wright. Du Bois demonstrated the extent to which the U.S. government had failed the freed slaves after the Civil War, and Wright portrayed the twentieth-century consequences of this failure. Du Bois sought to bring the Negro folk tradition together with a scholarly recovery of black experience that white historians had either missed or intentionally distorted (see Sundquist, *To Wake* 467–90). In *Souls*, Du Bois frames his chapters with musical notation meant to represent the sorrow songs. In a less schematic way, *Invisible Man* succeeded in dramatizing Du Bois's historical vision, which combined folk forms with erudition to address what happened after Reconstruction. This invisible history was also Ellison's preoccupation—it was the defining issue for the post–Civil War, pre-*Brown* black intellectual. As a work of invisible history that joined Negro folk wisdom to the latest achievements in narrative aesthetics, Ellison's great novel constituted a tradition unto itself. Like Du Bois, Ellison was writing to change history, not just represent it.

As Allen's work explains and Ellison recognized immediately, *Brown* and its aftermath marked a "reconstitution" of American society that symbolically returned his gun to *Invisible Man*'s grandfather in the form of legal redress. After nearly one hundred years, the 13th, 14th, and 15th amendments were at last to be applied to every American. Speaking of the cost required for each American citizen to achieve full "identity," Ellison noted that "we [Americans] have been reluctant since we first suspected that we are fated to live up to our sacred commitments or die, and the Civil War was the form of that fateful knowledge" (*Collected* 706). Allen follows Ellison's logic by arguing that the civil rights period restaged the Civil War. If "the U.S. Constitution devised institutions that went a long way toward solving the problem of radical distrust within a democratic citizenry," then the fact that "they could not solve the problem once and for all is proved not only by the U.S. Civil War of 1861 but also by the small civil wars of the 1960s" (xx). Allen chooses the integration of Little Rock's Central High as the symbolic moment of the nation's reconstitution, in part because photographs of the encounter became an immediate part of the national memory. Eisenhower had sent federal troops to Arkansas to act against Governor Orville Faubus's decision to use state troops to prevent black students from enrolling. To Ellison, and other black Americans, it was as if the withdrawal of federal troops from the South in 1877 had been rescinded. To white Southerners, such as William Faulkner and Robert Penn Warren, the period threatened to mark another Northern invasion and a violation of Southern integrity.

Ellison's illegitimate literary father, Faulkner, famously told a London *Sunday Times* reporter, "As long as there is a middle road, all right, I'll be on it. But if it came to fighting I'd fight for Mississippi against the United States even if it meant going out into the streets and shooting Negroes" (Blotner, *Faulkner* 2:1591). Robert Penn Warren wrote a book for *Life* magazine, *Segregation: The Inner Conflict of the South* (1956), which more circumspectly responded to the threat to the "old ways" that *Brown* provided. As Faulkner's public outbursts about "shooting Negroes" in the streets and Warren's *Segregation* suggest, though, even cultured, sophisticated white Southerners were skeptical that the federal government could make the reconstitution stick. The entire "strange career of Jim Crow," in the phrase of C. Vann Woodward, suggested that white Southerners, with the collaboration of a few Northerners, could evade the federal mandate of equal rights for black and white citizens. The Southern counterrevolt against *Brown*, led by Georgia senator Richard Russell, which Ellison feared would work, was not ultimately successful, Allen says, because a sufficient number of white Americans were ashamed of the treatment that blacks had to suffer. Allen does not discount the enormous courage and powerful impact of the protest movement, ably guided by a number of black leaders, but also insists that without white support the revolution for equal rights could not have happened. In part, this revolution was due to the resolve of the Supreme Court and Lyndon Johnson, but in the end it was also because enough white Southerners gave way that the public spaces in the South could, in the sudden blink of history's eye, become integrated.

Allen suggests that once the laws were in place and the government meant to enforce them, the next step required that blacks and whites learn to trust one another as fellow citizens. In a word, friendship became the new social goal, but attaining that goal would require more than calling off the dogs, turning down the fire hoses, and shaking hands. Many, like Faulkner or Baldwin, would understandably respond to the reconstitution with a version of what we now call identity politics. Allen, though, argues that what the reconstitution called for was a new model of democratic citizenship. "This democracy has repeatedly failed to develop forms of citizenship that help break down distrust and generate trust, a failing closely linked to a second failure to develop citizenly habits that can contend with the unequal distribution of benefits and burdens inevitably produced by political decisions" (xxi). Why? There is no one answer, but in terms of American history the most obvious answer—the one Wright gave in *12 Million Black Voices*— is the treatment of blacks as property or cheap, replaceable labor. *Brown* did not do away with the fact that blacks, among all Americans, would continue to be the most exploited group in American society but did make it possible to imagine a society where this exploitation did not have to be the case and, indeed, where blacks could rise to places never before occupied by any one other than whites.

After *Invisible Man*, Ellison worked to articulate a position that acknowledged and addressed the fears of blacks and whites about becoming part of a new, reconstituted American society. The question for Ellison, as it was for King, was how to make this possible. The answer, according to Allen, was "political," but not in the conventional sense of the term. If American democracy had repeatedly failed to generate models of trust between citizens, then what the new era required was for Americans to explore how "the ordinary practice of friendship provides all citizens with knowledge that can be carried into the political realm with good effect" (xxi). Allen's description aptly characterizes both how Ellison saw himself after *Invisible Man* and the strategies he pursued as a public black intellectual in light of his new visibility: "I ask all citizens to see themselves as founders of institutions," and as such they will become "mediums of trust-building." These are Allen's words (xxi), but they might as well have been Ralph Ellison's words, since they convey perfectly his post–*Invisible Man* vision.

If "friendship begins in the recognition that friends have a shared life" and that friendship "is not an emotion but a practice" (Allen xxi), then the challenge for Ellison was how to demonstrate and enact the new form of democratic friendship that the changing American society required. He never relinquished his position as a black intellectual with a privileged understanding of black life; however, he consistently acted against arguments that did not promote civic trust and the ideal of friendship as a hard-earned practice. He did not support the tactics of the Black Panthers, for instance, but he acknowledged that Malcolm X represented an authentic black perspective, however potentially dangerous that perspective may have been for comity between blacks and whites.[2] Ellison's post–*Invisible Man* essays affirmed Allen's argument that in a democratic society "our shared elements" are, "when considered at the political rather than the private level, made out of all the combinations of all our interactions with each other. We are always awash in each other's lives, and for most of us that shared life, recorded as history, will be the only artifact we leave behind" (xxii). Recognizing this shared life meant that Americans had to go beyond their historical comfort zones. One of the lessons of *Invisible Man*, insofar as that novel was a history of Jim Crow America, is that blacks leave the company of other blacks at their own peril. With *Brown*, however, blacks and whites were presented with an opportunity to risk and answer the question that Ellison's narrator poses at the end of his story. Why not see which frequencies we share and who might be able to speak for (and with) whom?

Allen's political reading of Ellison provides a broader frame for considering Ellison's career as an attempt to get beyond Jim Crow–derived identity politics and cultural wars to a point where civility—civic trust—is possible. In this context, among the most revealing aspects of Ellison's career were his friendships with those grandsons of the Confederacy, Robert Penn Warren and C. Vann Woodward. Each of them believed that the Civil War was the landmark event of American history, and each spent his intellectual life trying to explain why this was so. Woodward dedicated *The Burden of Southern History* (1958) to Warren, his colleague then at Yale. Warren's *Who Speaks for the Negro?* (1965) was in part a tribute to Ellison. The talk Ellison was working on at the time of his death had Warren's ideas at the heart of it.[3] Woodward paid perhaps the highest praise he could pay to Ellison when, at the 1968 Southern Historical Association meeting in New Orleans, he dubbed him a Southerner and a historian.

Ellison's crucial and crucially overlooked friendship with these two Southern intellectuals has received its most sustained attention in Rampersad's recent biography. For Rampersad—whose characterization lacks the sense of trust that Allen calls for—these friendships were merely instrumental: Warren was the means by which Ellison raised himself in white literary society. On this view, Warren was Ellison's patron (to the American Academy of Letters and then to its Century Club), and in return, Ellison vouched for the white man's social integrity. Undoubtedly, each man benefited from the friendship—a friendship that lasted nearly forty years and ended only with Warren's death in 1989. Such a reading, though, ignores the basis of their friendship: they were gifted literary artists consumed by the intersection between history and aesthetic representation. Moreover, not only did each believe the Civil War to have been the decisive event in American history, each of them thought he was witnessing its end in his own lifetime.

In 1989, when Warren was near death, Ellison wrote a letter to his friend Nathan Scott testifying to the deep bond he shared with Warren. He recalls meeting Warren at a party celebrating the release of *Invisible Man* but says that their friendship ripened four years when they were both in Rome for an extended period. During that time he saw Warren daily, and Warren "became the companion with whom I enjoyed an extended period of discussing literature, writing, history, politics—you name it—exploring the city, exchanging folk tales, joking, lying, eating and drinking." Ellison suggests that the two men's natural affinity for each other was enhanced by their mutual recognition that they became friends despite the historical traditions that had formed them. Rosanna Warren says that her father "saw Ralph as an equal who deserved every honor" and adds that "just about the last thing Father said before he died, was something about having to go with Ralph to buy a car. He was delirious, but Ralph was on his mind" (Rampersad 538). Ellison spoke at Warren's funeral, but he could not have been more eloquent there than in recalling to Scott their days in Rome when together they explored "historical sites, restaurants, and bars": "Through such pleasurable roaming," they found that "any bars to our friendship that might have been imposed by Southern manners and history went down the drain and left the well-known Fugitive poet and the fledgling writer and grandson of Freedmen marvelously free to enjoy themselves as human beings" (17 July 1989).

Ellison's deep friendship with Warren was the embodiment of his post-*Brown* political and social vision. Without denying the hardships that had faced blacks in the past and continued in the present, Ellison decided that the only way to get past the past was to make a truce with it, and a truce works both ways. If Warren helped elect Ellison to the American Academy of Arts and Letters and then to its Century Club, then this gesture also allowed Warren to integrate that organization, with the result that other blacks would be invited to join.[4] Ellison represented an opportunity for Warren to rethink his position as Southern white man in light of black political equality. In this sense, their friendship began before they ever met, when Warren first read *Invisible Man*. "The mere fact that this book is written by a Negro gives it a special force and significance," Warren wrote Albert Erskine. "To me it was more enlightening about one important aspect of the Negro's relation to our society than anything else I've ever read" (*Selected* 437). Warren praised *Invisible Man* because it helped him—a white Southerner who had lived a good portion of his life among blacks and thought that he knew them well—to understand something about blacks that he had *not* known. He sought Ellison out after *Invisible Man* was published, and their friendship blossomed in the way that Ellison describes.

Warren's friendship was part of a process by which he was renouncing a "militant" white Southern position he had once occupied as a member of the group known as the Southern Agrarians. In 1963 Martin Luther King told Warren that "the sacrifices and sufferings" that King's people had to face were something of which "your own people don't have an understanding, an appreciation," since Southern whites were "seeking to destroy [King's] image at every point" (Frady 127). King could not know that for Warren their meeting was an attempt by this chastened white man to redress historical wrongs he now believed he had committed. As a young man, he had published an essay in *I'll Take My Stand* (1930) which defended the logic of *Plessy v. Ferguson* (1896), the decision that institutionalized Jim Crow. In works such as *Segregation* (1956) and *Who Will Speak for the Negro?* (1965), Warren was completing the process of moral enlightenment that *Invisible Man* had demanded of him and that took on more urgency with the success of the Civil Rights movement.

The Ellison and Warren families became close friends. Fanny Ellison and Eleanor Warren wrote each other often, and Ellison earned the affection of Warren's children. When visiting the Warrens, the Ellisons stayed overnight. They liked the Warren-atmosphere. To Nathan Scott, Ellison praised the "Southern and yet cosmopolitan, intellectually sophisticated, but downhome friendly" atmosphere of the Warrens' parties, which were marked by an "easy Americanness" that may have "bewildered" some guests, "their talk of equality notwithstanding." It is probably not too much to say that Warren, at his best, represented Ellison's ideal post-*Brown* white American. In that same letter to Scott, Ellison notes that he and his wife were "delighted—though not surprised" to attend Rosanna Warren's wedding and find that the ritual was being performed by a black minister. It is tempting to suggest that Ellison, who spent forty years writing a novel that featured a black minister, sometimes may have thought of himself as one ministering to Warren's moral education—except that their obvious respect for each other as equals permeates their letters.

In 1970, when Ellison was being reviled by black nationalists, Warren wrote him to say that a position was being made available for him at Yale. Warren urged Ellison to consider it, since "as you well know, you have many friends and admirers here who would welcome the idea of having you as a colleague and who would welcome you" (27 Feb. 1970). Among those friends was the historian C. Vann Woodward, and by this point in his life Ellison, the former black militant intellectual, may have thought he had more in common with reconstructed white Southern intellectuals than with 1960s militant black intellectuals. Though their friendship was not as personal as the one with Warren, Woodward and Ellison too shared a passionate commitment to understanding what had happened to the South since the Civil War. Woodward passed along book manuscripts by other historians that he knew would excite Ellison's interest and commentary. He also invited Ellison to participate in gatherings with other historians. In inviting Ellison to the 1968 Southern Historical Association convention, Woodward joked that "the purposes would be the standard ones: the advancement of learning and the glory of God." There would "be no fee and no expense account" but the "fringe benefits" would be considerable: "the companionship of all concerned" (18 Mar. 1968). Woodward's note implies what Warren's invitation to come to Yale makes explicit: the sense that the three of them are fellow travelers who cherish their association.

Understanding Ellison's friendship with these two giants of twentieth-century Southern thought is as important to understanding Ellison's life and work as is his formative friendship with Richard Wright. For as Wright marked the way through which Ellison achieved his apotheosis as the novelist of Negro history, Warren and Woodward indicated that the enemy, as it were, could be won over. *Brown* made blacks visible within American society; thereafter, Ellison's role was to enact this visibility and to do so not only by protesting the legacies of discrimination. He looked for points of intersection and integration through which he began to transform the past. One way to do so was to reclaim Southern history as a type of black history. In the 1990 "Notes for a Class Day Talk at Columbia University," Ellison marvels at the incongruity of seeing a black man on the streets of New York wearing a hat with a rebel flag on it before deciding, "Ellison, the Confederates were also *Americans*, and, God help him, so is he!" (*Collected* 839–40). In his association with Warren and Woodward, Ellison likewise affirmed their shared identities as Americans, even as he was trying to co-opt their visions as versions of his own.

In introducing him at the 1968 conference, Woodward said that Ellison "has declared his allegiance to history, as well as his Southern identity, most clearly in his warning to a critic about the abstraction he would impose upon American reality" (Ellison, *Conversations* 143). In *The Burden of Southern History* Woodward had suggested that racial progress would come in the South not only when white Southerners surrendered the idea that the South's mission was to remain, as it were, Confederate but when the Negro offers "an acknowledgment that he is also a Southerner as well as an American" (22). I argue that Ellison's tortured "Tell It Like It Is, Baby" (*Collected*), along with his interview with Warren for *Who Speaks for the Negro?* (both published in 1965), answers Woodward's charge. Moreover, Woodward's career pursued a journey comparable to the one Ellison lived: he risked the disapproval of his peer group (Southern whites and Southern historians) to affirm a view of history that contradicted the status quo. Warren's case, however, was different because he had been more committed to an ideal of the virtuous South than Woodward ever was. Thus, the friendship between Ellison and Warren confirmed Ellison's intuition that democracy was a force of history that could change lives in almost unimaginable ways.

In a 1971 letter to Warren, Ellison describes "a fine portrait" of "Red" that Fanny had clipped from a magazine and that she and Ellison had placed on their bookshelves along with pictures of Mark Twain, Henry James, Tchaikovsky, Abe Lincoln, and Louis Armstrong. Ellison tells Warren that a black journalist had visited him recently and, looking at the pictures, wanted to know who Ellison had placed among these other luminaries. "That's just our old friend Red," Ellison replies casually. "*Warren*," the visitor exclaims, before adding "Well I'll be dam, you just never know." Ellison, amused by his visitor's confusion, agrees with the self-assessment. "No, you never do," he replies. Ellison notes that his visitor "waited for the wheels to stop whirling behind his astonished eyes." The letter suggests that the seeming incongruity of their friendship was a fact that Ellison and Warren both enjoyed, but for Ellison the friendship was more than a joke of literary history. As he tells Warren, "The next time the subject comes up (and I am sure it will) I shall explain something of the intricacies of our relationship and some of the ways in which friendship transcends abstractions. And I'll do it only because the guy is attempting to write American fiction" (1971).

Ellison spent his post-*Brown* career trying to explain the intricacies of American history and the various concealed relationships that that history comprised. In his 1989 letter to Scott, he praises an essay that Scott had written about Warren in which he confronted "our old historical problem" and in so doing made "a valuable contribution to literary criticism." Ellison clearly understood his friendship with Warrant to be a response to the "old historical problem" brought about by the enslavement of blacks, and he also clearly wanted the meaning of his friendship with Warren to be understood as a part of his legacy. What follows is an attempt to do justice to this friendship between a Fugitive poet and a grandson of freedmen, two of Faulkner's children, who together sought to transcend abstractions and centuries of prejudice. Their friendship, though largely invisible, remains one of the most remarkable in American literary history.

Their interview in *Who Speaks for The Negro?* marks the symbolic summit of their friendship. Before we can mount that summit, though, I turn to C. Vann Woodward, whose life and work as a historian exemplify the historical process that brought Ellison and Warren together.

The South's "Invisible" Historian

Woodward was the preeminent Southern historian and Ellison the preeminent black intellectual of the post–World War II era, but their intellectual intersection is largely unrecognized. There was a good reason Woodward and Ellison shared the stage during the 1968 meeting of the Southern Historical Association: each was committed to destroying the post–Civil War myth of the Confederate South. In the 1960s Martin Luther King, while he and his supporters were being jailed or maimed or killed by fearful whites, told his audience that in the face of violence one must still reach out to embrace and love one's enemy. In *Invisible Man*, Ellison anticipated King's strategy by inviting his readers, white and black, to see in his narrator's story a version of their own. Although *Invisible Man* communicated an in-group message that had everything to do with a specific Negro history of struggling for full expression and equal rights, the book also spoke to a historical situation that blacks shared with white Southerners and it challenged them to revise the version of history they thought was theirs.

Warren read *Invisible Man* and had his eyes opened to Southern black anger, but Woodward had been on a trajectory that would make his work consistent with the political objectives of King (and of Ellison). Works such as *The Origins of the New South* or *The Strange Career of Jim Crow* documented the same post–Civil War era that Ellison also covered in *Invisible Man* and attacked the same entrenched points of view that Ellison was attacking. If Ellison never marched with King, then Woodward in a fashion did, since King often praised Woodward's *The Strange Career of Jim Crow* as "the historical Bible of the civil rights movement" (Woodward, *Thinking* 92). Moreover, as a young scholar seeking a dissertation subject, Woodward had approached Du Bois with the hope of working with him. Du Bois declined to encourage him, yet Woodward's work would eventually affront the very old-time white Southern sensibility that Du Bois identified as the major block to achieving democracy. Although Woodward's orientation to Southern history was tilted toward "white" Southern history, his work would not make sense without the social transformation heralded by *Invisible Man* and brought to truth by King and the Civil Rights movement. As Barbara J. Fields points out regarding *The Origins of the New South*, Woodward never examined the condition of blacks "as a subject apart from the subjects of land, agriculture, and rural unrest; industrial development and political economy; class warfare, class alliances, and politics; and literature, the sciences, and the arts" (Fields 261). Woodward recognized that blacks were Southerners and Americans and that their historical situation could not be segregated from that of Americans generally.

Woodward's memoir, *Thinking Back* (1986), can be read as a Southern white intellectual's *Invisible Man*. His illumination is not as dramatic as that of Ellison's narrator, but the logic of his story was to dismantle and replace the racist pieties of Southern history. His intellectual coming of age coincided with the "most creative years of the Southern Literary Renaissance," which also influenced Warren, and he speaks of Faulkner as his role model. Where Faulkner and Warren struggled to preserve their ideal of the Old South, however, Woodward, the artist as historian, was ready to tear it down. Perhaps not coincidentally, Woodward, unlike Warren or Faulkner, was attracted to black culture. He was fascinated by "the continuous rebirth of jazz," and his appreciation of jazz, an art form "black in origin," was an important "part of the scene" that shaped him (*Thinking* 10). As a "surviving witness" of that period, Woodward speaks of being "thoroughly familiar with one side of the universally prevailing system of racial subordination." Without any of the defensiveness that marks Warren's sociological memoirs, Woodward says that he "would never have any cause for wonder at the little signs, White Only and Colored." His lack of defensiveness may have come from the fact that he was writing in 1985, not 1956 or 1965, or it may have come from the fact that by 1934 he, like Ellison, had been questioning the logic of segregation from within (14).

Woodward characterizes the segregated South of his youth by its "siege mentality" (*Thinking* 15). In *Who Speaks for the Negro?* Ellison and King would both tell a defensive Warren that from the Negro perspective white Southerners were imprisoned by their blind fealty to what they took to be their history. Woodward says that the South of his youth had what W. J. Cash properly called "'a savage ideal'" that was "not a sign or a consequence of unity," as Warren might argue, "but rather of regimentation" (*Thinking* 15). Woodward says that Cash defined this mood when he wrote that "criticism, analysis, detachment" were qualities that Southerners viewed as acts of "'high and aggravated treason'" (15). Thus, when Woodward determined that he would become a historian who subjected his native region, the South, to the very forms of analysis that Cash identified as treasonous, he knew that his work risked being received as "an affront" and an "insult" to "one's fellow citizens," who might very well "call in question one's very loyalty" to one's homeland (15). Like Ellison's, his interest in history was inseparable from his desire to change the present by exposing the casually accepted injustices of the past.

Woodward does not say that as a dissident white Southern intellectual, he was invisible. The metaphor applies to his situation, though, because he knew that along with his criticism of the South's "siege mentality," his intellectual work would alienate his core group. Woodward consistently had to reject premises of his birth region in his search for a higher (historical) consciousness. Understanding that "the system founded on the ruins of the Reconstruction called the New South" was corrupt, he hoped to redeem the South's history as something worth preserving in terms other than the racist ones in which it had been celebrated. This ambition recalls Du Bois or Ellison more than white Southern historians of the era. To Woodward, the practice of Southern history had become rotten because its goal was merely to reiterate and reconfirm "the enduring and fundamentally unbroken unity, solidarity, and continuity of Southern history" (*Thinking* 23). He acknowledges that Du Bois had tried to counteract the prevailing view in *Black Reconstruction* (1935), but the white Southern hegemony could not yet be compelled to entertain a Negro point of view, so Woodward was left to attack this tradition from the inside (24).

Like his hero Faulkner, Woodward understood the history he wanted to tell to be a search for the appropriate narrative form. Knowing that his "attack" would have to be "oblique"—that he would have to employ, as it were, underground tactics and rely on the boomerang of history to come back to him—Woodward sought subjects that would allow him as a historian to occupy "the omission and long silences that characterized the New South school" (*Thinking* 29). When he was invited by historian Maury Maverick to participate in a history-of-the-South project, Woodward accepted the job so as to be a "mole to subvert the establishment" (44). His work as a mole turned into a decades-long project that he eventually published as *The Origins of the New South*. Upon the publication of this landmark book, a friend asked him, "How can you possibly write so long a book about a period in which nothing happened?" (59). Woodward admits that "this question nicely captures the prejudice against this period of American history," a period that Woodward and Ellison understood to be critical for defining their present moment (*Thinking* 59). These are the same years implied by *Invisible* Man and aptly described in "Tell It Like It Is, Baby" as a realm of "equivocation . . . born of the Hayes-Tilden Compromise of 1877 and faintly illumined by the candle of liberty" (*Collected* 32).

For Woodward, the years 1877–1913 were a realm overlooked and misunderstood. Monographs on this period were "short, thin, primitive, and immature" and portrayed the South as an entity that had to be won again from the ravages of the "Northern Aggression" (*Thinking* 59). Woodward notes that by the 1940s, Southern historians were declaring victory—not over Germany and Japan but over Lincoln and Grant. Robert S. Cotterill's 1949 address before the Southern Historical Association, Woodward notes, proclaimed that "the New South" was "merely a continuation of the Old South. And not only in its economic life: the New South inherited, also, the spirit of the Old. There is, in fact, no Old South and no New. There is only The South. Fundamentally, as it was in the beginning it is now, and, if God please, it shall be evermore" (63). In "Tell It Like It Is, Baby," Ellison would hear a version of those words in Edmund Wilson's *Patriotic Gore* (1962), in which Lincoln is referred to as a tyrant, and of course also in the Southern rebellion against *Brown*, led by Senator Russell. The sentiment behind "if God please, it shall be evermore" justified the violence against Negroes that defined that period and created the illusion of white Southern unanimity. Woodward saw that the South's response to the humiliation of the Civil War was expressed not only by the Klan but at the highest level of the intellectual establishment. Only as restored Southerners, as people who had recaptured what the Civil War had taken away, could Southern whites renationalize themselves as patriotic Americans "in step with the U.S.A. in patriotism, progressivism, and prosperity" (62). And this could be achieved through one method: by repressing blacks.

As Du Bois and Ellison both demonstrate, the period of Southern renationalization marks the point where the post–Civil War hopes of Negroes were kicked to the curb. Woodward's account of Southern history during this period—in *The Origins of the New South*, *The Strange Career of Jim Crow*, and his memoir—complements the words of the narrator's grandfather in *Invisible Man*. In resisting the oppression of the white South's renationalization, Woodward occupied a position roughly analogous to that of post-Reconstruction Southern blacks. Each was fighting against the mythic power of the symbolic restoration of the Old South and did so as a spy in the enemy's country: a kind of invisible historian exposing that which was concealed his point of view from others.

Woodward's eventual strategy was to attack the illusory moral barrier that seemed to divide the North from the South. In *The Origins of the New South*, for instance, he argued that Northern capital funded the reconstituted Southern caste system (as Norton funded Bledsoe's college), because Northern industry depended on Southern labor practices (*Thinking* 65). Woodward's point is that the perceived conflict between a Northern moral code and a Southern ethos predicated on the exploitation of the Negro was largely "symbolic" or "cultural." (Norton serves this symbolic function in *Invisible Man*.) Although Woodward never explicitly defends the South and its systematic disenfranchisement of the Negro, his argument does undermine the proposition that the South alone is responsible for the betrayal of the 13th, 14th, and 15th Amendments. In exchange for "local control," the "Southern elite" acceded to the "federal" powers when necessary. The result was that white leaders of the North and South collaborated in creating "a colonial status for the Southern economy" (65). What conflict did exist in the South, according to Warren's *Legacy of the Civil War*, had to do with conflicts between rival business interests, which often took the symbolic form of questions about race and class. "To give things labels," Warren suggests, only in part facetiously, "We may say that the War gave the South the Great Alibi and gave the North the Treasury of Virtue" (*Legacy* 54). Despite occasional Populist revolts, however, Woodward's view was that the "industrial, capitalistic outlook" of the ruling class remained intact; the South sold itself to the North to preserve the disenfranchisement of blacks and poor whites. It was precisely for this reason that "nothing happened." Consequently, 1877 to 1954 was the "longest era of reasonable stability in the nineteenth and twentieth centuries," and the "old monuments of continuity" did not come down until the "rise of black nationalism" and "at the demand of a Southerner in the White House" with "a new and comprehensive Civil Rights Act and a Voting Rights Act" (*Thinking* 68).

The Origins of the New South was published one year before *Invisible Man* and touched off a fierce controversy among Southern historians. As Bethany L. Johnson explains, Woodward's work "located the South's troubles not in the Confederate defeat" or "in the oppressions and corruption of Reconstruction," as previous generations of Southern historians had, but "in the denial of democracy to freedpeople and white yeoman farmers; in the imposing strictures of Jim Crow laws and customs; in the debilitation of falling prices, debt, and agricultural failure; in the exploitation of land and labor" (20). It earned the praise of the black historian John Hope Franklin and the enmity of many others (19).[5] Despite his argument that Southern history was in part a story of collaboration with hypocritical Northern material interests, Woodward was attacked for not upholding the view that the South had remained unchanged since the Civil War. "One reputable member of the guild," Woodward notes, lamented that he "had not 'shown a greater measure of sympathy for Southern traditions and for the essential goodness of a long-suffering people'" (*Thinking* 66). The "long-suffering people" to whom this Southern historian referred were not slaves or their descendants but white Southerners. The most astute criticism to be directed at Woodward was that his history of the South ignored the extent to which the existence of legally free (in theory if not in practice) Negroes threatened the social order from within. Nor does Woodward's book suggest that one cause of this stable era's ending was Negro unrest. Yet as events and his next book would confirm, the existence of the Negro and the Negro people's quest to take their rightful place in American society were about to shatter the retro-myth of Southern exceptionalism.

It is fitting, then, that the publication of Ellison's *Invisible Man* was sandwiched between Woodward's *Origins of the New South* and the first edition of his *The Strange Career of Jim Crow*. Woodward recalls that he wrote that book during "the year of grace" the Supreme Court offered between the *Brown* decision and its eventual execution, and then he delivered its content as lectures at the University of Virginia (*Thinking* 83). Just as Ellison would rewrite *Invisible Man* as times changed, Woodward revised his most influential book as an evolving and tumultuous history kept changing the meaning of what he had just written. Ellison eventually framed his reader as a version of what he called "the little man at Chehaw Station," someone capable of recognizing the plurality of possible histories and identities contained in *Invisible Man*. Woodward understood *Jim Crow*'s first reader as an enlightened, educated Southern white; he had no idea that King would use the book for his movement. Originally, Woodward had wanted to explain to this white reader that segregation was not handed down by God to Jefferson Davis's descendants as the pillar around which they were to organize their society. Woodward wanted to disprove "the conviction" that "legal segregation" was of "ancient origins" and "entrenched in the folkways of both races" (*Thinking* 84). His initial thesis was that segregation in the South did not follow logically from the end of slavery but was created by the post–Civil War South, despite other possibilities, as an evolving, collective communal work that by 1954 had become an ossified relic. Yet despite this thesis and unlike the more visionary Ellison—who wrote explicitly to galvanize his reader to take action against the status quo—Woodward believed segregation to be "firmly entrenched" and "beyond the possibility of change by legal action" (83).

Woodward's own example, however, was proof that the walls were coming down, and despite his sense of himself as a spy, the point of view he was advancing was soon to become national doctrine. Woodward understood *Jim Crow* to mark the end of a long journey for its author away from the "siege mentality" of the New Old South. He recounts how in the 1920s he lived in the shadow of the Klan at Stone Mountain, Georgia, and through his uncle he met Dr. Will Alexander, head of the Commission on Interracial Cooperation in Atlanta. When he worked at Georgia Tech in the 1930s, he became friends with the black writer J. Saunders Redding (who would severely criticize *Invisible Man*). He met Langston Hughes at Columbia in 1932–33, just before Ellison met Hughes. As noted above, Woodward had sought the mentorship of W. E. B. Du Bois (*Thinking* 86). In 1952, as president of the Southern Historical Assocation, Woodward canceled a dinner at a Knoxville hotel that would not seat his friend John Hope Franklin, and he turned to Franklin for help in writing *Jim Crow*. Recalling that he first presented *Jim Crow* "at the invitation" of "one of the most respected Southern universities," Woodward marvels in 1986, "What sort of Southerner was this, anyway, and how did he go so thoroughly wrong"? The answer is that he went right and that his work as a historian proved it.

For Woodward, as for Ellison and Warren, history is a living thing, shaped by the narrative that the historian uncovers, or writes, depending on one's point of view. In his memoir, Woodward wants to say that as a historian he is not simply making things up but that he is getting to the actual truth. Yet he acknowledges that he is intent on overturning a specific understanding of Southern history in part because he feels that it justified a social order that he wanted to see changed. Woodward, like Ellison, became a kind of death messenger for the older white Southern values. As a white Southerner, Woodward was keen to the sense that he, like Faulkner's Quentin Compson, was born into a territory that had been conquered by outsiders, and that the history of the South was a constant rebuke to the habitual American "national self-image of innocence and moral complacency" (*Burden* 20). Thus, as a Southerner who defended the rights of Negroes, Woodward attacked the abstract nature of American history—the belief that Americans are "immune from the forces of history" (169). "America," he says, "has a history," and it may seem to be exceptional because "the tragic aspects and the ironic implications of that history have been obscured by the national legend of success and victory and by the perpetuation of infant illusions of innocence and virtue" (189). Woodward's work documents the hypocrisy of the North in attributing to the South *all* of the moral responsibility for the Negro's plight in an American society.

For reasons that had everything to do with his being sympathetic to the plight of black rather than white Southerners, Ellison greeted the Civil Rights movement with more optimism that did Warren or even Woodward. His people had risen where, in a sense, Woodward's people, without the grace of the Negro's sense of being the blessed carriers of progress, were perpetually fallen, and fallen in a sense that they knew to be biblical, which means damned. Ellison is necessarily on both sides of Woodward's "Southern" insight that American history involves the perpetuation of infant illusions of innocence and virtue. As a Negro, Ellison understood the pain of being an American, yet he also wanted American history to be redeemed through the collective intervention of Negroes. Woodward did not imagine that his account of the South's betrayal of the freed slaves or the federal government's eventual efforts to integrate the armed services could change the present. As Ellison often argued, however, the Negro, "as a symbol of guilt and redemption," has been part of "the deepest recesses of the American psyche" as "the keeper of the nation's sense of democratic achievement, and the human scale by which would be measured its painfully slow advance to true equality" (*Collected* 778). From an Ellisonian perspective, the Negro resides in the "deepest recesses' of Woodward's histories of the post–Civil War South. Ultimately, the Negro becomes the figure that confirms Woodward's achievement. Thus, through the leadership of King and the example of Negro leaders such as Ellison, Woodward's work became an instrument of racial progress and an answer to *Invisible Man*.

Ellison's Anxiety

From its beginning, Ellison saw his friendship with Warren as an opportunity to test his own vision and to gauge how quickly history was changing. In 1956, Ellison tells Murray that with Warren he can confirm his belief that a black intellectual who masters "his own sense of reality" "doesn't have to take a step back for anybody" (*Trading* 158). Knowing Warren allowed Ellison to test his own skills as a thinker. As the time of their meeting in Rome (1956–57), Warren had just published his response to *Brown* (*Segregation*) and was no doubt intrigued by Ellison's view. Ellison mentions to Murray in September 1956 that he has read Warren's piece as part of a *Life* series on segregation but does not comment on it. Six months later he tells Murray that he is considering writing a "piece on desegregation" and that, "at the suggestion of Robert Penn Warren," he is "hoping to make a short book of it" (*Trading* 157). Ellison and Warren met each other not only in the atmosphere they shared as successful American writers but also in the context of the Civil Rights movement. Ellison tells Murray that he is drawn to Warren as "a man who's lived and thought his way free of a lot of irrational illusions" (158).

When *Brown* happened, Warren and Ellison were stunned. Both found that not only was their sense of history at stake but so was their sense of personal identity. Warren leaves his response in *Segregation*. Throughout his voice aspires to wisdom and patience, but his anxiety concerning a suddenly changing history is evident. Thus, the question Warren proposes to ask is as urgent as it is fearful: *What's coming?* (*Segregation* 78; original emphasis). The answers Warren provides sometimes read like a parodic version of what Shreve envisioned with Quentin at the end of Faulkner's *Absalom, Absalom!* "Lots of dead niggers round here, that's what's coming," says one white man before adding, "But hell, it won't stop nothing. Fifty years from now everybody will be gray anyway, Jews and Germans and French and Chinese and niggers, and who'll give a durn?" (*Segregation* 85). Warren distances himself from the speaker—he speaks only as a "gradualist" and a (white) Southerner (114).

Ellison, by contrast, welcomes the transformation of society that *Brown* promises but doubts its reality. Like the blacks Warren interviewed for *Segregation*, Ellison wavers between outbursts of excitement and uncertainty about the new American reality. On the one hand, Ellison can praise those "NAACP legal studs" for "bullrushing the Supreme Court" but, on the other, worry that maybe this "desegregation thing is going too dam fast" (*Trading* 132). When *Brown* was threatened by Southern recalcitrance, Ellison became angry. During his time in Rome—when he was writing his second novel, which had at its center the assassination of a race-baiting senator—he felt that the meaning of the Civil War was literally at stake. "I read about these southern senators being such noble characters, à la *Time*, I want to load up a sock with shit and go to work on the editors and publishers" (*Trading* 175). As Ellison watched Senator Russell lead a cabal working to undo *Brown*, he said, "I want to see someone charge Russell and those other wild talking motherfuckers with treason because it is exactly the name for what they're playing with" (178). Here his language reaches a violence (however comic) consistent with his 1940 letters to Richard Wright. Then he had joked to Wright that if Roosevelt decided to arm black soldiers for the upcoming war, he hoped that they would know which direction to point the weapons (15 May 1940).

Warren's work offered a voice of moderation more "liberal" than Faulkner's. Ellison appreciated the efforts Warren was making and could contrast them with Faulkner's more reactionary perspective. In this new context, in which Negro political pressure demands the equal enforcement of U.S. law for all its citizens, Ellison—three years removed from having told Faulkner "his children" would soon be emerging from the shadows—is outraged by Faulkner's public admonition "to go slow." He writes Saul Bellow:

> Since Faulkner seems bent upon organizing his peon Negroes to fight the North, do you think I could persuade Ernest [Hemingway] to organize a guerrilla squad to oppose them? I'd go along as impartial foreign correspondent to report the thing. Understand Faulkner has removed his granddaddy's Civil War uniform from mothballs and is stocking up on minny balls. Seems he's been planning his strategy (over the proper bourbon, of course) for a long time. Still, maybe this time we win—NO? (4 May 1956).

To Murray, Ellison writes:

> Bill Faulkner can write a million letters to the North as he recently did in LIFE, but for one thing he forgets that the people that he's talking to are Negroes and they're everywhere in the States and without sectional alliance when it comes to the problem. The next thing he forgets is that Mose isn't in the market for his advice, because he's been knowing how to 'wait-a-while'—Faulkner's advice—for over three hundred years, only he's never been simply waiting, he's been probing for a soft spot, looking for a hole, and now he's got the hole. Faulkner has delusions of grandeur because he really believes that he invented these characteristics which he ascribes to Negroes in his fiction and now he thinks he can end this great historical action just as he ends a dramatic action in one of his novels with Joe Christmas dead and his balls cut off by a man not nearly as worthy as himself. . . . Nuts! He thinks Negroes simply exist to give ironic overtone to the viciousness of white folks, when he should know very well that we're trying hard as hell to free ourselves; thoroughly and completely, so that when we get the crackers off of our back we can discover what we (Moses) really wish to preserve out of the experience that made us. (*Trading* 117)

Ellison's remarkable reaction to Faulkner's public comments expresses the confluence of excitement and anger that Negroes in the 1950s experienced as they saw that the walls of Jericho might finally be tumbling down. To Faulkner's advice to "go slow," Ellison is saying, no, we're going to go faster because we have been ready since 1877. To Warren's nervous question "what next," Ellison insists that here at last is an opportunity to transform American society and the place of the Negro and the non-Negro within it. The chance to "discover what we (Mose) really wish to preserve out of the experience that made us" meant the opportunity for Negro leaders to redefine what it meant to be an American so that being an American meant accepting Negroes as vital and equal cocreators of the American scene. *Maybe this time we win.*

Ellison's 1950s letters reveal—his later critics notwithstanding—his utter identification with the Civil Rights movement. From Rome he followed the reports of the 1955–56 Montgomery bus boycott led by Martin Luther King Jr. and the 1956 protests at the University of Alabama involving Autherine Lucy's admission. He is overwhelmed by the protesters' resilience and courage: "Yes, man!," he exults, "they're talking sense and acting! I'm supposed to know Negroes, being one myself, but these moses are revealing just a little bit more of their complexity" (*Trading* 116). Ellison praises the protests because they have "turned the Supreme Court into the forum of liberty it was intended to be, and the Constitution into the briarpatch in which the nimble people, the willing people have a chance" (117). Ellison's language domesticates the Constitution as if it were an instance of Negro folklore and reinforces what other blacks will tell Warren concerning *Brown* and its attendant recent developments: enforce the law.

Yet Ellison's responses to the ongoing reconstitution also reveal an anxiety concerning how things will turn out, which may have something to do with why he never published a second novel. Kenneth Warren has suggested that Ellison's "incomplete transit from *Invisible Man* to the second novel" might be understood in terms of "Ellison's unsuccessful attempt to negotiate the difference between writing about segregation and desegregation" and that it "reflects the extent to which the Negro American novel as a cultural project was tied to the Jim Crow era" ("Chaos" 189). Where Faulkner wrote that the past was never past, and his most profound narrative consciousness, Quentin Compson, surrendered himself to a past that could never be transcended and was consummated as a form of self-annihilation, Ellison after *Invisible Man* lived in a future that he was trying to embody as the fulfillment of what to him was America's sacred history. Ellison's private response to Faulkner's defensive, self-contradictory pronouncements (a version of the screaming white woman in the Little Rock photo) suggests an uncertainty about what is happening. If, as his remarks about Faulkner indicate, Ellison's very identity as Negro, American, and artist was at stake, then he was obligated to put his shoulder to the wheel. Yet what work could he do beyond *Invisible Man*?

The answer is that Ellison's ambition and imagination ventured beyond writing novels and instead toward essays and speeches in which his voice could plausibly address the past, the present, and the future simultaneously. What Ellison wanted—a society dedicated to equality—could not be brought about by writing another novel, especially one that was rooted in the Jim Crow era, which was receding before everyone's eyes. In fact, it could not happen by any one person's efforts, and he knew that it might never happen at all.

The belief that the fight for a just, democratic society might be won was, in Ellison's view, the charge to Negro Americans, and he—one Negro among many thousands gone—had dedicated his life to pushing it along. *Invisible Man* embodied this quest, and after *Brown*, his strategy was to act as if the society he longed for was happening through the agency of his own will. Emerson said, "When my genius calls me," he "would write on the lintels of my door-post, Whim" and "hope that it is somewhat better than whim at last" (*Essays* 262). Ellison was practicing this insight on a grand level, but at inevitable personal cost, since no one—not even Lincoln or King or Ellison—can, by his very will, make history accord with his vision, whatever sacrifices he must endure.

The two works that most clearly reflect the overwhelming sense of historical anxiety that Ellison experienced in the aftermath of *Invisible Man* are the second novel and the essay, "Tell It Like It Is, Baby." Not coincidentally, neither of these was completed, though Ellison did publish "Tell," as he also published excerpts from the novel. Still, he did not collect "Tell" in either of his books of his essays; rather, like the second novel, it stands as a sort of orphan in the Ellison canon. I think that Kenneth Warren is right when he suggests that this essay was for Ellison a kind of coming to terms with his failure to complete his second novel ("Chaos" 190). Both works seem rooted in the same Jim Crow despair that also inspired *Invisible Man*; neither can imagine a path through the legacy of segregation that does not lead to the specter of white betrayal. Both works are consumed by Lincoln's meaning in American history and imagine blacks as the ones who fight to keep alive the meaning of Lincoln's sacrifice. Beyond Kenneth Warren's reading, I would suggest further that "Tell" represents Ellison's attempt to come to terms with the fact of his role as a symbolic actor in trying to shape a history that was beyond his control. The essay marked his tacit recognition that the role available for him within the Negro Freedom Movement was as an essayist, a speaker, and the author of *Invisible Man*.

The published version dates "Tell" "1956/1965 Rome, New York" (*Collected*) but is unclear how the essay evolved during the nine-year period between inception and publication. Initially, the essay responded to two events: the March 1956 "Southern Manifesto," signed by twenty-two Southern senators who were trying to repeal *Brown*, and a letter from his down-home friend Virgil. Yet it seems to address events after 1956, in particular King's 1963 "I Have a Dream" speech, as well as the Civil Rights marches generally. Although those nine years marked a period of almost unbelievable progress for the Civil Rights movement, Ellison's essay is gloomy. Responding to Virgil's request that he address the "Southern Manifesto," Ellison coolly remarks, "I confess defeat, it is too complex for me to 'tell it like it is'" (*Collected* 46). Of all Ellison's post–*Invisible Man* essays, "Tell" is the most despairing and arguably the only one that wonders whether the historical mission of Negroes to make good on the promises of the Declaration of Independence and the Civil War is doomed.

Most of "Tell" involves a complex, surreal dream that is framed by elliptical commentary from the fully awake, if still mystified, Ellison. In the second novel, the narrative repeatedly returns to the Lincoln Memorial to contemplate Lincoln's legacy. In "Tell," Ellison dreams he is a child seeking either Abraham Lincoln or his father or both. Throughout, the question of who Ellison is and what role he is to play in the bizarre drama he dreams is paramount if unclear, as is the question whether his father and Lincoln both perform the same function in Ellison's life. Thus, the deaths of Lincoln and Ellison's father become intertwined at the outset of the work. Lincoln's death lasts for years as Negroes and whites, led by a man whose description recalls Edmund Wilson and is probably an allusion to Wilson's *Patriotic Gore*, fight for control of the corpse. At the end of the dream, "the mysterious Negroes" who have tried to watch over Lincoln's body "motioned for me to look over the edge" where the dreamer assumes that the body rests. What he sees is "a multitude, some black faces among them, sitting at table making a ghoulish meal of some frightful thing that a white sheet hid from view" (*Collected* 44). He sees "something stirring and expanding beneath the sheet" as his dream is "plunging me screaming into a terrible wakefulness" (44). Having presented the dream as he received it, Ellison strangely comments that the corpse could be that of either Lincoln or Robert E. Lee. What Lincoln's body means and what its consumption has to do with contemporary events are the questions that Ellison's commentary haltingly tries to answer.

The dream conveys the dreamer's helpless sense that the conflicts that started the Civil War have not been resolved, and it continues to play over and over, as if American history were an endlessly recurring reel of film (one of the conceits of the second novel). Through the ritualistic defacing of Lincoln's corpse, the dream demonstrates how Americans after the Civil War refused to live up to the challenge of assimilating the freed slaves and their descendants into free American society. At stake for the dreaming Ellison, and all Americans in the wake of the Civil Rights movement, is whether Lincoln—killed for freeing the slaves—will be redeemed during Ellison's lifetime. In the dream, anonymous Negroes struggle to keep Lincoln's legacy alive and incur repeatedly the kicks of those who wish to see him forgotten. In the second novel, Hickman faces Lincoln's statue and thinks of what *"those sorrowful eyes reveal about what it means to be a man who struggles to reconcile all of the contending forces of his country out of a belief in simple justice. . . . Yes, that look in those eyes and the struggles which placed it there—those are what made him one of us"* (*Three* 575). Lincoln's story is Hickman's story, and the struggle that Hickman identifies in Lincoln's eyes is the same one that Ellison confronts in his dream and in this essay. *"Yes, he was one of us,"* Hickman affirms, because *"he became the one man who pointed the way for all who are willing to pay the hard price of true freedom—Yes!"* (*Three* 576). Although Ellison insists that in his dream he knew Lincoln could not die, the dream expresses his fear that perhaps Lincoln, and the historical vision that he represents to Ellison, *might* die anyway. What if the euphoria unleashed by *Brown* turned out to be only a dream and history returned to its 1877 course? What if the Edmund Wilson of *Patriotic Gore* were right? What if Lincoln were remembered not as the upholder of the Constitution for all Americans, including Negroes, but merely as the tyrant who destroyed the South to satisfy his own personal ambition?

At the center of this essay about history and the two slain patriarchs (Lincoln and Ellison's father) is an Ellison who occupies at least three roles: the writer framing the "failed" essay; the protagonist-dreamer who experiences the vision of the essay; the child-double of the dreamer who suffers the events dreamed. The one framing the essay sees that "there lay deeply within me a great deal of horror generated by the Civil War and the tragic incident which marked the reversal of the North's 'victory'" (*Collected* 30). The protagonist of the dream, unable either to identify the man he thought was his father or to join other Negroes wrestling for Lincoln's corpse, suffers an overwhelming feeling of uncertainty and guilt. "What had I done—what had I failed to do?," he asks without being able to answer (30). Throughout, there is the combined sense that he is a helpless witness to the drama unfolding before him and somehow responsible for what he witnesses. In his waking life Ellison is the master of his rhetorical situation, but in the dream he is reduced to being a child. Perhaps more tellingly, he is also a slave, albeit one who is "literate, a slave who could read" (37). The dreaming Ellison seems trapped by history rather than its triumphant exponent. Having left the coal mine of the Jim Crow world where he, like his novel's narrator, could view history from the relative anonymity of black experience, did Ellison after *Invisible Man* sometimes think he had conquered the literary world only to remain at heart a slave descended from slaves?

That his dream turns him into a slave seems to convey both his identification with the entire course of Negro history and his feeling of impotence to alter the course of events that he witnesses. The "anonymous" Negroes could refer to the generations of Negroes, like the grandfather in *Invisible Man* or Hickman's parishioners in the second novel, who struggled to keep alive their dream of themselves as enfranchised American citizens. They could also refer to the visible blacks of the Civil Rights movement whose nonviolent protests attracted the violence of angry whites, even as they affirmed the living legacy of Lincoln. This movement reaches its symbolic summit with King's 1963 "I Have a Dream" speech on the steps of the Lincoln Memorial—a real-life version of Hickman's affirmation of Lincoln's meaning in the second novel. When Ellison began the essay in "Tell" 1956, he could not have related to his friend Virgil everything of what was really happening because he did not know that the protests at Birmingham, Little Rock, and Selma, combined with the political adroitness of Lyndon Baines Johnson, were going to win the day against the traitorous Southerners. As "Tell" and the second novel both suggest, Ellison was imagining the historical process that had led to the present moment and trying to divine what would happen next.

Thus, Ellison put himself at the center of the dream within an essay portraying a black artist trying to understand his role in this decisive moment in American history. He was uncertain of where history was tending and what his role was to be, but the tortured ambivalence of his position also suggests that his sense of identification with an evolving black history was—more than being a novelist—what made Negro life most meaningful to him. Virgil, a black person but not a black intellectual, had asked Ellison to respond, as a black spokesman, to what was happening. Although Ellison undercuts this ethos by being characterized as "home-boy done gone intellectual," his dream reveals the seriousness with which he accepts Virgil's charge. Ellison is duty bound to respond as "a writer who is American, a Negro, and most eager to discover a more artful, more broadly significant approach to those centers of stress within our national life wherein he finds his task and being" (30). Yet his dream tells him that he is an "orphan" who has been "fatally flawed and doomed" by his father's premature death. His task is to find redress for his father's death and redeem the history that has orphaned him. The child in the dream cannot act. Redemption is sought by writing this essay, but only history itself, and not Ellison's intervention, can bring the desired end.

Whereas Ellison found the key to organizing *Invisible Man* in the works of Lord Raglan and Kenneth Burke, here he suggests that the answer to the dream-hero's dilemma may be found in Gilbert Murray's *The Classical Tradition in Poetry* (1927), noting that he fell asleep while reading Murray's chapter on Hamlet and Orestes. The child in the dream, Ellison observes, was afflicted by a Hamlet-like sense of inaction, while Lincoln suffered the martyr's death of Orestes, who was destroyed by those his art had most inspired. Kenneth Warren says Murray shows that the essay "reveals the composing process for the second novel to have been an extended effort to discover whether or not the elements of classical tragedy could be produced from the ninety-year history of post–Civil War American society" ("Chaos" 197). In this view, the critical task that confronts Ellison becomes a question that he could answer only in his second novel: "What effect could Ellison as a novelist, working in a form that many scholars had declared defunct, have on a nation still at war with itself over the status of the Negro?" (197). Kenneth Warren's question may help explain why the dreamer suffers from an uncanny intuition that he is responsible for something that he cannot name. At the dream's outset he hears a voice from a loudspeaker ask, "Is he the one?" (*Collected* 34), and the tension that this question creates builds without resolution until the horrifying moment when Ellison is startled "screaming into a terrible wakefulness" (44).

One cannot know whether this "terrible wakefulness" occurs in 1956, when he began the essay, or 1965, when he published it, and knowing the difference is crucial to understanding what the essay reveals about its author. If it occurs in 1956, then the dream may convey Ellison's fear that the reality of *Brown* is illusory. If it occurs in 1965, then it may well reflect Ellison's growing uncertainty as a black novelist and intellectual. One wonders why the dreaming Ellison is isolated from the other Negroes trying to save

Lincoln's body. Does this isolation reflect his growing divide from 1960s "militant" Negroes or perhaps even the Civil Rights movement? I think it more likely that Ellison's identification with the movement is such that he knows its success does not depend on him, even if his own success is perhaps an indication that history is moving in the right direction. As he well knew, *Brown* would have happened without *Invisible Man*. Likewise, no novel Ellison wrote could stop Strom Thurmond, Richard Russell, and other Southern senators from trying to overturn *Brown*, any more than one had prompted Thurgood Marshall to argue the winning side of *Brown*. Ellison's greatness as a novelist was extraordinary, but the power to change history did not reside in this greatness. Rather, history would change, if it could change, through the combined efforts of otherwise anonymous men and women such as those who marched to hear King deliver his 1963 address in Washington and prevailed upon the president to acknowledge that their dream was actually truth and that Americans should commit themselves to seeing it happen.

Despite its many interpretive levels, "Tell It Like It Is, Baby" can be seen to mark the point at which Ellison began to acknowledge that he need not finish his second novel to contribute to the cause of civil rights. This is not to say that he did not harbor hopes of publishing the novel, but the fact of the case is that he never did. Yet his essays show that his engagement with history and its incarnations in the ongoing present remained acute and alive. Interpreting his dream though his reading of Gilbert Murray's account of classical tragedy, Ellison recognizes Lincoln as "the hero-father murdered (for Lincoln *is* a kind of father of twentieth-century America), his life evilly sacrificed and the fruits of his neglected labors withering some ninety years in the fields; the state fallen into corruption, and the citizens into moral anarchy, with no hero come to set things right" (*Collected* 46). This is the same insight he gives to Hickman in the second novel, just as "Tell" is a compressed version of the historical dilemma that the second novel portrays. What Ellison does not say is that perhaps King became history's symbolic actor who completes the dramatic action that the dream leaves unfinished—perhaps because it was still too early to say. The same unresolved situation the dream names defined the status of the second novel too. Ellison never could decide to complete the drama of the long death of Bliss/Senator Sunraider, whose life clearly diminishes the meaning of Lincoln's death.

Ellison says the essay "Tell" fails (as he said *Invisible Man* failed and tacitly said his second novel failed too), but actually it was more creative and successful than he imagined it to be. If the essay and the unfinished novel are failures, then they fail because what he demands of his writing is impossible. No piece of writing can contain history's meaning. In *Ralph Ellison in Progress* (2010), Adam Bradley argues that with time the second novel's unfinished state may be a warrant of its continuing interest. Better than any other work of American literature I can think of, the second novel shows that "the Negro question" is at the center of American history, yet its resolution seems forever to be hanging in the balance. Thus, Americans can elect a "black" president or have a "black" head of the armed forces, yet the lives of the majority of black Americans, especially those living in jails or below the poverty line, remain "invisible" to most post-*Brown* Americans. In the second novel, the members of Hickman's flock question his devotion to Lincoln. But if Lincoln's sacrifice means nothing, Ellison seemed to think, history is merely a series of violent acts securing no moral except the unending assertion of power. As an intellectual and an artist, Ellison believed in form, and for him Lincoln's death, like American history, was the tragic underpinning of the epic Negro struggle to become American.

In Gilbert Murray's book Ellison read that an artist's genius unblocks the "stream" of "desires and fears and passions, long, slumbering yet eternally familiar, which have for thousands of years lain near the root of our most intimate emotions and been wrought into the fabric of our most magical dreams" (Warren 196). Arguably, Murray's description applies to *Invisible Man*, since that work about the problem of Negro leadership was so clearly trying to imagine a visible hero who could lift the cloak of invisibility that blighted so many lives. The second novel confronted the same situation that *Invisible Man* did and also aspired to this form of "genius," but Hickman's hope for a hero, Bliss, failed the community, and no hero arrived unless it was Bliss's assassin. As he watched history solving his narrative dilemma, Ellison gradually surrendered the idea that he could write the narrative that would solve his people's historical dilemma. Instead, he found more modest ways to push history forward. When he was close to Wright, his letters consistently addressed "the Negro problem" from an in-group perspective. His perpetual question was, what are *we* (blacks) going to do? *Invisible Man* dealth with a version of this question, but the book tacitly looked beyond the group as well—and did so just as the group was making dramatic, visible progress toward the goal. Even at his most "American," Ellison never vacated his Negro perspective, but he saw that becoming "equal" did not mean simply victory in the present but also a transformation of the past.

In "Tell," Ellison says that "when a Negro American novelist tries to write about desegregation, he must regard, in all its torturous ambiguity, the South" (*Collected* 31). If blacks were going to have a place in society equal with whites, then blacks were at some point going to have to surrender their status as victim. Ironically, this gesture would mean raising whites to their moral level, which could be accomplished through forgiveness. In the second novel, Love New suggests that whites and blacks were equally the victims of "State history" and that both groups would have to surrender the prejudices they had inherited through slavery and its aftermath. Speaking of the "great man," Lincoln, and the "sacrifice" he suffered, New says that "when he's killed the land gets sick, and to cure the sickness proper things must be done to redeem his sacrifice and appease his spirit." Thus "not only did they fail to do the proper things to appease his spirit, they *lied* about it! And that's what made for this deep sickness that's in this land and in all the State people—Yao!" (*Three* 815). Ellison's task as a post-*Brown* intellectual was to confront this "sickness" in "all the State people" and try to suggest a cure.

"Tell It Like It Is, Baby" responds, Ellison says, to the discrepancy "between the ideal of equality and the actuality of our society in which social, educational, and economic inequalities are enforced explicitly on the irremediable ground of race" (*Collected* 31). For Ellison, to understand that black history was American history meant solving the race problem. His historical vision aspired to a rapprochement between "white" and "black" versions of American history—what *Invisible Man* tentatively imagines. Ellison's sudden sense in the 1950s that his work has been accepted within an American culture that would not have included him even ten years earlier obligated him to rethink his relationship, as a Negro, to the past. *Brown* could only confirm this self-reappraisal. Rather than locating his identity in the past, where black identity had to create itself despite white oppression, Ellison looked to the future and an integrated society that would, contrary to Faulkner's dictum, render the past as past. In the future he was trying to meet, the one implied by King's vision, Ellison met Robert Penn Warren. On 1 June 1963 he wrote Warren that "with the rapid developments in the South I am sure there will be much to talk about." By then, he and Warren had been friends for seven years, and their conversations had evolved to a point where they were willing to risk friendship in public. Warren's interview with Ellison, published in *Who Speaks for the Negro?* the same year as "Tell," defines Ellison's view of the Civil Rights movement. He suggests that King's heroism is in its deepest meaning a group achievement, and he also addresses the anxieties that white Southerners are experiencing as society changes. Warren approaches Ellison not quite as a suppliant, but it is clear that together they are working through a historical dilemma confronting all Americans. It is hard to say who has traveled farther to meet the other.

Warren's Southern Odyssey

In his 1968 essay "The Myth of the Flawed White Southerner," Ellison, thinking of Lyndon Johnson, speaks of the Negro mythology that imagines a white person who, though guilty of discriminatory and possibly violent acts against blacks, nonetheless is capable in a moment of inspiration of transcending that history and meeting blacks on equal ground. He may also have been thinking of Warren, who seemed to him to have made a difficult journey through and away from Jim Crow America. The *Brown* decision, says Woodward, "gave way early in 1956 to something near panic across the South" (*Thinking* 90).[6] Profoundly shaken by *Brown* and the escalating Civil Rights movement, Warren in *Segregation* and *Who Speaks for the Negro?* presents himself as one bidden by history to confront a past that is changing everything he knows. "I went back," he says, because "going back this time, like all other times, was a necessary part of my life" (*Segregation* 3). The South is a territory that occupies Warren wherever he goes, and any change there means that something is changing in him.

Despite Warren's appreciation of *Invisible Man*, *Segregation* suggests that in 1956 he is reluctant to meet Ellison's people on equal terms. Returning to the South in the wake of *Brown*, listening to "the voices in my own blood," Warren sees not Lincoln's body attended by Negroes but his two grandfathers at Shiloh, that "morning of April 6, 1862," traversing "the lethal spring thickets" before the great battle after which "they had fallen back on Corinth, into Mississippi" (4, 8). Where Ellison's "Tell" confronts the losses after the Civil War, Warren's *Segregation* summons the Civil War before the South had surrendered. Hence, Warren remarks, "History, like nature, knows no jumps," before adding "Except the jump backward, maybe" (114). The events he documents are sweeping away his cherished understanding of the South's past and his relationship to it. He encounters a white Mississippi girl who, sounding like a Faulkner character, tells him, "I feel it's all happening inside of me, every bit of it. It's all there." "I know what she meant," Warren avers (4). The language conveys fear and a sense of something being suffered helplessly. An inner revolution happening against one's will.

In Warren's personal history, the new reconstitution was not at first a drama for Negro equality but a challenge to an exceptionalist white Southern identity. The white Southerners whom Warren meets collectively want "to preserve," as a former Klansman tells him, "what you might name the old Southern way, what we was raised up to" (*Segregation* 23). An "official of one of the segregation outfits" fondly recalls to Warren having known Civil War veterans who "talked their war, they had something to remember and be proud of, not like these veterans we got nowadays, nothing to be proud of" (36, 37). Standing before a replica of Fort Nashborough, Warren meets a "fine-looking boy, erect, manly in the face," who has traveled from Alabama to see the fort and commune with its heritage. "I like to go round seeing things that got history, and such. It gives you something to think about," he tells Warren (17). Yet when prompted by Warren to speak about the emerging Civil Rights movement, the "fine-looking boy" says, "I hate them bastards" (18). Summing up his encounter with this kind of double to his own quest, Warren aptly remarks that "somehow the hallowedness of the ground he stood on had vindicated, as it were, that hate" (19). Old ways die hard. Warren reports another remark from a white Southerner who identifies Warren's theme: "It is hard to claw out from under the past and the past way" (12). At stake for the grandchildren of the Confederacy is the suspicion that Negroes are "spitting on their grandparents' grave." Warren says of these white Southerners that "they feel some connection they don't want to break," and he proposes that this feeling be called "piety" (56).

The Civil Rights movement threatens this piety and the dream "to be Southern again." In this manner white Southerners wish "to recreate a habitation for the values that they would preserve, to achieve in unity some clarity of spirit, to envisage some healed image of their own identity" (*Segregation* 96). Warren's book affirms one white Southerner's statement that "there's something you can't explain, what being a Southerner is," even if it also reveals that being a Southerner precludes being "a nigger," since this piety does not include the Negro as either an object of or participant in its veneration. In 1956 Warren is reluctant, despite his budding friendship with Ellison, to sympathize with the insecurity expressed by blacks. He will characterize a black woman's fear of retaliation from a white man who had been acquitted of killing her husband as "a cliché." He adds that her story is a "cliché of fear" that has "come alive," but his complacent sense that such acts of violence are to be taken for granted mars the sympathy his account tries to evoke (15). Ellison would not see this woman's pain as clichéd. Yet were it not for *Brown*, Warren would not have been compelled to make this journey home to meet this woman.

Recording the white Southerner's pain regarding the Civil War, Warren says, "We are the prisoners of our history" (*Segregation* 109). His white interlocutors reiterate this point. They seem prisoners of the past who cannot or do not want to see the future. To Warren's question, "What does the Negro want?" a Negro answers, "We want the law" (56–57). The answer makes Warren uncomfortable. He asks if they want the law "right now," and when someone refers to "the Supreme Court decision," Warren cuts the speaker off before he can finish: "It says all deliberate speed . . . or something like that" (58). "All deliberate speed" raises the question of what is coming next yet also seems to justify a position of patience, moderation. By the end of *Segregation,* Warren has given the classic Faulknerian response to the historical dilemma that confronts him. Interviewing himself, he says that he does not think "the problem is to learn to live with the Negro" but "to learn to live with ourselves" (111). Such a formulation accepts moral failure as it evades confronting the social consequences of that failure. Whether the Negro's place in society is improved matters less than that the white Southerner rectifies his conscience. Only then will the "race problem" subside. "I don't think you can live with yourself when you are humiliating the man next to you" (111). Warren creates a context of self-confrontation and self-forgiveness that permits him to hope that "the South, because it has had to deal concretely with a moral problem, may offer some leadership" (115).

This position allows no place either for Negro leadership or for significant Negro interaction in American society. By framing the Negro's position in terms of the question "What does the Negro want?" (*Segregation* 56), Warren risks implying that the Negro can give no answer that will not strike others as demanding too much, too soon. Warren's position unwittingly echoes Ellison's insight in *Invisible Man* that American society during the Jim Crow era has worked because blacks have been made to sacrifice their civic equality in exchange for white stability. As Warren knows, *Brown* unsettled this balance. He advances the view that history is "deliberate" in order to slow down the demands that a social order still indebted to slavery be overturned "with speed." Warren affirms that he supports desegregation but says that it will occur "not soon" and will arrive only after people "realize that desegregation is just one small episode in the long effort for justice" (113).

What Warren feared in 1956 did come to pass. The law was enforced. In 1957, the federal government through President Eisenhower intervened to ensure that schools in Little Rock, Arkansas, would be integrated. This act effectively ended the period of Southern history that had begun with the Hayes-Tilden compromise of 1877. Woodward suggests that not only did Eisenhower's intervention mark "the first breach of the Compromise of 1877 in eighty years and the end of an era in Southern history"; it also killed "the myth of Negro contentment with the 'Southern Way of Life'" (*Strange* 91). *Invisible Man* had described the death of this myth, and Warren, one of Ellison's most astute readers, met the situation bravely: nine years later his *Who Speaks for the Negro?* gave black leaders a chance to speak. There is no way to know whether his friendship with Ellison prompted Warren's more direct confrontation with the present and the Negro's active role in carrying the body of Lincoln forward. Nevertheless, his efforts went far beyond the "go slow" advice of Faulkner, who did not live to see the successes of the Civil Rights movement. Warren's remarkable work of journalism integrated a chastened Confederate perspective with the multiple perspectives of black leaders.

Warren's quest embodied what Ellison called on white readers to do at the end of *Invisible Man*, just as C. Vann Woodward's work was often a self-conscious repudiation of the dominant ethos of Southern history after the Civil War. At the outset of *Who Speaks*, Warren explains, "I have written this book because I wanted to find out something first hand, about the people, some of them anyway, who are making the Negro Revolution what it is—one of the dramatic events of American history." Warren acknowledges that as a young man, living in England, he had written an essay defending segregation and "dimly sensed" that rereading it would "make me uncomfortable" (11). He also tells a revealing story about a racial encounter he did not quite have. Once, in Baton Rouge, he saw a white man beating a Negro boy and wondered what he should do. Intervene? But then what? Struggling with his conscience, Warren felt invisible and inadequate. His immediate moral dilemma was solved when a large LSU football player reacted unreflectively: "Hey, what you doen to that nigger?" Warren, lacking the physical courage and the moral eloquence of this football player's gesture, is at first relieved—"I had been saved. I had not had to get 'involved'" (13)—but also ashamed that he waited for someone else to solve his moral quandary. The story stands in for Warren's involvement in the Civil Rights movement, and this book enacts his "reflective" action on a situation that has engulfed him since before memory.

In *Who Speaks for the Negro?* Warren questions his own assumptions about his understanding of the history that has made him who he thinks himself to be. His quest to find which "frequencies" he shares with these black leaders requires that he modify if not outright reject his position as a white Southern male. He describes the difficult evolution of his views on race. Following the examples of his father and grandfather, he had argued as a young intellectual (associated with the Southern Agrarians) for "full legal protection" for the Negro, including "equal pay for equal work" and "equal economic opportunities" (11). He recalls that his father, also a version of the flawed white Southerner, would say, "If you treat a Negro right, he'll treat you right," and that during the Depression his father would not evict a Negro renter because "you can't do that to a man who has no place to go" (11). Yet the younger Warren apparently never considered what it meant to have a place in society that was defined as off limits for others. He says that if someone in his father's house had let slip the word "nigger," then "the roof would have fallen" (11). A white person's attitude toward a black person was what counted, not what the black person might do, free of whites' perceptions.

Warren recalls how as a child in Kentucky he would gaze at "an oak tree that stood by the decrepit, shoe-box size jail" that he could not walk past, as he did often, "without some peculiar, cold flicker of feeling" (*Who* 11). In 1965, reflecting on the end of segregation and the rise of the Negro to a place of visibility in American society, Warren confesses that "the image of that tree which I still carry in my head has a rotten and raveled length of rope hanging from a bare bough, bare because the image in my head is always of a tree set in a winter scene. In actuality it is most improbable that I ever saw a length of rope hanging from that tree, for the lynching had taken place long before my birth. It may not, even, have been that tree. It may, even, have been out in the country" (11). Warren's recollection is belated—and confused—testimony that his father's "humane" response to the Negro was not and had never been enough to protect him from that tree. Delicately, Warren is trying to suggest that the image of the lynch mob, and the mutilating murder of an innocent Negro, is the tortured memory not only of African Americans such Ellison or King but of some Southern whites as well. By admitting that his father's gentility and his loyalty to "tradition" are sustained in part by the memory of atrocities he can neither repress nor, finally, deny, Warren implies how searing this post-*Brown*, post–*Invisible Man* confrontation with one's heritage was for white Southerners.

Warren recalls only one lynching, one that happened just before his memory could place it, and it lacks the gruesome detail that a true eyewitness account would have. Instead of recounting what happened, according to family legend or local newspaper reports, Warren chooses to leave the incident vague, as his imagination creates and represses the memory all at once. He says that he does not "remember how I first heard about the lynching, certainly when I was a very small child, for I do remember how it had to be explained to me, probably by an older boy" (*Who* 11). Warren's studied incomprehension recalls Ellison's brilliant 1937 story, "A Party Down at the Square," which recounts how a white adolescent about Huckleberry Finn's age witnesses a lynching. Ellison's story, written well before he and Warren had met and probably unknown to Warren, can be read as a version of the sort of repressed moral awakening that Warren's book acknowledges. In the story the moral horror of the witnessed lynching is present to the reader but not quite to the narrator. That discrepancy accounts for the story's power. At the end the white narrator is left with a grudging respect for the "Bacote Nigger" he has seen burned, but he has also been initiated into a social custom that may not seem so horrible to him the next time he sees it.

Clearly modeled on *Huckleberry Finn*, Ellison's story illuminates the struggle it was for whites to repress their human identification with the black victims of their social rites. Getting past one's sympathy with the sacrificial black body was itself a rite of initiation into white society. In contrast to Ellison's story, Warren's description of his first lynching is willfully vague, but the repressed moral discomfort is palpable. *Who Speaks for the Negro?* is a way of releasing this repression—a letting-off of pressure as the writer confronts both the legacy of his white ancestors and the possible shapes of new social structures to come. Warren's book is all the more fascinating because it earned the tacit approval of his friend Ellison, who was keenly aware of how difficult this moral awakening was for someone of Warren's background.

Where Warren's reminiscences about his attitude toward blacks in his youth assumed a kind of friendship between whites and blacks, Ellison's generosity toward Warren demonstrates that that friendship could continue even after whites had been disabused of their stereotypes about what blacks want. Warren's fear, as his questions to other black leaders indicate, is that blacks will use their new social position to exact an eye for an eye. Ellison's role is not quite to assure Warren that Confederates are forgiven but to show the way to a history in which such questions are no longer pressing because the aggrieved parties have gotten past that bad shared "State history" (in Love New's phrase) and found new things to think about. In reaching out to whites, Ellison is not trying to earn his "moderate" credentials, as some might suggest, but demonstrating that he understands the sacrifice others are making to recognize him. Without this gesture—without acknowledging Warren's acquiescence—there could be no social reciprocity, regardless of what the laws decreed.

Once Warren, however tentatively, acknowledges the limitations of his past views, then it is possible for him to hear what blacks are saying to him about their shared society. He can truly answer the call of *Invisible Man*. If Ellison's novel had at its core the question of Negro leadership in a segregated society, then *Who Speaks for the Negro?* allows living Negro leaders to speak out in the context of the nation's reconstitution. Not unlike *The Human Stain*, *Who Speaks* is in this sense a sequel to *Invisible Man*. Warren's book, though, is written in a time when the abstract questions of Ellison's novel are being answered every day as a form of living history. From this perspective, the book reads like a kind of question-and-answer follow-up to *Invisible Man* in which different voices from the narrative—Bledsoe, the Vet, Clifton, Ras, and the narrator—take turns answering Warren's questions. Warren's book thus emphasizes what some later Ellison critics generally obscure—that Ellison's work should not and cannot be isolated from the Civil Rights era and its leadership.

By including Ellison in *Who Speaks*, a book that also offered the views of King, Stokely Carmichael, James Farmer, James Forman, Malcolm X (interviewed shortly before he was killed), Bayard Rustin, Roy Wilkins, Whitney Young—of virtually all of the prominent black political leaders of the day—Warren clearly indicated his understanding that Ellison's work was part of the national, social, and political reconstitution happening after *Brown*. The book's title implicitly pits its many speakers against one another as the reader is asked to judge which of Warren's interlocutors articulates the most compelling vision of American society. For Warren, Ellison's vision is a literary equivalent of Martin Luther King's, and these two figures speak a language that compels the white Southerner to respond.[7] The views that Ellison expresses to Warren do not sound out of key with those of the other leaders Warren talks to; in particular they frequently echo the remarks of Roy Wilkins and Whitney Young.[8]

Wilkins tells Warren that the Negro is actually an old American and that Negroes are "liberal" only because the politics of race has forced them to take this position (*Who* 152). Wilkins sounds like Ellison when he stresses the sense of "responsibility" that characterizes Negro experience (164). He praises whites who have fought for increased liberty for all (153–54). He says that compared with Malcolm X or Robert Moses he is a "moderate," but defends this position because as a moderate he has been committed to the most radical political position of the American twentieth century—"the idea of eliminating racial segregation" (155). Again, reiterating a crucial theme of *Invisible Man* and Harold Cruse's *The Crisis of the Negro Intellectual*, Wilkins argues that the white power structure effectively manipulates the Negro question and thus makes it difficult for genuine Negro leadership either to appear or to be recognized. The clear implication of Wilkins's remarks is that without cooperation from the white power structure, Negro leadership is able to create beautiful rhetoric but not necessarily social change. Here Wilkins's position, like Ellison's, explicitly echoes King's comment to Warren that "in this revolution the quest is for the Negro to get into the stream of American life. It's a revolution calling on the nation to live up to what is already there in an idealistic sense" (*Who* 218).

Warren places the disparate black voices of *Invisible Man* in conversation with living history and includes among them a voice that *Invisible Man* could only invoke—that of the white Southerner. The drama of *Who Speaks* inheres in the friction between the Confederate Warren and the Negro leaders he addresses. Warren admits to feeling "cold rage" when he is praised for being "courageous" by one of his interviewees (232). With Kenneth Clark, he argues about the historical significance of John Brown. Where Warren sees Brown as a psychopathic murderer, Clark sees a Christ-like martyr and suggests to Warren that "apparently rational, reasonable men" rarely change "the status quo." History is changed, Clark says, "by irrational, unreasonable, questionable men" like Brown (322). What is at stake in such exchanges, though, is Warren's self-diagnosed condition of being "shot through with Southern defensiveness" (320). The exchange with Clark over John Brown indicates Warren's fear that a resurrected "black" John Brown may still rise to exact vengeance. Yet Warren looks to the Negro to affirm his point of view and his good intentions. He did not seek such assurance in *Segregation,* and it is precisely the kind of social and political reconciliation that Ellison sought in *Invisible Man.* Warren affirms James Baldwin's claim that the Southerner needs to believe that an Eden once existed between blacks and whites, while agreeing with Baldwin's assertion that the Southern mob does not equal the Southern majority (74). *Who Speaks* shows that Warren was coming to the recognition that his Southern Eden no longer existed, if it ever did, and that a moral obligation required him to reach out to those whose perspectives he had never truly acknowledged or taken into account. As the conversation with Clark suggests, Warren had some testy exchanges with black leaders who could not but view him with irony—as he well knew. Nonetheless, the book presents an extraordinary tableau that is the inversion of the ending of *Invisible Man*: a Southern white man asking black man after black man for recognition. Of the many eloquent speakers Warren addressed, Ellison was the one who saw what Warren needed and, without either humbling himself or humiliating the vulnerable Warren, recognized him as a white Southerner trying to lay down the arms that had made their shared history a war.

Healing History's Wounds

After *Invisible Man*, Ellison published, or allowed to be published, many interviews. Staging these interviews became a kind of art form for him and an effective way to promote his ideas about art, politics, and culture. The interview with Warren in *Who Speaks* stands out as one of his most essential because its context gives his words a different weight: rather than being asked to explain *Invisible Man*, or to respond to some critical attack on his work, or to reveal the progress he has made on the next novel, Ellison is assumed to be speaking as a Negro leader. Warren labels Ellison a "leader from the periphery," which means that Ellison as a novelist and cultural commentator can hardly be expected to make a political difference in the way that a King or a Johnson could. Nonetheless, Warren recognizes that he and Ellison understand what is happening differently because Ellison is a Negro and Warren is not. Moreover, they approach one another as ambassadors, as it were, of opposing historical perspectives who know themselves in part through their dialectical engagement. Warren's description of Ellison recalls Ellison's description of Warren to Murray. Struck by how Ellison's face conveys "calmness and control," Warren surmises that this "calmness has a history, I should imagine, a history based on self-conquest and hard lessons of sympathy learned through a burgeoning and forgiving imagination" (326). This "self-conquest" may be read as a veiled allusion to the self-control required of the Jim Crow–era Negro, just as the journey of this book requires of Warren a type of "self-sacrifice." At one point Warren directly asks Ellison if he can understand that "a white Southerner feeling that his identity is involved may defend a lot of things in one package as being Southern, and one of those things is segregation. He feels he has to have the whole package to define his culture and his identity" (334).

Warren's question is a more nuanced version of Faulkner's public remarks that had so animated Ellison ten years earlier. His answer is not angry or dismissive, as it might have been, but subtle and sympathetic. Ellison suggests that such a Southerner need be seen not as racist or stuck in the past but as a version of the logic that King would enact in praying for the souls of the white Southerners who were attacking Negroes for wanting equal rights. Ellison says that Warren's Confederate anxiety "makes a lot of sense to me" because what he sees "when I look at the Southerner who has these feelings, is that he has been imprisoned by them, and that he has been prevented from achieving his individuality, perhaps more than Negroes have" (*Who* 334). Rather than denying white Southerners a sense of identity rooted in their own complex view of the past, Ellison suggests that one of the potentially dangerous aspects of the Civil Rights movement is that white Southerners are made to feel that they are being rendered invisible. "I wish," he says as if speaking to white America generally, "that we could break this thing down so that it could be seen that desegregation isn't going to stop people from being Southern, that freedom for Negroes isn't going to destroy the main current of that way of life, which becomes, like most ways of life when we *talk* about them, more real on the level of myth, memory and dream than on the level of actuality anyway" (334). Setting his eyes on the future and not the past, Ellison judges that "what is valuable and worth preserving in the white Southern way of life is no more exclusively dependent upon the existence of segregation than what is valuable in Southern Negro life depends upon its being recognized by white people" (335).

Ellison's analysis of what desegregation will bring is reassuring in its suggestion that white Southerners have a culture worth preserving, one that need not and does not depend on repressing Negroes. He also indicates that white Southerners should not fear any closer association with Negroes than they already have, since Negroes are not looking to white Southerners for approval. Ellison mixes reassurance with an assertion of Negro cultural independence. To emphasize that Negroes are less concerned with their own cultural welfare than they are with the achieving and preserving equal rights before the law, Ellison adds, somewhat pointedly, that much of the white Southern "way of life" is "structured in a manner which isn't particularly attractive to Negroes" (335).

Here we do not see an Ellison removed from the conflicts and risks of the Civil Rights movement but one Negro voice among other Negro voices, enacting a logic that in effect makes him a leader of whites as well as blacks. He insists that Negro culture does not require white appreciation to survive. He playfully remarks, "There is, after all, a tiny bit of truth in the story which Southern whites love to tell, to the effect that if a white man could be a Negro on Saturday night he'd never wish to be white again" (335). For Ellison, as for King, the critical issue that confronted Negroes after *Brown* was not to find their authentic voices (the goal of the Black Arts movement) but to demonstrate that Negroes were as capable of leading as whites were. "It's just very hard," Ellison says, "for Governor Wallace to recognize that he has got to share not only the background but the power of looking after the State of Alabama with Negroes who probably know as much about it as he does" (336). To reinforce this point, Ellison refers to his own success as a Negro artist. He mentions friends—presumably whites—who know him "as an individual" but cannot know "the experience behind me." Their inability to know his background matters not because they cannot achieve a meaningful friendship with him but because their perception of his success may prevent them from understanding the devastating social inequality that blacks have been made to suffer and have tried to overcome. Ellison is "'different' or a 'special instance'" insofar as "I'm a fairly conscious example, and in some ways a lucky instance, of the general run of American Negroes" (336–37).

Ellison's assertion that he is a *fairly conscious example* once again speaks to his sense that his story is part of a broader and longer one that has to do with being born black after the Civil War. Warren, the white Southerner, understands the historical context of Ellison's modest claim. He notes that Ellison is not unaware "of the blankness of the fate of many Negroes, and the last thing to be found in him is any trace of that cruel complacency of some who have, they think, mastered fate." Warren remarks that Ellison would not stress "the values of challenge in the plight of the Negro, any more than would James Farmer, to justify that plight." Rather, to Warren, Ellison speaks "in a spirit of pride in being numbered with those other people who have suffered" the challenges of being a Negro in the United States. Indeed, to suggest, as so many of Ellison's African American critics have done, that he was insufficiently sympathetic to hardships faced by Negroes not as talented or as lucky as he is to misread *Invisible Man*. As Warren stresses, no Negro or other American "has made more unrelenting statements of the dehumanizing pressures that have been put upon the Negro," and Ellison's novel "is the most powerful statement we have of a Negro under these dehumanizing conditions." Thus, Warren concludes, Ellison has made "a statement of the human triumph over those conditions" (*Who* 354). His continued presence on the American scene, risking the slings and arrows of others, reinforces this statement.

For Warren, Ellison confirms a central humanist truth. Perhaps this formulation unduly blunts Ellison's achievement of its political edge; fellow humans meeting in the sacred realm of art need not concern themselves with the messiness of history. For Ellison, though, American history and the Negro's role in it are what shaped his artist's will. Warren's "human" recognition of Ellison's "invisible man" is a political insight too. Indeed, its political component is what supplies its aesthetic power. Warren affirms that Ellison's view of the artist is of one who, "by opening our eyes to life, not by merely giving us models of action and response, but by, quite literally, creating us," would help to change the society he confronts through his readers (*Who* 348). In his post–*Invisible Man* career, Ellison presented himself as a living symbol of that triumph, a version of the creator turned into his own living creation. Yet as he says to Warren, that individual triumph meant little to him unless it was understood as a small episode in the greater drama of black history in America, which was itself part of the drama of American history. Ellison pointedly tells Warren that Negroes are rejecting "the old traditional role of national scapegoat" in a heroic effort "to bring America's conduct in line with its professed ideals" (339). If the past treatment of blacks has indicated that "the nation has been rotting at its moral core," then Ellison's stance is that the successful reconstitution of American society will require blacks as well as whites to accept new roles (339).

As King used Thomas Jefferson's words to confront the American nation during the 1963 March on Washington, Ellison insists to Warren that "Negroes are forcing the confrontation" between ideals and practice, "and they are most American in that they are doing so" (*Who* 339). With this rhetorical shift, one that he would employ over and over in his essays and lectures after 1965, Ellison connects the Negro's heroic quest for freedom to America's search for an ideal republic. Inspired by or willing to follow the Negro's actions, "other Americans are going to have to do the same thing" (339). This statement is Ellison at his most visionary. He is not accommodating either himself or Negroes generally to the existing American power structure. He is offering to lead other Americans willing to submit themselves to the same ideals that he advocates as a Negro and as an American. Whatever power Ellison assumes himself to have is not the result of a monstrous egotism on his part but is vested in him by his experience as a Negro influenced by American experience and history.

In 1955 Ellison said that *Invisible Man* was in part his response to Lord Raglan's study of the hero myth. His narrator, involved in a quest to become a type of Negro leader-hero, cannot quite triumph over his story's other characters in such a way that they will recognize him (as the gods recognize Odysseus). As discussed in the next chapter, the narrator is a hero because he repeatedly enacts a ritual of communal sacrifice and survives. In the context of the Civil Rights movement, Ellison suggests, Martin Luther King is a hero because his leadership is understood to be the embodiment of the aspirations of a people. Warren mentions Kenneth Clark's view that King's doctrine of forgiveness establishes an unrealistic standard for blacks and whites to meet and puts almost unbearable psychological pressures on the Negroes, who are being asked to forgive the very people who most hurt them. Ellison replies that "Dr. Clark misses the heroic side of this thing" and its role in motivating "Southern Negroes" (340). Ellison discerns in King's strategy a version of the insight that one also finds with Dostoevski or Christ: "There is a great power in humility" that is also "a form of courage" (*Who* 341). In "Richard Wright's Blues" Ellison defined this courage as the blues, which gave the Negro the knowledge that the mastery of what threatens you only makes you stronger. Thus, Ellison argues that King "is working out of a long history of Negro tradition and wisdom"—the same one that inspired Ellison—and therefore understands that his "people have been conditioned to contain not only the physical pressures involved in their struggle, but that they are capable, through this same tradition, of mastering the psychological pressures of which Clark speaks" (341).

Ellison frames King's leadership in the same mythic terms of a heroic struggle as he did for his narrator in *Invisible Man*. In this sense, King continues his protagonist's story, and Ellison's novel provides a context for understanding King and the movement he led. Perhaps because he is talking to a representative white Southerner who he knows cannot understand his own experience in the way that virtually any Negro intellectual might, Ellison expresses here as nowhere else the pride he takes in the Civil Rights movement and his sense of himself as a small part in the history that is being made. In his effort to explain to Warren how Clark misreads King, Ellison reaches for the terminology of his novel to clarify King's heroic role. "I'm referring," he says, "to the basic, implicit heroism of people who must live within a society without recognition, real status, but who are involved in the ideals of that society and who are trying to make their way, trying to determine their true position and their rightful position within it" (*Who* 342). Ellison found the words to name this situation in *Invisible Man*, but the people King represents and leads now must "act it out." Acting it out successfully requires a double assertion on the part of Negroes. Negroes have to show whites that "you are being dishonest," yet accept that rising "above a simple position of social and political inferiority" necessarily "imposes

upon Negroes the necessity of the other man," which means accepting that
"they have the obligation to themselves of giving up some of their need for
revenge" (343).

Arguably alone among Ellison critics—black and white—Warren understood that Ellison had "arrived, I take it, at his own secular version of
Martin Luther King's *agapē*" (*Who* 353). His subsequent essays and speeches
advanced this point of view as a practical matter of American citizenship.
In 1982 Woodward sent to Ellison for his review a manuscript called "Black
Masters: A Free Family of Color in the Old South" (1986). Ellison's detailed,
marvelous reply to one of its authors, James L. Roark, speaks to his sense
of his own evolution as a post-*Brown* black American. In their book, the
authors told the story of some black South Carolina slaveholders named
Ellison. Ralph Ellison thought their history revealed the complexity of
American experience—in which blacks could be not just slaves but slave-
owners. He playfully imagined the black slaveholding Ellisons running into
Henry James during one of their visits to New York City and the irony that
not even James could fully understand the "American joke" being performed
before him. Woodward and Roark thought Ellison might have been related to the slaveholders, but Ellison explains that he was not. Nonetheless,
Woodward's suggestion prompts him to acknowledge that he must confront the unpleasant proposition that he might have been descended from
slaveholders. In confronting that possibility, he must further acknowledge
that the past should incite not only his anger but also his forbearance, since,
as he told Roark, "there was no more disgrace in one's being related to a
black slaveholder than to those who happened to have been designated
'white'" (23 Nov. 1982).

Eight years before this exchange, in an address to the Harvard class
of 1949, Ellison developed the logic of his friendships with Warren and
Woodward. Speaking to a group that had graduated during the time that
he was struggling to write *Invisible Man*, Ellison related an epiphany he
experienced while strolling Harvard's grounds the year after he published
his novel. After giving his talk he was approached by a woman who praised
his speech and further confided that she was in communication with intel-
ligences from outer space. Disoriented by this encounter, and wondering
what he might have to do with extraterrestrial communication, Ellison was
struck by a vision as he stood before a monument to Harvard men who
had died in the Civil War. "And it was then that it happened," he recounts.
"As I stumbled along, my attention was drawn upward and I was aware
of the marble walls, somber and carved with names," and he experienced

"a moment in which perception leaped dizzily ahead of the processes of normal thought" (*Collected* 419). Looking back on something that had happened to him more than twenty years before, Ellison portrays this moment of dizzy perception as the birth of his recognition that the Civil War had been fought, in a very real sense, for him. In *Invisible Man*, the narrator refers to the Civil War when he remarks that his existence had been in the cards eighty-seven years earlier. When *Invisible Man*'s author confronts this Civil War memorial in 1953, though, he says that "the shock of recognition filled me with a kind of anguish. Something within me cried out 'No!' against that painful knowledge, for I knew that I stood within the presence of Harvard men who had given their young lives to set me free" (419).

One of those men was Colonel Robert Shaw, who volunteered to lead the first black Union troops to fight in the Civil War. As Ellison elsewhere noted, Shaw served with Henry James's brother, Wilky, in the 54th Massachusetts Negro regiment, and after being killed Shaw's "body had been thrown into a ditch with those of his [black] men" (*Invisible* xxi). In assessing Shaw's legacy, William James argued that even greater than Shaw's willingness to die in battle was the "civic courage" he showed in his willingness to serve with the black troops the Civil War was working to free. "The nation blest above all nations is the one in whom the civic genius of the people does the saving day by day, by acts without external picturesqueness" (Lewis 142). Instead of shouting "no" to the sacrifice of Shaw or Wilky James, Ellison realized that the burden of slavery and its legacy was shared by all Americans. This sense of "civic courage" describes perfectly Ellison's stance as a Negro intellectual. After *Invisible Man*, he expanded his vision to recognize the shared sacrifices made and being made by all Americans to transform society. He recognized that even the Confederates had died for his "freedom" and their sacrifice must be acknowledged too. Foregoing the position of black anger, Ellison's courage consists in its lace of picturesqueness and its humane recognition that others will learn to make the daily sacrifices heretofore required only of Negroes. In 1965, with Warren before him and the vanguard of 1960s Negro leadership surrounding him, Ellison dramatically enacted this position as he confronted "the individual white Southerner's task of reconciling himself to the new political reality" (*Collected* 31). Neither he nor Warren nor Woodward could put to rest America's history of violent race relations, but through their friendship and intellectual work they explored what it might mean to do so.

4

Invisible Man's Political Vision
Ellison and King

> It is in this fact that we must look for an explanation of the phenomenon of the last chapter: namely, that though the hero gains his throne by a victory, he never loses it by defeat.
>
> LORD RAGLAN, *The Hero*

> I have attempted to show that traditional narratives are never historical; that they are myths, and that a myth is story told in connection with a rite. . . . Traditional narratives show, by their form and their content, that they are derived neither from historical fact nor from imaginative fiction, but from acted ritual, that is to say, ritual performed for the benefit, and in the presence of, a body of worshippers who either take no part in it, or a very small part.
>
> LORD RAGLAN, *The Hero*

> So on a farm in Vermont where I was reading *The Hero* by Lord Raglan and speculating on the nature of Negro leadership in the United States, I wrote the first paragraph of *Invisible Man*, and was soon involved in the struggle of creating the novel.
>
> RALPH ELLISON

ELLISON'S WORK as a novelist and his career as a public intellectual emerged out of his conception of Negro history and its relationship to the fluid social processes of American democracy. In particular, Ellison understood the Negro's quest for social equality to be the mechanism by which United States history would fulfill its utopian ideal of creating a society in which everyone enjoyed an equal stake. As Ellison often explained, *Invisible Man* was in part an attempt to define the limits and possibilities of Negro leadership in a society that seemed unable to accept any Negro leader who challenged the necessity of segregation. *Invisible Man* showed how American social structures worked to reinforce a status quo in which white and black Americans remained invisible to each other—an inevitable consequence of centuries of racial oppression. The narrator repeatedly challenges this status quo—he has "gone out into the world; he has gone out into it; and into it; and into it," as Philip Roth says (*Reading* 191)—but can achieve only a limited success. Finding neither a constituency he can lead nor an institutional authority he can persuade, he is left to tell his story to himself and to anyone who might happen upon its telling. His act of leadership, which is also an act of revolt, is to turn his story into a ceremonial offer of his own self-enlightenment. This consummately Emersonian gesture evades solipsism insofar as its gesture is accepted and transformed by those who read or hear his story. The hero's narrative act does not insist that others follow him so much as that they find themselves in his example. His tale of how he came to understand his "invisible" place in American society is also an invitation to his ideal readers to transform their invisible community into social reality.

Significantly, the hero fails his quest to become an effective Negro leader; he succeeds only as the ironic messenger of his failure. Any immediate triumph that can be ascribed to this narrative performance may seem decidedly *aesthetic* rather than political. The narrator has mastered his self, and that mastery is expressed through the artistry of his narrative. Indeed, it may be more accurate to say that his literary mastery makes possible his self-mastery. From this perspective, *Invisible Man* follows the modernist narrative model established by Proust's *In Pursuit of Lost Time* or Joyce's *Portrait of the Artist.* Yet perhaps because *Invisible Man* is so embedded within the premises of a Negro and American history, it has rarely been seen as "merely" an aesthetic achievement. As John Hersey noticed in 1974, many years after the question of when Ellison would publish another novel had become tired, "the argument, as old as art itself, over the question: 'What use has art?'—hounds Ellison perhaps more than any other first-rank novelist of our time, unless it be Alexander Solzhenitsyn" (*Collected* 785). At the time of Hersey's comparison, Solzhenitsyn was the world's foremost political dissident, a living monument of revolt against the totalitarian regime of the Soviet Union and a champion of the individual artist's moral obligation to be true to the dictates of his or her individual conscience. Ellison too championed the integrity of the individual, despite attacks from critics who mistakenly regarded his politics as a form of complacency.

In retrospect, to compare Ellison to Solzhenitsyn may seem overstated, but it accurately conveys the feeling that Ellison projected of being an artist alone working to transform his society through his art. For some readers, Ellison became stranded from black history, just as Solzhenitsyn seemed stranded from twentieth-century Russian history. Yet Ellison never stopped arguing for the necessary visibility of blacks in American society. Robert Penn Warren's recognition that Ellison's vision of African American history mirrored King's vision suggests how inevitably connected to his historical times Ellison truly was. This is a point that Eric Sundquist reiterates when he notes that in Ellison's comments in the 1960s "his reasoning is nearly identical to King's" (*King's* 87). As Sundquist argues, "King's greatness, as well as the greatness of his [Dream] speech, lay in his ability to elevate the cause of civil rights and the cause of America at the same time" (10).[1] Like King, Ellison insisted that blacks and whites were equal Americans. Like King, Ellison understood that to enact this point of view would require blacks and whites to perform roles in American society different from those they had historically been allowed to play.

King and Ellison were both visionary figures. As King's various biographers remind us, King was often attacked by other Civil Rights leaders for being too conservative in his tactics. His decision to turn the march around on the Selma bridge or his concession to Johnson regarding the 1964 Mississippi Freedom Democratic Party delegation are two famous instances where some of King's allies felt that he had fallen short as a leader.[2] As a political leader, King's role was different from Ellison's. King could "do more" than a novelist, but, as Aldon Morris and Nick Kotz have shown, his action depended on the concerted efforts of thousands of committed people, not least Lyndon Johnson. No one would argue that King was out of step with history, even if some critics said he was too conciliatory with white America or that he was wrong to protest the Vietnam War.[3] Ellison, by contrast, was an intellectual whose role was to frame the cultural and political issues that King confronted, and to do so from an inherently black political position. In this context, Nicole A. Waligora-Davis is right to argue that "to delineate Ellison's racial philosophy," one must see it "as much an expression of black nationalism as it is the formation of an ethical system for human interaction and accountability" (386). She adds, "Ellison's racial ethic or nationalism expresses a critical cosmopolitanism deeply critical of both the historical cycle of State-sanctioned human and civil rights abuses and the complicity and sometimes collusion of the black subject in his/her colonization" (389). In attacking the moral hypocrisy of the white power structure, Ellison and King each sought to inspire his people to affirm the humanity that they had achieved in the face of, and despite, brutal oppression.

Reviewing the entire course of Ellison's career as a public intellectual, one should not forget that it was Ellison *himself* who initially judged *Invisible*

Man to be a failure and "not an important novel" (*Collected* 217). It is unclear whether he meant that his work was an aesthetic failure—unless he was suggesting that his literary technique did not surpass that of Joyce, Faulkner, or Proust. Given his exacting standards, such a reading is possible, although I think unlikely. "I failed of eloquence," he confesses, because "many of the immediate issues are rapidly falling away. If it does last, it will simply be because there are things that are going on in its depth that are of more permanent interest than on its surface. I hope so, anyway" (217). The immediate issues that Ellison mentions almost certainly referred to the historical and political condition of being black in America. He is speaking one year after *Brown* and can see already that the period in which "visibility" as defined by the Jim Crow context is over.

At the time Ellison made this remark, he was more than knee-deep in the second novel. Adam Bradley has suggested that the second novel was in a sense a version of *Invisible Man* since its story hinged on the character of Bliss, whom Ellison conceived as a version of *Invisible Man*'s Rinehart. One of the paradoxes of Rinehart's role in *Invisible Man* is that he is a character crucial to the development of the narrator's consciousness, yet technically, he never truly appears in the novel. He exists only as the projection of other characters' misperceptions. In his notes for the second novel, Ellison does explicitly connect the two novels through Bliss: "Bliss Proteus Rinehart returned to his part very much as a man to his mother or a dog to his vomit, and that's no lie." He also notes that Bliss's role, "secondarily and psychologically," is "to manipulate possibility and identities" of the other characters in order "to take revenge on his own life" (*Three* 975–76) In *Invisible Man*, Rinehart seems to be a Harlem operator, almost certainly black, and seeking personal profit rather then revenge. Rinehart provides moments of reversal and recognition through which the narrator sees that his life is one of utter possibility, and through Rinehart he rejects the false roles that have been put upon him. How interesting to think, then, that the first appearance of Bliss is in the other novel in which he is more clearly a cynical exploiter of others' beliefs (or that *Invisible Man*'s hero sees himself in Senator Sunraider). Moreover, as Bliss is neither black nor white, or he is both, or is he one pretending to be the other. One cannot tell. What is clear is that as a United States senator he represents a historical process by which white Americans have betrayed black Americans. In this context, B. P. Rinehart is not a gateway to unlimited possibility but a bar to progress for blacks in American society. The same character—if a shape-shifter can be described as one character—conveys opposed meanings, depending on which novel contains him: in one, the character's meaning is the key to the story's completion; in the other, his meaning blocks its conclusion.

Ellison told Murray that he was starting his second novel even before he finished his *Invisible Man*, and it may make sense to think of the two novels *as versions of the same novel*. Bradley comes very close to making this suggestion when he notices that *Invisible Man*, like the second novel, had many conflicting drafts and thus wonders if it would make sense to open up readings of *Invisible Man* to these other versions. I do not think that *Invisible Man* can be opened this way without violating Ellison's achievement or our sense that novels are individual works fully realized by the author. I do believe, however, that these writings should be read and used to open our understanding of Ellison—especially since I think it is likely that Ellison's judgment of *Invisible Man*'s topical belatedness was almost certainly the same as his judgment of the second novel. Both novels expressed the rage that blacks felt within the seemingly static Jim Crow historical era. Where *Invisible Man* imagined a way for individual blacks to come to terms with their humanity despite social structures that denied this humanity, the second novel imagined a social structure impervious to change and anchored in the ongoing betrayal of blacks by whites. In the second novel the resourcefulness and wit of blacks is never questioned. What is questioned, through Bliss, is the belief that whites can merit the love and forgiveness of blacks. Insofar as Bliss represents the ability to transform himself across racial lines, the second novel is pessimistic about the possibilities for blacks in a post–Jim Crow society.

Think of the two novels as one and that Ellison treated them as a wishbone: two directions, or endings, extending from the same (American) root. If *Brown* had not happened, Ellison probably would have published his second novel. Bliss's ending, Rinehart's demise, would complicate *Invisible Man*'s "optimistic" conclusion, since it would deny the reality that the fluid American society seemed to represent. If Proteus is dead, then shapes may no longer shift and everyone is stuck being where and who they are. Before he could finish the second book, though, history broke Ellison's wishbone and left him—and his readers—holding *Invisible Man*. That book became his charm, his mojo hand, and he held it up to divine the shifting American present and uncertain future. But in 1955, the "immediate issues rapidly falling away" indicated that the brilliant metaphor of "invisibility" already referred to a time no longer present. The brilliant framing of the novel, its Prologue and Epilogue, nonetheless seemed to speak from a surreal space beyond the hard Jim Crow reality between them. This dream world in which history boomeranged into something else became the space of American reality. Jim Crow logic was repudiated, and suddenly American history was turned inside out. Bliss Proteus lived.

Perhaps Ellison was being disingenuous when he said his novel failed of eloquence, but he may also have been frustrated to find himself being outwitted by history—and in a sense by other living "moses" too. It took him a long time not to publish the second novel—to learn to hold only the half of the wishbone that history had given him. Here he was, a novelist obsessed with American history and utterly committed to the endurance and wisdom of the black folk tradition, yet he could not see in his fiction that the Civil Rights movement was about to break through in ways that neither Jack the Bear nor Hickman could imagine. While Hickman was sitting at Bliss's bedside through the 1950s and then 1960s, with Ellison as sole witness, King was persuading Lyndon Johnson to risk the electoral future of the Democratic Party (and his own political future) to sign legislation that consolidated the gains of the *Brown* decision. *Invisible Man* had exposed the traps that would confront and overwhelm any black leader, but it did not see a way out of them except through individual enlightenment not sanctioned by politics or society. Ellison knew on some level, of course, that change might happen; he just did not know how close it was. He also knew, I would hazard, that the second novel's plot was not in step with either contemporary reality or, more important, his own reoriented sense of that reality.

If one thinks of Ellison's two novels as drafts of the same book, then it is possible to think of him as having written thousands of pages of fiction and then choosing to repress all but those that became *Invisible Man* and the eight segments he published from the second novel. Those segments for the most part express a shared black cultural history and perspective that are rooted in the past. *Invisible Man*, though, differs from its hidden twin because it looks forward and backward at the same time, which is why Ellison decided to claim it rather that continue questioning its worth. As an aesthetic achievement, it continued (and continues) to speak to the American present and future in a way that I think no other "classic" American novel quite can. Ironically, the deserved emphasis on *Invisible Man*'s aesthetic achievement, consistently abetted by Ellison, has veiled us from understanding the extent to which *Invisible Man* prophesies and in a sense anticipates the Freedom Movement's victories of the 1960s. The second novel lacked *Invisible Man*'s element of prophecy (unless one says it foretold a doomed armed revolt) and instead looked back to a moment that seemed to be intractable.

From this perspective, those who have argued that Ellison was a failure as a political visionary have missed something essential to his achievement. H. Williams Rice sums up a tradition of Ellison criticism when he asserts that "despite his attempt to be responsible for democracy, Ellison ultimately failed as so many other American writers have done. As good a historian as he was, Ellison did not in hibernating Invisible Man account for Martin Luther King, Jr. or Malcolm X or the bizarre chaos of events that made Birmingham possible" (140). John S. Wright, though, suggests that "critical responses to the novel remain fettered to radical cliché" but have "all but ignored *Invisible Man*'s central concern with political power and the problems of black leadership" (22). Morris Dickstein is on the right track when he observes that "in the typology of *Invisible Man*, Marcus Garvey foreshadows the Black Panthers, thirties Marxism anticipates post-sixties Marxism, and a mid-century conception of America's cultural diversity, marked by a fluid, malleable sense of identity, proves remarkably germane to an end-of-the-century debate over pluralism and multiculturalism" (146). Rampersad notes that by the mid-1960s, "almost uncannily, certain dramatic features of *Invisible Man* . . . now seemed to be not so much a fictional world created by Ralph as his inspired prophecy" (406). As Dickstein and Rampersad suggest, readers have occasionally recognized that *Invisible Man*'s story is intertwined with the future, but this point of view has not yet been embedded in most understandings of Ellison's work. (Indeed, Rampersad's observation occurs in the midst of his broader argument that Ellison was not engaged with the Civil Rights movement.)[4] In fact, *Invisible Man* was in the tradition of Martin Delany, Nat Turner, Frederick Douglass, Harriet Tubman, A. Philip Randolph, and, finally, Martin Luther King, and its author wrote that tradition as a mythic story that aspired to prophecy. Someday, we will overcome.

Ordinarily, critics use history to interpret fiction, but with Ellison one can use fiction in order to interpret history. We can reclaim the political implications of Ellison's novel by asking this question: what happens to Ellison's novel if we read it not in terms of its failure to imagine King's eventual success but in terms of King's successful completion of the narrative gesture that Ellison's hero left open? Reading *Invisible Man* through King's movement tells us that Ellison's novel is not just a Jim Crow artifact or an aesthetic masterpiece but a living text that helps us to understand why King succeeded as a leader and how Ellison's anti–Jim Crow commitment to equality was the basis of what made the Civil Rights movement effective. At the end of *Invisible Man*, the narrator has galvanized his people but failed to lead them to a changed society. What to do with the energy he has tapped and by what mechanism (ritual) to release and organize that energy is the novel's open question (see Callahan "Frequencies"; "Democracy"). King and the movement he led solve the riddle of the Negro leader that Ellison's hero enacts. Eventually, Ellison would enact strategies for confronting the new society that King's work helped to make possible. Before he did that, though, Ellison had his own narrative riddle to solve: how to invent a black hero who could act "heroically" within a social structure that seemed to deny him agency. Thus, the "uncanny" element that Rampersad correctly identifies makes sense, because Ellison's "inspired prophecy" was predicated on a narrative genius that was able to identify and dramatize *the mythic structures* scripting the heroic saga of blacks in America. Lord Raglan gave him the clue he needed—to finish his first novel if not his second.

From History to Myth

In his own words, Ellison began *Invisible Man* when he was "on a farm in Vermont where I was reading *The Hero* by Lord Raglan and speculating on the nature of Negro leadership" (*Collected* 218). There are a number of Negro leaders in the novel—Bledsoe, Barbee, Clifton, and Ras the Exhorter are the most prominent. Moreover, characters such as Trueblood, the Vet, Tarp, Wrestrum, and Rinehart offer conflicting strategies whereby black American men can try to negotiate the perils of invisibility within American society. Furthermore, historical figures such as Frederick Douglass, Booker T. Washington, W. E. B. Du Bois, and Marcus Garvey cast their shadows over the narrator's story. Absent a society committed to enforcing its legal principles for everyone, though, black leaders are likely either to collaborate with a corrupt white power structure in order to keep their position (Bledsoe) or to inspire forms of violent revolt that put the community at risk. Politics—as the Brotherhood sections suggest—is a club from which the black masses are excluded and with which they are endlessly beaten. Instead, black expression becomes most persuasive through cultural forms such as music, dress, or storytelling. Without political visibility, the narrator's community can rely only on its own folk rituals to ensure its preservation and vitality.

Of the many black leaders subjected to critique by the narrative, the figures of Booker T. Washington and Frederick Douglass perhaps most stand out. The narrator's first portrayed attempt to be a leader finds him quoting without evident comprehension the words of Washington. Near the end of the novel, the narrator stands beneath a portrait of Douglass and tries to imagine a connection between his own life and Douglass's example. Arguably, Douglass better speaks to the narrator's situation and ambition than Washington. Like Douglass, the narrator leaves the initial site of his bondage to recreate himself in a region (the North) that seems to afford him more freedom. Like Douglass, the narrator finds his voice and thus his self in mastering his story and sharing it with an interested audience. The resolution of his story, however, does not solve the question of Negro leadership that it raises any more than Douglass's memoirs solved the historical problem of slavery. Thus, he rejects Washington's example but can offer nothing better.[5] The hero has discovered his own story, but he has not participated in a social action that clearly improves the condition of his people. Ironically, his success can be recast as a version of Washington's famous advice that the narrator quoted in his high school valedictory address. Those inspired by his completed story must now, as he has done, cast their bucket where they are and hope it brings up something good.

On this reading, Negro leadership in 1952 had not progressed (perhaps could not progress) much beyond the situation confronted by the narrator after the first chapter Battle Royal. Yet Ellison by his own admission was telling this story in order to figure out how to transcend the historical situation that inspired it. The Battle Royal establishes the ritual of identity creation (and suppression) that is enacted in virtually every encounter between blacks and whites in American history. For Ellison, the Civil War, followed by the brief period of Reconstruction (after which his grandfather had to surrender his gun), was the only period in which this ritual was challenged. When the hero gives his speech, this aspiring Negro leader does not understand that he is being initiated into a situation that he is powerless to change. Ellison's extraordinary double-voiced narrative conveys the narrator's submission to the social codes of segregation with his almost unconscious desire to break those codes. No words (except the blues) he speaks can change the degradation—the humiliation—of the rhetorical situation he inherits. His "triumph" as a student cannot be separated from a ceremony commemorating the shared condition of being born into a society that divides its material goods and social honor according to the color of one's skin.

Speaking to an audience at West Point in 1969, Ellison characterized the Battle Royal as a "rite of initiation" that the narrator had to undergo in order to understand "that American society cannot define the role of the individual, or at least not that of the *responsible* individual" (*Collected* 528). He points out that the Battle Royal, an event perpetrated throughout the

South of his youth, "was a rite which could be used to project racial divisions into the society and reinforce the idea of white racial superiority" (529). Ellison's young hero, while no doubt abstractly aware of the power that whites held in his society, apparently did not understand that power circulated continuously through all levels of society in ways that could not help but influence his own attempts at self-affirmation. But what would such an understanding imply?

A leader such as Booker T. Washington understood very well how this power worked and that understanding became the premise for his choices as a leader. The narrator's home community probably believed that any future success he might hope to have as a Negro leader, or simply as an individual, depended on his learning this lesson as quickly as possible. At the very least, they may have been concerned that his ignorance would embarrass and thus potentially harm the group. Thus, although in *Invisible Man* it is the white community that runs the ritual that "initiates" the hero into "the idea of white racial superiority," it is the black community that instigates his initiation. This does not mean that its members affirm "the idea of white racial superiority." To the contrary, the narrator's initiation—the symbolic action that he enacts and that is enacted upon him—must precede any progress he or they can make in their quest to eradicate the society's commitment to the idea of white superiority. Nonetheless, his refusal, however naive, to accept this "superiority" constitutes his heroism. One can say that his heroism is unconscious or even stupid, but, as King proved, society cannot be changed unless the premise of white superiority (legal, moral, and social) is rejected. The narrative that is the novel is a more sophisticated version of this refusal and suggests why the narrator might one day, circumstances permitting, be an effective Negro leader beyond the Washington model.

The most famous attack upon the Washingtonian position was Du Bois's *The Souls of Black Folk*. Rather than accommodating black interests to the white power structure and working safely with what the society gave them, Du Bois argued that Negroes should seek to transform that structure through the achievements of what he called the talented tenth. Ellison's narrator aspires to be a member of Du Bois's talented tenth (his success in education suggests that he will be), but nothing in his experience suggests that the sort of social integration Du Bois envisioned will be possible in the world that the novel portrays. On *Invisible Man*'s logic, neither the Washington nor the Du Bois position will be adequate to further the interests of the hero's community—a point of view that is reinforced by the description of the Founder's statue at the beginning of the second chapter. This stone version of a Washington-like figure is described in imagery that also evokes Du Bois. The narrator sees a "cold Father symbol, his hands outstretched in the breathtaking gesture of lifting a veil that flutters in hard, metallic folds above the face of a kneeling slave; and I am standing puzzled, unable to decide whether the veil is really being lifted, or lowered more firmly in place" (*Invisible* 36). By alluding to Du Bois's famous metaphor of the veil, while emphasizing the narrator's skepticism that progress from slavery is possible, Ellison conflates the two opposed leaders into one. The intractable fact that the narrator, as an aspiring leader, confronts is that the historical situation he has been born into seems so perfectly static—like the statue in which it is impossible to discern whether the motion being depicted is that of rising or falling.

In this context, can black leaders be realistically expected not to exploit their group in exchange for the illusion of power? Bledsoe is the logical answer to this dilemma as he works to lead and keep his people in place at the same time. He cannot serve his people without being subservient to the white power structure. Negroes who will not play by his rules—that is to say, by "white" rules, characters such as Trueblood or the narrator—are beyond the pale and cast out of the community. As is the case for all the black men in the novel, however, the subsequent roles the narrator enacts are only versions of the one that Bledsoe has mastered. The narrator must consistently reject the historical double bind that traps Bledsoe, since this rejection is his only hope that history may one day change and that he will be ready for the change when it comes.

In that same 1969 address at West Point, Ellison reiterates that when writing *Invisible Man* during the decade that preceded King's 1955 emergence on the national scene with the Montgomery bus boycott, he "was very much involved with the question of just why our Negro leadership was never able to enforce its will. Just what was there about the structure of American society that prevented Negroes from throwing up effective leaders?" (*Collected* 525). *Invisible Man* expressed Ellison's sense that Negro leadership was inadequate to the will of the Negro people, and he wanted to figure out why that was so. Thus, he adds, "it was no accident that the young man in my book turned out to be hungry and thirsty to prove to himself that he could be an effective leader" (525). One event that provoked Ellison's frustration was the U.S. government's refusal to allow black military personnel to serve on an equal basis with whites. Although he dropped the project that was explicitly concerned with this issue to follow the call of *Invisible Man*, his outrage that the assertion of "equality for all" was a statement that did not in practice apply to black Americans drove the logic of the narrative as powerfully as did his inquiry into the nature of Negro leadership.

Ellison's remarks to Warren about King indicate his respect for King, but Ellison continued to believe that the heroic toughness King embodied would be required of his people in perpetuity. Once *Brown* showed that movement was possible, his people's heroic toughness could play a productive—not defensive—role in the struggle. Until that moment, though, if the Negro leader could enact only the choices afforded Clifton or Ras or Bledsoe, then best to reject them and, like some Kerouac character, go underground and plot one's next move. As a novelist and not a politician, however, Ellison could still forcefully portray the hypocrisy of the nation's commitment to "equality" and the disingenuous ways whites exploited blacks to consolidate their own positions as "Americans." Ellison need not risk being lynched or losing a high position by vividly portraying how American history or identity, whatever its true origins and acts, expressed the "right white" point of view and celebrated the "optic white" success of cynical innocence. After *Brown*, King and other leaders could say—in public and on television—versions of what Ellison portrayed in *Invisible Man*.

I have characterized Ellison's point of view in more bitter terms than Ellison allowed himself to express after the book was published. Litwack argues that the American South from 1877 to 1954 was in effect a totalitarian state, and *Invisible Man* affirms this claim. That the Brotherhood, despite its progressive politics, offers him no better place *as a Negro* than he could have acquired for himself had he remained in the South underscores the inherent nihilism of his social and historical position. When a West Point student in 1970 asked Ellison if his intention was "to show this white domination over the Negro and of keeping the Negro in his primitive state," Ellison responded, pointedly, "The answer is no" (*Collected* 536). Ellison's "no" likely reflects his sense that Negro culture, especially in its vernacular forms, was complex and sophisticated, and also his defiant belief that without Negro culture American culture would be bankrupt. He was answering it again several years after passage of the Civil Rights Act, and Voting Rights Act, and he knew—as racist as American society still was—that the law was now on his people's side in ways it had never been before.

Yet the student's question very easily could have been answered by a "yes." Fifteen years earlier, Ellison had remarked that at the heart of his novel was the wisdom of the black folklore rhyme: "If you're black, stay back; if you're brown, stick around; if you're white, you're right" (*Collected* 215). Thus, whatever inadequacies of personal vision the narrator's valedictory speech may have revealed, his failure to lead is insignificant once one understands that no achievement of eloquence on his part could seemingly change either his or his people's historical condition as Israelites born into political bondage. Ellison's novel, in his words, failed of eloquence because, as a political document, it could only name and replicate the historical epoch symbolized by the Battle Royal. Although the novel elsewhere celebrates blacks' capacity for communal self-invention, the Battle Royal chapter portrays a black community that has been ritually degraded and can expect only more of the same. The narrator subsequently addresses his audience with his mouth leaking blood. So did Ellison when he spoke to the *Partisan Review* in 1955 or West Point students in 1969; he just didn't let it show.

Besides the narrator, Ras the Exhorter is the only black leader who seems ready to reject the existing power structure and also the only one prepared to meet it with acts of violence. As Ellison told Robert O'Meally in 1976, though, Malcolm X's rhetoric was understandable and perhaps necessary, but it risked bringing more violence down upon blacks. Ellison also rejected Marcus Garvey–like cultural nationalism, but he still counted on cultural resilience (and even genius) to make the best history and especially *Brown's* new possibilities (*Living* 280–81). Thus, while the Battle Royal exhibits the black hero's initiation into a racist society, it also reveals his almost unconscious perception that such a society must be overturned. The scene rejects this possibility as "realistic" even as it raises the specter of equality as something that haunts and animates American history.

The ones who presume to orchestrate the narrator's initiation into American society are easily identified: "the town's big shots" "in their tuxedos, wolfing down the buffet foods, drinking beer and whiskey and smoking black cigars," who sadistically brutalize young black boys by blindfolding them and making them punch one another's lights out and then further humiliate them by forcing them to ogle a similarly exploited naked white woman (*Invisible* 17). The Marxist orientation that Barbara Foley discerns in *Invisible Man* is evident in this description of a privileged group enjoying the material excess they have extorted from the social and economic class beneath them. To borrow a phrase from a blues refrain, how can a poor boy get home? How can a poor boy hope to confront or transform an audience that so piggishly and matter-of-factly denies him, and his black peers, the expression of their own humanity? Analogously, what kind of leadership will allow the descendants of slaves to come together to overthrow these men in their tuxedos and achieve their rightful place in an American society truly dedicated to equality for all? Especially when it is the black community that sends them to the slaughter?

The narrator provides the answer, or the answer is providentially placed in his mouth: true "social responsibility" is impossible without a shared commitment, at every level of society, to "equality." What occurs at this moment is one of the most remarkable exchanges in the novel and, arguably, provides the key to understanding Ellison's assessment of his group's foreseeable political future. At last getting to address the group he so desperately wants to impress, the narrator speaks by rote a speech that seems "a hundred times as long as before" (*Invisible* 30). The phrase "social responsibility," words that to his audience signify black submission to the status quo, elicits a demand for him to repeat himself.

> "What's that word you say, boy?"
> "Social responsibility."
> "What?"
> "Social ..."
> "Louder."
> "... responsibility."
> "More!"
> "Respon—"
> "Repeat!"
> "—bility." (*Invisible* 30)

The exchange evokes and mocks the call-and-response format of the black church that Wright depicted in *12 Million Black Voices*, except that here the communal power ordinarily represented by such sacramental forms between and among blacks is being usurped by the whites and deployed against the black speaker. Rather than leading his audience, he is being led by them. As a representative of the black community, he is powerless. His audience is laughing at him.

The rhetorical context changes, as does the relationship of power between the speaker and his audience, when the narrator unaccountably breaks the pattern by substituting the word "equality" for "responsibility." The effect is as if to freeze time, except that within that instant history is revealed to be something that is alive and thus capable of being transformed. "The laughter hung smokelike in the sudden stillness," the narrative states (*Invisible* 31). I do not think it is too much to say that for the moment—perhaps for the first time in the memory of anyone present—a black person and a group of white people see each other differently. At the very least, the whites recognize the prospect of being compelled to recognize the speaker—a black person—as being human, as they are human, and not merely the prescribed social function of a denigrating racial epithet that they are free to abuse as they please, and do. The word "equality," which the narrator says is a word he had "seen denounced in newspaper editorials," requires the two sides for a moment to have an exchange that is not prescripted. The initiation ritual is violated. Although further conversation quickly seems to restore the original order of things, Ellison has brilliantly conveyed the power that the invocation of "equality" has in American politics. This moment portrays a collision between historical epochs—the 1877–1954 Jim Crow era (which incorporates the pre–Emancipation Proclamation period) and the shocking transformation of American society about to occur with the Civil Rights movement.

Ellison surely knew that that he was portraying a collision of histories when he wrote this scene. The expansion of the notion of "equality" to include Negroes would help make possible the successful protests of Martin Luther King. One cannot quite say that Ellison's aspiring Negro leader has failed in this moment because the lessons he learns do not, within the novel, have a context in which they might have a second life. "I was swallowing blood," he says to excuse his slip (*Invisible* 31). Political "equality" between blacks and whites is not possible in the universe that *Invisible Man* imagines. Yet, read retroactively, this famous symbolic scene of ossified Jim Crow social stasis becomes prophetic because it foreshadows how King and others would consolidate a mass movement predicated on the premise that "equality" was something more than a word and that Negroes had a stake in it as legitimate as that of any other American. Just as Ellison's narrator was subjected to the violence of the white community, King accepted that violence as the price he was willing to pay for the remission of white people's sins against equality. King's strategy of nonviolence *usurped and appropriated to his people's advantage* the ritual of violence that Jim Crow required and that the Battle Royal depicts. Thus, King's "humility" was not the same as that of Booker T. Washington, and it heralded a radical new form of successful Negro leadership that has arguably been without sequel.

As King wrote in 1956, "We Negroes have replaced self-pity with self-respect and self-depreciation with dignity" (*I Have* 5). King's point—which differs from Ellison's post–*Invisible Man* pronouncements—was that blacks could begin to reverse history only by reversing the image of themselves that they had inherited from the white men. Ellison's perpetual assertion that *Invisible Man*'s hero had to see himself first before he could become a leader is consistent with King's message in "Our Struggle." Articulating precisely the historical logic revealed by the Battle Royal, King describes how generations of post Civil War whites allowed "the triumph of their lesser instincts" to rationalize the belief that the "Negro, being less than human, deserved and even enjoyed second-class status." From this rationalization came the belief that an "inferior social, economic and political position was good for" the Negro. This belief became institutionalized and thus accurately "reflected the Negro's innate and true nature." Moreover, King suggests, Negroes internalized this arbitrary social arrangement as the natural order of things. However, "once we discovered that we had never really smothered our self-respect and that we could not be at one with ourselves without asserting it," genuine social change for Negroes became possible to imagine—and to realize (*I Have* 5).

Ellison, by contrast, never made the concession to black self-doubt that King did in his remarks above, and would likely argue that had those assessments been correct, the Civil Rights movement could never have happened. For Ellison, as it was for Du Bois and Wright, being black and American constituted a heroic action. To define this heroic action in his novel, Ellison drew on traditional narrative forms such as the epic, in which myth, more than history, structured the action being depicted. Writing within a historical context in which the emergence of an authentic black heroic leader seemed impossible, Ellison looked to myth to redeem the seeming nihilism of his historical moment. Ultimately, *Invisible Man* imagined the mythic necessity of King, that is to say, the necessity of the role that King would play. In Lord Raglan's *The Hero*, a study of the relationship between myth and ritual in traditional narrative, Ellison found the key that helped him structure his hero's story so that "history" or "the present" was less important than how that hero, and through him the group he represented, could survive and perhaps master history. For Ellison the very survival of American blacks, along with the culture they created out of slavery and its aftermath, constituted a "heroic" action in a sense that was mythic before it was historic.

According to Lord Raglan, "traditional narrative, in all its forms, is based not upon historical facts on the one hand or imaginative fictions on the other, but upon dramatic ritual or ritual drama" (278). In this context, both the "historical facts" and the imagined action dramatized in *Invisible Man* matter less than identifying the ritual that will complete the drama of the hero's story in a satisfactory way. The historical facts and Ellison's many reinventions are "true" only insofar as their meaning is organized according to the dramatic ritual by which they are enacted and symbolized. For the narrator, that ritual is the Battle Royal, and once he has been initiated into his drama by that ritual, his heroic status is assured.

Lord Raglan notes that "though the hero gains the throne by a victory, he never loses it by a defeat" (199). It may seem ironic to characterize the completion of the Battle Royal as the hero's victory, since on so many levels it seems to be a defeat for him and the community that he represents. Moreover, as Ellison's hero undertakes his quest for a more obvious victory—visibility—the completion of this quest seems possible only as a form of perhaps questionable self-invention. Yet if we understand the ritual of the Battle Royal to mean that through it the narrator has discovered the wherewithal to confront his destiny, regardless of what dangers beset him, then what matters is that somehow through this ritual the hero, and the community whose story he represents, will complete the drama than enacts his—their—ultimate triumph. The hero's lasting victory is sanctioned by his successful completion of the ritual that symbolizes the community's commitment to perseverance, regardless of the forces opposed to their survival. In this mythic context, it is crucial that the black community identifies him as the one of "ours" who had to endure the ritual of the Battle Royal. Thus, every "failure" that the hero suffers in his quest to become visible is, paradoxically, a success, since for him it confirms the resolve required to continue his quest. As long as his acts are true to the communal resolve that the ritual symbolizes, he remains the hero of the group's myth.

In this context, the victory that captures the throne would be one that transformed the ritual enacted by the Battle Royal so that the hero—and others like him—could become visible within the entire society. That the narrator can claim visibility at the end of the novel is in part a function of his recognition that his capacity to endure in his quest inheres in the ritual he enacted at his story's start. When he confronts his unseen audience with the fact of his "heroism," which is his willingness to risk his life and the meaning of his life in an encounter (that may also be a battle), he is once again performing a version of the Battle Royal. Now his mouth is no longer bloody when he speaks, and he has even contrived for himself a safe space from which to join the battle again—and it surely is a battle that he will be joining. This last gesture to the reader is the final version of the many speeches he has given throughout the novel. Over and over, he speaks to audiences eager to confront the meaning of equality, and only through a commitment to that word's meaning can his group expect to prevail in their communal quest. The hero's "assertion of equality" in the face of his antagonist foreshadows the community's ultimate victory.

On Lord Raglan's terms, "the hero of history and the hero of tradition are really two quite different persons" (205–6). For Lord Raglan, the hero is never truly a historical figure (a person who actually lived and died); the hero is a mythic figure created by communal ritual and revealed in narrative form. In chapter 3, Ellison explained to Robert Penn Warren that the Civil Rights protests and marches, whether led by King or by the children of Little Rock, were the embodiment of a communal resolve in which risking one's life was a sacrifice required of anyone asked to perform it in order to preserve the community's existence. In this respect, the "hero" is never quite an individualized character but the symbolic enactment of a communal ritual. The relative anonymity of Ellison's narrator accords with this principle, but this point also suggests that King's role is more "mythic" than "real." To join others and risk lives by marching against dogs, fire hoses, clubs, and guns requires the same sense of bloody resolve that the Battle Royal had required of Ellison's hero. In these marches, members of the black community are not being made to fight among themselves, but they all have to endure and risk a conclusion to their protest that is the same as the conclusion to the Battle Royal. As "Tell It Like It Is, Baby" suggested, success was not guaranteed. All that could be guaranteed was the collective will to carry on.

During the Civil Rights movement, Martin Luther King Jr. performed the heroic role that had been demanded of Ellison's hero. One can conceivably say, as I have said in different sections of this book, that King succeeded where Ellison's imaginary hero failed because King encountered a historical context in which success was possible. But heroism from the mass of blacks was necessary too. Before blacks could attend schools of their choice, have a fairer chance at equal housing or employment, be better represented in local and national government, or even select which water fountain to use, they had to enact a mythic drama or ritual in which the undue sacrifice required of them could be performed and symbolized by a particular hero's actions. As King was the hero and leader of the Freedom Movement, though, his life was less important than the mythic drama that the narrative he was enacting required him to perform.[6] In this way, his life and his role as mythic hero came together in the moment of his death—a death that was but the "heroic" version of the progression of uncountable deaths since the slave ships first came to America. Before King died, the movement's success had been ratified, as it were, by the U.S. Supreme Court, the work of three presidents, and two stunning acts of Congress. From the "mythic" perspective of *Invisible Man*, however, King's heroism consisted in the role assigned to him within a communal drama in which he would continually risk his life to sustain the group.[7] It was that will which made the Civil Rights movement possible. The actual politics that made the hero-ism that King embodied meaningful to those outside the group—to Warren or Lyndon B. Johnson—so that "history" could be changed was another, not to say incidental, matter.

From *Invisible Man* to Montgomery

In exploring the problem of the Negro leader during the Jim Crow era, Ellison, through his encounter with Lord Raglan, was writing the narra-tive that King eventually enacted within history: to consolidate and release the power of the black community into viable political action. As Barbara Foley's work laments, Ellison revised his novel to disguise the Marxist origins of his critique of American society. I think that he did this in part out of his recognition that the Communist position was not then a viable one in American politics. Ellison placed his faith in the ingenuity of black folk wisdom—codified in blues and jazz—and also in Lincoln's legacy. He hoped that (white) America could accept "equality" as a principle that ap-plied to all its citizens. *Invisible Man* is a living history of the mythic spirit of black revolt against their oppression, and the narrator's unconscious tie to his folk roots sustains him through his many misadventures. As Ellison insisted in 1958, "Negroes" view their "slave past" as "sources of strength" and in their "spirituals" voice "their birth as a people" (*Collected* 298). This per-spective distinguished him from Wright and made him understand black culture as something more than a Marxist economic integer. From Ellison's perspective, "the desegregation struggle is *only* the socio-political manifes-tation of this process" (298; emphasis added).

Ellison's logic roots the black political movement of the 1950s within the ritualized folk tradition of the slave tales and the blues. As Ellison told Warren, King was a figure out of Negro folklore: High John the Conqueror returned to redeem his people. Ellison was thus fascinated that King found himself in "the realm of politics while trying to stay outside it," since in a sense that fact revealed how an earlier narrative demanded King's ap-pearance rather than King himself scripting the story in which he must play hero (*Collected* 814). For Ellison, King served a function similar to that performed by singer Jimmy Rushing when he was belting out the blues along his home street Deep Second in Oklahoma City. Rushing's music, Ellison notes, was related to the church and "helped to give our lives some semblance of wholeness" (*Collected* 275). Hidden away "from the great white world," Rushing's singing "expressed a value, an attitude about the world for which our lives afforded no other definition" (273). For Ellison, King's achievement was that he was able to bring the sense of community that Rushing's singing affirmed into "the great wide world" that knew little of the blues but recognized the moral authority of King's voice and his cause.

Invisible Man's exploration of Negro leadership also reflects Ellison's sense that for black Americans, cultural affirmation had to precede political action. The group had to preserve and name itself through folk ritual in order to act together effectively. Yet this synthesis between communal knowledge and effective leadership (political action) that King represented is precisely what the novel portrays as broken. Arguably, the narrator's awakening to his relationship to his own story begins when he hears "a record shop loudspeaker blaring a languid blues" that may as well be Jimmy Rushing singing (*Invisible* 436). But the process that leads to the narrator's self-illumination cannot be replicated on a broad, communal scale, even if in his desire to become one with the black audiences he addresses causes him to wonder, "How else could I save myself from disintegration?" (346). He cannot quite become High John the Conqueror; rather, he is the embodiment of a folk-historical process that created High John.

Despite moving from South to North and meeting representative black leaders as distinct from each other as Bledsoe and Tarp, the protagonist cannot discover or create a context that significantly replaces the one he encounters at the Battle Royal. His double bind, one that reflects his historical condition rather than his personal failure, is that he cannot galvanize the black masses by cowering before whites, yet he cannot advance among whites without in some sense betraying the black masses. Like Douglass, the narrator leaves the South behind. In the North, he finds a measure of individual freedom and advances himself (as Douglass did) through a political organization that is run by white men. These men, however, exploit the black masses as cynically as the white Southerners did in the Battle Royal. Outside the novel, though, King's success would depend on organizing the energy of the already politicized Southern black masses. Except through its folk roots, Ellison's novel does not suggest the political revolution that was building within the black South. Yet the novel is explicit in suggesting that the narrator's chances for establishing an effective black political movement must occur outside the Brotherhood's supervision. The first of these encounters is telling because it predicts the mode of social protest that King, with the help of television, would eventually master.

The failed political drama begins when the narrator encounters an old black couple being evicted from their home. The narrator is struck by the betrayal of hopes and promises he sees in their removal, and he intuits that their story is also his story. "The old woman's sobbing was having a strange effect on me," he relates (the sobbing woman recalls the slave woman he dreams in his Prologue), and he is moved to act. But how and to what end? He chooses to start speaking—to improvise on a theme. The improvisational nature of the speech indicates the need to invent new political strategies and new political contexts for confronting what has become a static historical situation. The disenfranchisement of blacks by whites is a calcified fact of American history, and it will be changed only by a creative black leadership that can draw on its vast cultural resources to change the context of this struggle. Ellison's narrator, however, has only his goodwill and his eloquence to rely on. He risks himself in an improvised act of courage, but he lacks the organization—the narrative structure—through which his action can be translated into effective leadership.

To a makeshift audience of mostly stray blacks, he recounts shared truths embedded in their history, and his allusion to their shared history, represented by the eviction of the couple, excites them to action. A community has been called together by his words and recognizes itself as such. But this recognition again raises the question, what to do and to what end? The narrator is trying to orchestrate an effective street protest. His protest anticipates the better orchestrated street protests that the Civil Rights movement would engineer with the 1960 lunch counter boycott in Greensboro, North Carolina, or the boycott in Nashville, Tennessee.[8] His protest elicits the same communal energy that those highly planned "improvisational" protests would require, but his effort lacks the television cameras and the authority of the U.S. Supreme Court that made those actions so effective.

What Ellison's narrator enacts is not a planned version of an improvisational protest but a spontaneous reaction to a random event that is actually part of an ongoing historical pattern: black people being denied their homes. Ellison portrays the encounter as one more anonymous incident of disenfranchisement among hundreds of thousands of others—but this one is happening in a novel pretending to record the event for posterity. Absent television cameras and court injunctions, the incident's shape comes from Ellison's narrative organization, and its power derives from the reader's recognition that the injustice taking place is long-standing and ongoing. In this moment, tension rises quickly. "There's plenty nerve," one anonymous man observes to the narrator. "All they need is someone to set it off. All they need is a leader" (*Invisible* 262). The "nerve" is as important as "the someone," and the narrator briefly becomes that "someone," but what "setting it off" might mean and what a leader could accomplish other than inciting the crowd to immediate violence is unclear.

The narrator's initial reaction to the eviction is outrage. He pretends that such things happen only in the South. But what provokes his action is not the violence of the evictors but the moral fury of the old woman being removed. In an important sense, her anger and hurt fuel the action. She yells, "Take your hands off my Bible" and "This here's the last straw. They ain't going to bother with my Bible" (*Invisible* 263). Her outrage concerning her Bible speaks to her sense that the evictors are appropriating not only her material possessions but *the history of who she is* as well. Something sacred is being taken from her as she is removed from a home that could hardly be imagined to be luxurious or—if we go by Wright's account in *12 Million Black Voices*—even comfortable. Her cry of protest identifies a historical condition, a recurring everyday situation, which calls for an ingenious gesture of redemptive redress. She refuses to excuse the white lackeys evicting her because "it's all the white folks, not just one. They all against us. Every stinking low-down one of them" who have united to continually dispossess her. Who is going to stand up to "these white folks"? (263).

Arguably, the novel suggests that the question cannot be adequately answered, though asking it is itself a type of revolt. *Invisible Man's* authority inheres in Ellison's ability to voice the black community's need to affirm and reinvent its bonds, despite the malignant interventions of white American society. The narrator's last gesture invites readers of all colors to join those whose story he enacts, but the consequence of his invitation is left in the dark. Ellison is often wrongly thought of as a "blocked" writer, but what *Invisible Man* reveals is how "blocked" by society American blacks were. Once the situation became unblocked by *Brown* and its aftermath, then the assumptions of what made one "black" or "white" were fundamentally changed. Ellison recognized this when he said the novel had "failed of eloquence," but his novel nonetheless provided the most eloquent expression in American literature of American blacks' will to overcome the blocks placed before them (and on which they were originally placed).

This anonymous woman's cry—more powerful because she is anonymous and thus her situation is so utterly emblematic—presages a remarkable spilling out of Negro history in the form of her possessions tumbled into the street. Like the slave woman the narrator dreams of in his Prologue, she is an embodiment of the spirit by which blacks survived the middle crossing and slavery on this continent. She may also be seen as a version of Rosa Parks or Fanny Lou Hamer, who led the protest when the Mississippi Freedom Democratic Party tried to seat their delegates at the 1964 Democratic National Convention.[9] In the novel, the character's demand for redress is unanswered (except through the book's narrative), but her demand is eloquent and will not disappear. She is the living voice of the black past and of the black future, and for Ellison she is indomitable.

This woman's eviction prompts the narrator to reflect on the history he shares with other blacks. He discerns "an oval portrait of the old couple when young" and then thinks of the "nineteenth-century day" in which they had faced their future with a "grim, unillusioned pride" (*Invisible* 264). The history of Negro experience since before the Civil War tumbles forth in the scattering of "knocking bones," "the wooden block of a set of drums," "a High John the Conqueror" lucky stone, a card reading "God Bless Our Home," a "small Ethiopian flag," "a faded tintype of Abraham Lincoln," and "a yellowing newspaper portrait" with the "caption: MARCUS GARVEY DEPORTED" (265–66). He finds crumpled in "the dirty snow" a "fragile paper" proclaiming: "*Be it known to all men that my negro, Primus Provo, has been freed by me this sixth day of August, 1859. Signed, John Samuels. Macon*" (266). The narrator beholds a living material record of promises made and broken between the U.S. government and the freed Negro slaves. This woman, like Toni Morrison's Pilate in *Song of Solomon*, has carried with her the remains of her history as if she were a spirit seeking rest. Such bones were what walked the slaves into a perilous freedom and through the Jim Crow era that Ellison memorialized. Such bones would also walk their descendants through the marches of the Civil Rights movement and into the uncertain post-segregation future.

The novel asks what "freedom for blacks" has come to mean. Is it only and always a version of the Battle Royal and its recurring lesson "to keep this nigger boy running"? Is it possible that this freedom must be claimed, or earned, by Primus's descendents and not merely granted by John Samuels or even Abraham Lincoln? Isn't the woman in effect being evicted by a descendant of Samuels or Lincoln? The pathos of the history that the woman's eviction represents moves the narrator to action. He gives a speech that riles the crowd. He proves his mettle as a "rabble-rouser." Yet no matter his eloquence, his response is insufficient to what he witnesses. He cannot solve the woman's problem. He cannot prevent her from being evicted or restore her possessions so that their meaning and promise are not lost. He cannot persuade the "trusties" dispossessing her to leave. This eviction summons but cannot portray the political resolve that would appear in Greensboro, Nashville, and the Tallahassee bus boycott (see Morris 63–68).

The narrator's dilemma is also Ellison's as a political novelist. The situation he so beautifully evokes will be solved, if it can be solved, only by history. "In relation to their Southern background, the cultural history of Negroes in the North reads like the legend of some tragic people out of mythology," Ellison wrote in 1943, "a people who aspired to escape from its own unhappy homeland to the apparent peace of a distant mountain, but who, in migrating, made some fatal error of judgment and fell into a great chasm of mazelike passages that promise ever to lead to the mountain but ever end against a wall" (*Collected* 323). In Ellison's lifetime, the historical situation that he names would be transformed by Roosevelt's integration of the war factories, Truman's executive order to integrate the armed forces, *Brown*, and—when King brought his people to the mountain—the Civil Rights and Voting Rights Acts of 1964 and 1965. Ellison's 1943 "Harlem Is Nowhere" clearly indicated his belief that the unfair social contract between American whites and blacks could not hold much longer: "When Negroes are barred from participating in the main institutional life in society," Ellison says, "they lose one of the bulwarks which men place against themselves and the constant threat of chaos" (324). The plot of *Invisible Man* concludes with a vision of that chaos, a riot—a "Blow-Top Blues" (to name a song from that era)—suggesting that the angry will of the black masses is on the verge of erupting. The question that concerned Ellison, however, was not where the political will of blacks would come from—it was readily evident in the endurance of Negroes through their folk culture—but how that will would take shape in a leader or leaders who could advance the Civil Rights movement without bringing down pointless violence on blacks.

In the eviction scene, Ellison foresaw what would be the most effective symbolic protest action of the Freedom Movement, even if he could not foresee the Freedom Movement itself. The woman's outraged protection of her Bible points to the power of the black church as an organizing force of communal memory and action. Just as her refusal to surrender her Bible touches off the moving documentation of the many living artifacts of blacks in America since Reconstruction, so would the refusal of the black church to let any force "turn me around" become the galvanizing political agent that made possible the enforcement of the new laws requiring full integration in American society.

As Aldon Morris argued in his crucial history of the period, the "modern civil rights movement" represented "the first time that larges masses of blacks directly confronted and effectively disrupted the normal functioning of groups and institutions thought to be responsible for their repression" (xi). Moreover, discounting white cooperation, the fact of their success can be attributed almost solely to the power of a black church whose agency went back to slavery times when sermons were apt to focus on Moses leading his people from the enslavement of the Pharaohs. Other factors besides the church were relevant in the Civil Rights movement's success. *Brown* was a legal victory earned largely by the NAACP, and it was crucial in creating a context for what would come later. The Freedom Movement, however, was essentially a grassroots effort, improvisational in nature, which could work only by building on feelings and institutions already prevalent within the black community. Its effectiveness relied on the ability of people to cooperate under pressure with almost no previous political training. What political training they had was the history they already knew and shared as an oppressed people who had survived and invented a language of survival. As Morris notes, "For all the widespread sympathy and support it has enjoyed in the black community, the NAACP has never been able to organize a mass base," and "its membership seldom included more than two percent of the black population" (15).

The desegregation of the Montgomery, Alabama, bus lines "began" (actually, a symbolic act made explicit an already ongoing revolt) when a single woman, Rosa Parks, refused to give up her seat to a white person. In Ellison's eviction scene the legal system supported the eviction of the black woman, not her protest. Nor could the protest led by Ellison's hero prevent her from being evicted. When Brother Jack hears the narrator's speech, though, he recognizes power that resides in the hero's "moving them [the people] to action" (*Invisible* 298). The presumption that the narrator (and perhaps his creator) surrenders to is that discovering his true, authentic voice will instigate a collective social action, even though, as subsequent history outside the novel would prove, the social revolution that became the Civil Rights movement had already begun. As a reflection on how history works and the mysterious power it conveys, the woman's response to her eviction in *Invisible Man*, and her possessions that tumble into the street, suggest how powerfully Ellison's novel imagined the possibility of black protest. Although her act is presented as one episode within hundreds, the historical situation that her eviction evokes contains and provokes the

rhetorical act that is the novel. If the novel suggests that no singe political act can redress this woman's pain, it also suggests that only a renewed
commitment to group resolve will make the future better than the present.
Invisible Man gives form to that resolve.

History Breaks

The future that *Invisible Man* hoped to create was happening fast, and it
was not coming from the Brotherhood. As Ellison intuited when writing
Invisible Man, black people, not the Communists or truly either political
party, would provide the inspiration and resolve that made *Brown* the living
law of the land. It is easy to forget that the protest of Rosa Parks was no
isolated or spontaneous protest but one element of a long, continuous action
on the part of Parks and others. She in fact had made the very same gesture
of protest for which she became famous in 1955 during the early 1940s, with
the hope that the organizations to which she already belonged could help
her. By the time of the successful Montgomery protest, she had served as
a secretary for the local NAACP, and she knew important Negro leaders
such as Ella Baker, A. Philip Randolph, and Roy Wilkins. Moreover, at the
time of the boycott, Parks was an adult adviser to the Youth Council of the
local NAACP and had helped them borrow books from the white library.

A look at the organization behind the Montgomery boycott reveals a
network of activists considerably more sophisticated and effective than the
Brotherhood or Bledsoe's regime—with, of course, goals different from
those of Ellison's characters. As Morris argues, E. D. Nixon, not Martin
Luther King, escalated Parks's rebellion and devised the plan for the mass
boycott that eventually ended segregation on the city buses. Nixon was
known as "a militant and the person to see whenever blacks" were willing
"to fight against racial domination" (52). Some women had approached him
earlier about the bus situation, and he was not surprised when he learned
of Parks's arrest. Indeed, "This is the case!" Nixon is reported to have said
(Frady 31). Members of the Women's Political Council (WPC), a group of
professional black women, then began to initiate the boycott. Claudette
Colvin permitted herself to be arrested for the same offense that Parks
committed, and soon the citywide protest was on. Nixon recruited ministers
willing to lend aid to the cause because he knew, as he said at the time, that
the ministers "had their hands on the black masses," and it was they whose
power the movement meant to ignite (Morris 54). Thus, before King could

arouse his people and the political machinery of Birmingham to action, an entire structure of social and political relations was in place and already activated within the black community.

The boycott still needed a leader—a face for the movement—who could employ eloquence to keep the action going. Ralph Abernathy, who would emerge as King's lieutenant during the movement, asked Nixon to be the leader of the new organization. Nixon refused the chance to lead the emerging coalition, deciding that the symbolism of having a minister as the leader would be more powerful than having a Pullman porter in front. As things turned out, King was perfect for the role. King was able to employ language based in the Bible and the nation's sacred documents, and such language, as Morris observes, spoke to "the educated as well as the uneducated and downtrodden" (80). This is precisely the lesson that Ellison's narrator employs when he finds that his speeches work best when he draws on the rhetoric he had learned from black preachers. And of course Ellison's other protagonist, the one in the novel he never published, *was* a preacher (who could play jazz trombone).

The narrator alludes to his method of inspiration when he says that before one of his "extemporaneous" speeches "I had to fall back upon tradition. . . . I selected one of the political techniques that I had heard so often at home: The old down-to-earth, I'm-sick-and-tired-of-the-way-they've-been-treating-us approach" (*Invisible* 334–35). The power of King's speeches came from the same folk origins and was what allowed "the masses," as Morris notes, to recognize King's presence as proof that "protest was right and even divine" (80). Moreover, coming from the black church, which E. Franklin Frazier had famously characterized as a kind of "nation within a nation," King's authority as a leader conveyed an almost preternatural power (80). When he preached the power of nonviolence, he could draw on the fact that "the religious doctrines of the black church [had] provided the ideological framework through which the doctrine of nonviolence was disseminated to black Montgomeryites" (Morris 62). King happened to be—and this surprised King too—a brilliant, once-in-a-generation leader such as Ellison could not imagine in *Invisible Man*, even though both his hero and Tod Clifton predicted some of his qualities. To be expressed fully, King's gifts required a narrative to set them to work, and that was provided by history—and by the black community.

King's willingness to lead marches, go to jail, and continually stand as a lightning rod to attract anger (and inspire support) gave the protest a sense of inevitable momentum. Thus, he enacted a kind of street theater in which his powerful ethos concealed the fact that this was a movement from the ground up. Ellison's narrator, despite his eloquence, did not possess the narrative structure that made King's success possible. He was willing to bleed through his words, but he did not have the moral authority of the Supreme Court or television. Placing his story in a novel, which could be read by others, was the most dramatic representation of his plight possible. And the most effective action of a persuasive book is to move the reader. In so-called real life, endings considerably less inspiring were the rule. Ellison thus focused attention on how easy it was, in the context of Jim Crow, to manipulate black leaders. Seeing Ellison's hero leading the failed riot over the eviction, Brother Jack tells him, "Booker T. Washington was resurrected today at a certain eviction in Harlem. He came out from the anonymity of the crowd and spoke to the people" (*Invisible* 301). Jack asks, "How would you like to be the new Booker T. Washington?" (299). Jack insists that Washington is "still a living force," but the narrative says otherwise. To change the status quo would require white help, to be sure, but it would also require the sacrifice of black lives. Ellison might have chosen to kill his narrator, rather than leaving him in a basement affirming the promise of the Declaration of Independence, but to do so would have undermined the sense of defiant black endurance that his narrative portrayed.

King, however, fulfilled his role by offering his life to change the status quo. His end was predicted when his house was bombed after the Montgomery protest. King's father begged his son to consider backing off: "Better to be a live dog than a dead lion!" (Frady 47). The language that King Sr. used recalls the language of *Invisible Man*'s grandfather, who urged his heir to be "a spy in the enemy's country." By this logic, one fought segregation as one could but also survived to fight another day. Instead, King urged his supporters to love those who would kill them. Arguably, this was a logical extension of the tactics of *Invisible Man*'s patriarch, but it took place in the open, and it assumed that those watching, not the segregationists, would recognize that King's people occupied the moral high ground. Ellison's hero, like his grandfather, worked to find that high ground, and he too sought solidarity with strangers whose goodwill he could only imagine. By novel's end he is sustained by black folk culture and the Declaration of Independence, two crucial supports for King as well. Since he can neither lead nor incite a black mass movement, the narrator commits the most radical, courageous act he can imagine. Expressing the logic of one of King's favorite texts,

Thoreau's "On Civil Disobedience," he asks his reader of whatever color to affirm what neither he nor his audience could affirm after the Battle Royal: Jefferson's proposition of equality.

During the 1963 March on Washington, King would quote Jefferson's words while standing on the steps of the Lincoln Memorial, speaking to a national television audience larger than the *Invisible Man* narrator could confront. Although King employed a rhetorical strategy similar to that of Ellison's narrator, one that in fact goes back at least to Frederick Douglass's Fourth of July orations, he did so in a context utterly unimaginable to Ellison's protagonist. The Montgomery boycott, like the Freedom Movement, had benefited from factors beyond even the organization of the Negro masses. Through the media, King could orchestrate a morality play that brought national pressure to bear on the Montgomery community, along with the economic effects of the boycott. Finally, there was the November 13, 1956, decision of the United States Supreme Court, which took place nearly a year after Parks had refused to move, which reinforced the *Brown* ruling and led Eisenhower to send federal troops to Little Rock to integrate the schools and thus uphold the law of the land.

No federal troops come to Clifton's aid when he confronts the white cops or to the narrator's side when his speech for Clifton ignites the Harlem riot. The potential meaning of Clifton's sacrifice is invisible, and so is the narrator relating it. The example of King, however, obliterates Ellison's metaphor of invisibility as a code for being black in America. Where Ellison's narrator extends his grandfather's logic to create a context of enlightened invisibility, King's strategy, like that of the Freedom Movement, was one of maximum visibility. Before television cameras, radio microphones, and legions of scribbling journalists, King led marches into raging fire hoses, snarling dogs, swinging clubs, and sometimes murderous bullets. The grandfather in *Invisible Man* devises his strategy to "overcome with yesses" in order to subvert white authority but also as a way *to stay alive*. King too overcame his enemies with yeses—he affirmed the Negro's place in American society as a legal equal—but he did it in the open, and eventually his yes came at the cost of his life.

In *Invisible Man*, open protest can at best bring about the social turbulence such as the riot unleashes and, at worst, death to the protester. The cry of the evicted woman is unanswered and Clifton's sacrifice unredeemed. Because of *Brown*, King and his movement saw that the time had come when the political rewards to be achieved were worth risking the lives of his group. They were being killed anyway. King, like Ellison, understood that only a collective commitment to "equality" as a national principle could bring about the change in history which his protagonist so desired. Blacks had been committed to this principle since the Civil War and had been continually sacrificed in its name. For the terms of this sacrifice to be changed, though, its meaning would have to become symbolic as well as literal. Before *Brown*, blacks were "sacrificed"—killed—whether they wanted to be or not. After *Brown*, blacks could choose, as it were, to be sacrificed in order to dramatize their plight and then change it. Once the United States confronted the idea that equality must apply to everyone, then King's presentation of the nearly 400-year sacrifice made by blacks for American "equality" would have an almost unimaginable dramatic resonance among people who had previously taken the sacrifice of blacks for granted. The power of the Civil Rights movement resided in its ability to transform the ritual of the Battle Royal into a national rite, one that ultimately abolished the Battle Royal and what it represented altogether.

Ellison's conversation with Warren in 1965 implied that the Freedom Movement was the logical extension of the cultural processes and narrative ritual depicted in *Invisible Man*. The novel reveals the element of sacrifice that was essential to the success of the movement and, as I have suggested, stages a number of encounters between the narrator, as orator, and an audience seeking a hero to complete their drama. The final confrontation between the narrator and an audience, before the act that completes the novel, occurs at Clifton's funeral. The riot that this event touches off is either another literal reenactment of the Battle Royal or the solvent that will give a different ending to the ritual the hero has been performing throughout. However one interprets the riot, it releases a chaotic, turbulent energy that Ellison's narrator transforms into the revolutionary political act his story means to make possible. In this sense, the novel scripted in advance the controlled riots that King would so masterfully bring to bear on a white power structure that was losing its grip on the Jim Crow era.

Communal Sacrifice

One might say that the Civil Rights movement began with Rosa Parks refusing to be moved and King's intervention to safeguard her right to a seat in the front of the bus. By the logic of *Invisible Man*, however, to specify a point of origin for the Civil Rights movement is as misleading as to insist that *Invisible Man* began as Ellison's focused reaction to the single fact that the American armed forces remained segregated during World War II.

A local, daily outrage such as occurred on the bus lines of Montgomery can be said to have instigated a broader movement only because that broader movement was already latent in the collective will of black Americans to see themselves and their children through to a better day. This sense of communal discipline was what made the political success of the Civil Rights marches effective. Although I have portrayed the Battle Royal in terms of the black and white communities organizing themselves to preserve the logic of the color line, it is also true that the point of that ritual was to initiate Ellison's hero into the practice of Negro discipline necessary to sustain him and his community through dangerous times.

In 1957 black parents in Little Rock exhibited this discipline by putting their children at risk so that their kids might attend integrated schools. The children faced insults, rocks, and the threat of being shot by angry whites. In turn, blacks pressured President Eisenhower when he was slow to help resolve the situation. No one was more eloquent than one of Ellison's heros, Louis Armstrong, who denounced the president for having "no guts" and being "two-faced." Armstrong threatened to withdraw from a goodwill tour to the Soviet Union that he was undertaking at the State Department's behest if Eisenhower refused to act. "The way they are treating my people in the South, the government can go to hell," Armstrong said. He added that he would tell the Soviets the same thing: "The people over there ask me what's wrong with my country. What am I supposed to say?" In *Invisible Man*, Armstrong's art inspires the narrator's narrative action, and here Armstrong was part of the political process that forced Eisenhower's hand. That Armstrong, who normally steered clear of explicit political commentary, would be so direct suggests how committed the entire black community was to making equal rights happen once it became socially possible. When asked if he wanted to soften his comments, Armstrong told the reporter, "Don't take nothing out of that story. That's just what I said, and still say." After reviewing the reporter's copy, he wrote "solid" at the bottom and signed his name (Margolick).

Black Americans no longer had to hibernate and new roles were available to be played. Eisenhower rewarded their persistence (and Armstrong did go to the USSR as an American representative) by sending the national guard to the South to uphold equal rights for blacks for the first time since 1877. The courage and will to sacrifice themselves which blacks displayed startled even the most sophisticated observers of mass movement and political revolt. Hannah Arendt, for instance, was surprised by the militancy of the resistance and appalled that black children were being put in harm's way by their parents; as Danielle Allen observes, Arendt thought that the Civil Rights movement failed "to rise to the level of political action" (25). Ellison was compelled to respond, suggesting that the brilliant political theorist did not understand the extent to which the desegregation movement was an instance of decades of underground resistance now rising above ground. He argued that Arendt's ignorance of Negro tradition made it impossible for her to understand that the logic of the Negro resistance movement came from a long-established strategy for confronting tyrannical power, a strategy rooted in blacks' conception of sacrifice (which he had portrayed in the Battle Royal). As he told Warren, the courage driving the Civil Rights movement emerged from the preservation of a type of group discipline that had taken place "when the country was not looking at Negroes, and when we were restrained in certain of our activities by the interpretation of the law of the land, [but] something was present in our lives to sustain us." Blacks in America had been engaged in "political action" for centuries (Warren, *Who* 329).[10]

Ellison's response to Arendt is echoed by Morris's observation that the "Montgomery movement" contrasted "sharply with the charismatic movement described by Max Weber, where the leader attracts a revolutionary following because of his extraordinary personality and compelling vision" (54). In other words, King's charisma mattered only because it had been forged by the same ritual of communal sacrifice that Ellison's narrator had to complete. In confronting the nature of Negro leadership, Ellison, reader of Lord Raglan, settled on a hero whose journey to the underworld was a preparation for a future action—a role out of hibernation—which the narrative declined to name. As if confirming the "charismatic" thesis that Morris rejects, Eric Sundquist says that "King proved, through his catalytic personal witness in key civil rights campaigns and the majesty of his words, especially at the March on Washington, that the conscience of a nation, and ultimately its laws, could be changed by a single citizen" (*King's* 11).

Ellison, though, understood the leader to be less important than the drama that he was enacting. Consequently, he stressed the "the heroic side" of the Freedom Movement and praised King for "working out of a long history of Negro tradition and wisdom." Ellison certainly understood that King, or the movement, was carrying the story of *Invisible Man* forward, just as *Invisible Man* had been an attempt to tap into the kind of communal story that can be made true only by history. Attributing to King the same insight that his narrator learned through the Battle Royal, Ellison says that King understood that Negroes "have been conditioned to contain not only the pressures involved in their struggle, but that they are capable, through this same tradition of mastering the psychological pressures" that concerned Arendt. Through the years of struggle that preceded King's movement, Ellison says, each Negro has had to learn from conflict "to determine at what point and over which specific issue he will pay the ultimate price of his life" (Warren, *Who* 342). King, like so many others in the movement, would pay this price.

In *Invisible Man*, Ellison portrayed the Negro ideal of sacrifice not only in the Battle Royal but also through the martyrdom of Tod Clifton. Where the Battle Royal confirms the hero's resolve, Clifton's sacrifice conveys the sense that even senseless death must be transformed into meaningful social (political) action. The facts surrounding Clifton's death—his selling Sambo dolls on the street—are grotesque. Yet Clifton—this "black prince," as Ras calls him—dies a martyr's death in that he is killed because he punches a white police officer. His death also indicts the cynicism of the Brotherhood's exploitation of blacks for their political ends. The narrator's funeral oration emphasizes the ritualistic meaning of Clifton's sacrifice. The narrator recognizes that Clifton can be seen to have been sacrificed for someone else's history, and he wants to change the pattern that makes such wrongful sacrifices possible.

Usually interpreted as a version of the Communist Party and rooted in Ellison's knowledge of Richard Wright's experiences within that party, the Brotherhood actually represents Ellison's critique of an American political process that treats "the Negro question" only as a tactic for groups seeking to preserve their own power. In 1969 Ellison remarked that the "political patterns" embodied by the Brotherhood "still exist in and of which our two major political parties are guilty in their relationship to Negro Americans." He added that "it was very important for this young man, this would-be leader, to understand that all political parties are basically concerned with power and with maintaining power, not with humanitarian issues in the raw and abstract state" (*Collected* 538). Danielle Allen notes that "for decades, readers of *Invisible Man* have assumed that in it the Brotherhood party is a stand-in for the American Communist Party. It isn't" (108). More than critiquing the Communist Party of the 1930s and '40s, Ellison's Brotherhood critiques a political process in which the Republican and Democratic Parties both manipulated black political interests for their own ends.

On the premise that Clifton's gaudy death comes from his involvement with an organization that exploits charismatic black men for the preservations of its own power, one can argue that *Invisible Man* advocates political organizations run for and by black people. This is the position that Ras, the proto–Malcolm X figure of the novel, expresses to Clifton in an exchange that ends in a fist fight. "You young black men with plenty education; I been hearing your rabble rousing. Why you go over to the enslaver? What kind of education is that?" (*Invisible* 364). Their fight foreshadows the conflict between Malcolm X and King, a conflict embedded in the history of black intellectual thought and politics. Ras is portrayed as a force for destruction, but his argument to Clifton proves correct. "We sons of Mama Africa, you done forgot? You black, BLACK! You—*Godahm*, mahn!" (364). In fact, Clifton cannot answer Ras's charges except with fists or the weak command to "shut up." Since the Brotherhood did not care about Clifton or the narrator, and spurned the black men and their ideals, the novel does not altogether reject Ras's point of view. Moreover, the Civil Rights movement explicitly rejected the Brotherhood's model of leadership. As histories of the period remind us, white and black Civil Rights advocates agreed that leadership positions should be occupied by blacks. The social revolution would not be engineered by a white political party; rather, the two predominantly white political parties would be co-opted by a black political movement in order to ratify equal rights for all Americans.

In *Invisible Man* this social revolution cannot happen except by means of the republic it creates through its readers. Yet the novel's depiction of the intractable social and political patterns that an effective Negro political movement would have to overcome was accurate. Thus, although *Invisible Man* does not imagine precisely how the Civil Rights social revolution will occur, it does convey the sense that society is about to erupt and suggests the basis on which that eruption might be turned to a new political reality. The eruption occurs through the riot, though that in effect begins with Clifton's funeral, and points the way to King's triumphs of the 1950s and '60s.[11] Significantly, the riot is touched off by the narrator's recognition that subjecting himself and his people to the usual requirements of American political organizations will no longer suffice. As Allen suggests, the narrator wants "practices of reciprocity that democratize sacrifice and develop 'something like brotherhood' into a real feature of citizenship" (112). When such reciprocity does not occur, some combination of social and political violence to the existing system is inevitable.

As the crowd for Clifton's funeral gathers at Mount Morris Park, a site picked "to attract the largest possible number," the narrator sees that a diverse audience representing a wide range of the black community is present. "Young zoot-suiters, hep cats, and men in overalls and pool-hall gamblers" could be seen "stepping into the procession" (*Invisible* 443). As in the eviction scene, Ellison evokes a panorama of black history and style to convey the power of the gathering Negro masses. To the strains of "There's Many a Thousand Gone" (a song that would be sung at King's funeral), the narrator wonders about what could be bringing everyone together. Was it Clifton's death or something else? Amid his speculations the singing, accompanied by a euphonium, compels the mourners as if to a march, and suddenly the narrator is struck by the music made by a man who "sang with his whole body, phrasing each verse as naturally as he walked, his voice rising above all others, blending with that of the lucid horn" (445). The narrator realizes that the singer's performance, beautiful as it is, coincides with the song because the song that he sings precedes the singer. The song sings him. "The song had been there all the time," the narrator muses, "and he knew it and had aroused it" (446). Perhaps *his* song—his oration—will do the same with the energy of the crowd. Perhaps their song will sing his words.

As "the brothers and sisters" join in, whites included, the narrator experiences a vision. He understands that the familiar words of the song, "the same old slave-borne words," carried a version of history toward which the group was collectively marching. How they would get there, and who they would be on arrival, is not yet clear to him, but the possibility that a history different from the one that Clifton had known, yet one embedded in the collective experience they share, seems suddenly possible. The narrator "stood there trying to contain it as they brought Tod Clifton's coffin into the tower," a feeling that enlivens the funeral rite (446). The narrator's task is to convert this feeling into an address that will inspire those gathered to appropriate action.

What happens is, again, a mixture of success and failure. Using the language that King would also employ, the narrator shouts, "Listen to me standing up on this so-called mountain!" and "Let me tell it as it truly was!" (451). His language works to make the secular world a version of the sacred community that the church sanctions. He employs a tactic of building repetition that focuses on Clifton's name and the iteration of the bare facts of Clifton's "short bitter life." His incantation builds until his speech climaxes by resurrecting Clifton as one who can now lead them. He ventriloquizes Clifton's voice and addresses the crowd as if Clifton were speaking through him: "'Tell them to get out of the box,' that's what he would say if you could hear him. 'Tell them to get out of the box and go teach the cops to forget that rhyme. Tell them to teach them that when they call you a *nigger* to make a rhyme with *trigger* it makes the gun backfire'" (451). Here his language is closer to that of Malcolm X than to Martin Luther King's characteristic invocation to "let us pray that God shall give us strength to remain nonviolent though we may face death" (*I Have* 11). The hero's intemperate words—"I had let it get away from me," he admits—help to trigger the riot that engulfs the Harlem community and for which its residents will likely suffer. Yet the conflation of Clifton's martyred voice with the narrator's urgent call to immediate action foreshadows the symbolic tactics that King employed and that would make the Civil Rights marches so effective.

As Nick Kotz recounts in his penetrating *Judgment Days: Lyndon Baines Johnson, Martin Luther King Jr., and the Laws that Changed America* (2005), the march from Selma to Birmingham, which helped President Johnson acquire the political capital to get the Voting Rights Act passed, was a response to protesters who had been slain. The prelude to this march was provided by the burial of James E. Chaney, Andrew Goodman, and Michael Schwerner—the three Civil Rights workers whose murder had electrified the nation. When their bodies were found in August of 1964 and charges brought against nineteen white men, all members of the Klan, an FBI case inspector aptly assessed the likelihood of achieving justice for the murdered: the Klan "owned the place," he said, because "in spirit, everyone belonged to the Klan" (Kotz 187). The FBI's description complements the logic of Ellison's Battle Royal. Had one of the young black men been killed during the Battle Royal, no one would have been held culpable. In this case, the fact that Goodman and Schwerner were white underlined how the Civil Rights movement was transforming the political context of segregation: now whites were being sacrificed to protect the aura of white superiority.

In the context of *Invisible Man*, the deaths of two young white men cannot be squared with the many thousands of black lives gone. At Clifton's funeral, whites are present, and there is the suggestion that blacks are not the only one's outraged by what has happened. But the narrator's speech, in form and content, is directed at his black listeners. Goodman and Schwerner were whites who joined the movement and became martyrs; their deaths were necessary to awaken whites to black suffering. The effectiveness of the Freedom Movement still depended on unleashing the full force of black communal power. The funeral for Chaney, the black companion of Goodman and Schwerner, was a real-life version of Clifton's funeral in *Invisible Man*. The situation it confronted was the same: who is to be blamed and what it to be done about this murder of a young black man by white authorities? Kotz related that David Dennis, the leader of CORE (Congress of Racial Equality) in Mississippi, was the one who summoned

Chaney's spirit for the community. The words he spoke over the body of James Chaney set the stage for the Selma march and defined the element of sacrifice that drove the Freedom Movement. The cadences of his language and the rawness of his emotion echo and extend the frustration and style of Ellison's hero's funeral oration for Clifton. His eloquent words deserve full citation:

> As I stand here, I not only blame the people who pulled the trigger or did the beating or dug the hole with the shovel. I blame the people in Washington, D. C., and the state of Mississippi for what happened. I'm sick and tired of going to the funerals of black men who have been murdered by white men. I've got vengeance in my heart tonight, and I ask you to feel angry with me, I'm sick and tired, and I ask you to be sick and tired with me. The white men who murdered James Chaney are never going to be punished. I'm tired of people in this country allowing that to continue to happen.
>
> We've got to stand up. The best way we can remember James Chaney is to demand our rights. Don't you just look at me and go back and tell folks you've been to a nice service. Your work is just beginning. If you go back home and sit down and take what these white men are doing to us. If you take it, and don't do something about it—then God damn your souls! (*Judgment* 188)

As Kotz explains, when King came to Selma, fresh on the heels of Johnson's landslide 1964 victory, he knew that the stars of history had aligned to make possible an extraordinary victory for the Freedom Movement. As in Montgomery, King at Selma had to harness the communal energy already activated and ready for action by eloquent actors such as James Chaney and David Dennis. He was in a realm that *Invisible Man* could not even quite imagine as a utopia. He had recognized that in the White House sat the personification of what Ellison referred to as "the myth of the flawed white Southerner," and that the power of the black masses behind him were ready to follow King's lead. What was required, by the Lord Raglan logic of *Invisible Man*, was to enact the ritual drama that would complete the narrative being scripted. The story of how this was achieved at Selma and then through Johnson's getting the Voting Rights Act passed has been told too many times to be recounted in full here.[12] I would emphasize only the extent to which those events enacted the implications of Dennis's oration for Chaney, since it allows us to see Ellison's prescience in making Clifton's death the narrative trigger that leads to the conclusion of *Invisible Man*.

One other real-life sacrifice deserves mention in this context. During the Selma protests, Cager Lee, an eighty-two-year-old black protester, was attacked by white troopers and chased into a café. His daughter, Viola, and grandson, Jimmie Lee Jackson, tried to protect him. Both were beaten, and Jackson would eventually die as a result. King had time to commune with Jackson before he died, knowing that Malcolm X had been killed two days earlier and that his own death seemed closer than ever. On that night, King announced that his people would march to the state capitol in Montgomery to tell Governor Wallace that "we aren't going to take it anymore!"

Nine days later Jimmie Lee Jackson died. James Bevel, the SCLC project director for Alabama, asked the grieving family if they would be willing to participate in the upcoming march. Bevel's question was asked and answered in the spirit of sacrifice that Ellison identified to Warren and that his novel portrayed. Arguably, no moment in *Invisible Man* is as powerful as Cager Lee's two-word response to Bevel's request: "Oh, yeah," Lee said (Kotz 277). Bevel aptly summed up the logic of the boy's death: "The blood of Jackson will be on our hands if we don't march" (277). At Jackson's funeral, King reinforced Bevel's words and echoed Ellison's hero's words at Clifton's funeral, indicting the white society that allows such deaths to occur over and over without acknowledgment or remorse. "Jackson was murdered," King said, "by every white minister of the gospel who has remained silent behind the safe security of his stained glass windows." King called out "politicians," the "federal government," "sheriffs" and finally the "cowardice of every Negro who passively accepts the evils of segregation" (277). Like Dennis and Ellison's narrator, King called on the community to transform a black man's death into political action. Although in *Invisible Man* the riot that followed the narrator's incendiary words led to no satisfactory political conclusion, in the Freedom Movement, King's words, echoing those of Dennis and Bevel, were part of an action that helped to secure the enfranchisement of the black vote.

Over "many a thousands gone" did King and so many anonymous, invisible others enact the Freedom Movement, a version of which Ellison portrayed in his masterpiece, *Invisible Man*. Ellison and King were part of the same movement, and each made his contribution as he could. To ignore the vital, necessary historical and spiritual connection between Ellison and the Freedom Movement is to deny the logic of each. Ellison told that 1969 audience at West Point that "as a Negro writer" who was "fighting for a certain orientation," he accepted that he would have "to master" what were "the major motives of American literature, *even when written by people who philosophically would reject me as a member of the American community*" (*Collected* 527; original emphasis). If his narrator begins his address to an

unseen audience with a story that stresses his restraint in not killing someone who had insulted him, then he hopes that by its end readers will overcome their possible social antipathy toward the teller and join the "beloved
community" that his story aspires to create. Shortly after the Montgomery
bus boycott, King noted that "a boycott is not an end within itself" but "a
means to awaken a sense of shame within the oppressor and challenge his
false sense of superiority. The end," he stressed, "is reconciliation; the end is
redemption; the end is the creation of the beloved community" (*I Have* 22).
As Ellison told uncounted audiences for nearly forty years, this "beloved
community" is the true ending to *Invisible Man*.

Ironically, King's movement, like Ellison's novel, worked because it was
devised within a Jim Crow framework. Through his street protests, King
made visible the kind of social conflict that was the ground of virtually
every episode of *Invisible Man*. Once King's movement had obliterated the
legal basis on which the Jim Crow society had been built, King also lost the
moral foundation of his political action. The mysterious spiritual incarna-
tion of history that Ellison's narrator pursued and courted seems to have
found King in Montgomery in 1955 and then abandoned him once Johnson
contrived to get the Voting Rights Act passed in 1965. "King's victory in
Selma," Frady observes, "effectively constituted the end, the benediction, to
the classic Southern phase of his movement" (166). After 1965 King had no
other obvious political victories except possibly the Civil Rights Act of 1968
(Fair Housing Act), which Johnson passed in the aftermath of King's death.

Invisible Man had memorialized the Jim Crow era and also demanded its
destruction. In a paradoxical sense, King reached the climactic ending point
conveyed by *Invisible Man*'s narrator at the close of his story. King's success
ended the story that *Invisible Man* told, and with that ending, the future
was uncertain. The rituals that had sustained the black community in their
bondage were not appropriate in a context where "Negro" and "American"
were no longer legally opposed terms. In 1952 Ellison said he had written
the book primarily for blacks, but not long afterward he was insisting that
it was for whites too. Lyndon Johnson probably never read the novel—
despite asking Ellison to be one of his advisers—but he enacted its message
when he addressed a New Orleans audience on October 9, 1964, a month
before the presidential election. Although cautioned against speaking too
forthrightly on the subject of Civil Rights, since doing so might risk victory in Louisiana, Johnson nonetheless departed from his prepared remarks
to decry the logic of Southern politics which obligates those who want to
be elected to yell "Nigger, Nigger, Nigger" instead of trying to address the

South's more material political difficulties (Kotz 224). "I am not going to let them build up the hate and try to buy my people by appealing to their prejudice," Johnson said. Then, before a stunned audience of white Southerners, he employed the language of King to press his claim for social justice now: "Whatever your views are, we have a Constitution, and we have a Bill of Rights, and we have a law of the land (the Civil Rights Act), and two-thirds of the Democrats in the Senate voted for it, and three-fourths of the Republicans. I signed it, and I am going to enforce it, and I am going to observe it. And I think that anyone who is worthy of the high office of President is going to do the same thing" (225).

Arguably, for the first time in American history, a sitting U.S. president told a potentially hostile white audience that the United States was committed to equal rights for African Americans. This former master of the Senate, this white Southerner, was in his actions departing decisively from the betraying Senator Sunraider of Ellison's secret novel, responding instead to the historical moment as a version of *Invisible Man*'s ideal reader. Once Johnson was elected, he elevated his rhetoric so that it addressed not merely a local audience but the entire nation. Prompted by King's victory at Selma, a victory won through the combined efforts of people such as Cager Lee and his daughter, Viola, Johnson convened Congress to present his urgent legislative message. It was the first time in nearly twenty years that a president had appeared before Congress to present new legislation. Johnson had wanted King to sit with Ladybird Johnson during the speech, but King declined because he had a memorial service to perform in Selma.[13] While King buried his dead, Johnson prepared to lift them into citizenship.

In his speech Johnson alluded to the "good man, a man of God," who had been killed before delivering a message of what Ellison would likely call supreme eloquence: "There is no Negro problem. There is no Southern problem. There is no Northern problem. There is only an *American* problem. And we are met here tonight as Americans—not as Democrats or Republicans—we are met here as Americans to solve that problem" (Kotz 309). And that problem, Johnson explained, using the language that King employed in his speeches and that Ellison also would employ in his subsequent essays and lectures, has been "the failure of America to live up to its unique founding purpose—a purpose defined in phrases still found in every America heart." Those phrases include: "all men are created equal," "government by consent of the governed," and "give me liberty or give me death." Having insisted upon the right of blacks to be counted as equal citizens, Johnson then committed the extraordinary gesture of absorbing the Civil

Rights movement's language as his own. "Because it is not just Negroes, but really it is all of us, who must overcome the crippling legacy of bigotry and injustice. **And—we—*shall*—overcome!**" (311).

Johnson's remarkable act of communion symbolized and ratified the aim of King's movement. It also reportedly moved King to tears. David Garrow, one of King's biographers, called Johnson's speech "an emotional peak unmatched by anything that had come before, nor by anything that would come later" (Kotz 314).[14] According to Frady, King's tears marked the first time any of his aides had seen him cry (163). His tears enacted his recognition that his ritual drama was completed: his people were being made visible to American society. Ellison's gratitude was such that he supported Johnson's doomed foreign policy in Vietnam—to the scorn of most of his writer peers. Ellison also published "The Myth of the Flawed White Southerner" to explain the sacrifice that Johnson made in "betraying" his group (white Southerners) and identifying himself with the cause of Negroes (*Collected*). In a sense, Johnson was Bliss gone good—the ambiguous white-black political hero Ellison had killed in his second novel risen to heroic life despite Ellison's despairing imagination. So Ellison endorsed Johnson in print and left the full measure of Bliss's story in his desk. I submit that what mattered more to Ellison than the recognition that the published second novel might bring was his recognition through Johnson and King of how many readers were recognizing their own stories in the drama of *Invisible Man*. One can say, as historians such as Frady do, that "it was Selma bridge that had really brought all this to pass" (63), but only because Selma apotheosized decades of the invisible work that Ellison's novel portrayed and without which Selma could not have happened.

Johnson's open identification with the Freedom Movement as an agency enacting the will of all Americans was a confirmation of Ellison's narrator's declaration that "the invisible victim is responsible for the fate of all" (*Invisible* 14). The reciprocity he and King achieved was precisely what the political act of *Invisible Man* sought to make possible. To Johnson, King noted the "irony" that "after a century a southern white President would help lead the way toward the salvation of the Negro" (314). Ellison, as we have seen, explained this irony in "The Myth of the Flawed White Southerner," and fulfilling this role was something that Johnson, as president, embraced. As if he were mirroring Robert Penn Warren following Ellison's lead with *Invisible Man*, Johnson told King: "You're the leader who is making it possible. I'm just following along, trying to do what's right" (314). At the moment that Johnson affirmed his place—and the place of white Americans—within the ritualistic drama that *Invisible Man* and King both enacted, the definition of the community was broadened as well. The ritual drama enacted, a new narrative, a new history, was suddenly required. Such a narrative Ellison wrote not in his second novel but in his essays, speeches, and interviews. He committed—one might say sacrificed—his post–*Invisible Man* career to living the post-*Brown* narrative in which cultural diversity, not the cultural authenticity of the Jim Crow era, was the shared and acknowledged ground of American social reality. In his case, the invisible author, who was also the invisible victim, was willing to be responsible for the fate of all Americans. No other great American author of the twentieth century risked more in his or her fiction

After Ellison, Toward Obama

My problem is not whether I will accept or reject American values. It is, rather, how I can get into a position where I can have the maximum influence on those values.

RALPH ELLISON

I personally think in the post–Civil Rights period a black person is wasting his (or her) time, the preciously few years of their lives, by devoting their energy—as a "spokesman"—to explaining so-called "black" things to white people. Whites can—and should—do their own homework.

CHARLES S. JOHNSON

ELLISON SAW almost as soon as his novel was published that the second half of his life would allow him opportunities unimaginable during its first half. His 1950s letters to Murray express a cautious confidence about the possibilities opening up to a pair of talented "moses" such as Ellison and Murray. His optimism can be attributed in part to the startling and imme- diate success of *Invisible Man* and in part to the social revolution occurring beyond the confines of his study. They seemed to be related phenomena. With awe and admiration he watched the Montgomery bus boycott and Autherine Lucy's attempt to integrate the University of Alabama. "I feel a lot better about our struggle," he tells Murray from Rome in 1956, because "mose is still boycotting the hell out of Montgomery and still knocking on the door of Alabama U" (*Trading* 116). Two years later Ellison is ready to forget Jim Crow altogether, telling Murray that whenever he sees blacks settling for less than they can receive "it makes you want to kick their be- hinds and then go after Roy Wilkins and that crowd that don't see that Civil rights are only the beginning" (196).

Once the legal victories were won, however, Ellison's position did not always differ from that of Roy Wilkins. Wilkins criticized King's stance against the Vietnam War, probably for the same reason that Ellison never publicly opposed it: both wanted to be loyal to Lyndon Johnson, the white

Southerner without whose help neither the Civil Rights Act nor the Voting Rights Act would have been passed when it was. Ellison was concerned that King's Vietnam protest would cause the Civil Rights movement to lose its momentum. In the 1930s and '40s Ellison had aligned himself with the Communists because they seemed committed to advancing blacks' interest in American society. In the 1960s he aligned himself with Johnson for the same reason. Shrewd like his famous narrator's grandfather, he recognized that political realities shift and that therefore so must the tactics of minority groups looking to increase their holdings in the American game. Roosevelt had declined to integrate the armed forces; Johnson integrated the Supreme Court with the lawyer who had helped to win *Brown*. Once the Jim Crow cover was blown off the lid of American possibility, new opportunities came rushing out, and the strategy for advancing blacks' interests changed as well.

As Danielle Allen has argued, the changed status of blacks in American society required a new form of citizenship in which blacks would no longer be required to sacrifice themselves for the social cohesion of others (whites). This radical realignment of social roles meant that blacks and whites would see each other—and themselves—differently. Ellison bravely met a society in which the social and political assumptions of the first half of his life were obliterated by his occupying a position where he could speak for all Americans as well as black Americans. Of course, allowing blacks to occupy places that they had not "officially" been allowed to inhabit—whether seats in white restrooms or in white boardrooms—did not mean that historical conditions of poverty and social neglect would be addressed effectively or soon. Johnson's War on Poverty attempted to make good the promises of the Civil Rights Act and the Voting Rights Act, but the American political system recoiled at this gesture—as it had recoiled at giving forty acres and a mule to freed slaves—and systematically worked to displace it. The revolt against Johnson's programs was carried through over a thirty-year period in the elections of Nixon, Reagan, and, finally, Bill Clinton, whose administration effectively ended the welfare program for the poor that Johnson had tried to establish. Along with the reaction against Johnson's poverty programs came also a revolt against *Brown*. The Warren Court, which had unanimously passed *Brown*—with the support of top army officers—was systematically replaced with justices who promised to uphold "states rights" and, as it were, social responsibility. Legalized equality for blacks in American society could not quite replace the code words from the Civil War, but neither could the Civil Rights movement be eradicated. American social space was integrated, and programs such as affirmative action helped to diversify American universities and American corporations, if not the U.S. Senate.

In the 1930s and '40s the Communist Party appealed to American intellectuals who were committed to social justice because it was the political party most committed to confronting and redistributing the obscene disparity in wealth that characterizes American society. American Communists were a logical extension of the Wobblies, Debs's Socialist movement, and other labor groups that had successfully fought to increase workers' rights and brought about the eight-hour workday, child labor laws, and the minimum wage. After World War II, though, the Communists were destroyed as a viable political party, and, as Barbara Foley has shown, the reception history of *Invisible Man* was a part of this process. In the context of the McCarthy hearings, Ellison distanced himself and his work from his fellow-traveling youth. His novel's "Brotherhood" was understood, simplistically, to be an attack on the Communist Party; as Ellison acknowledged during the Vietnam War, though, his conception of the Brotherhood included (and attacked) the logic of the two major American political parties, which each sacrificed the interest of some its members (blacks, especially) in order to advance the party's interest. And of course this reading of the Brotherhood is instructive for understanding what has happened to "black identity" in American politics since *Brown*. As a group, blacks have continued to be a political football kicked back and forth between the two parties, and, given the rate of black unemployment and the disproportionate number of black men in American prisons, it is difficult to say that either party has done much to improve the collective interests of blacks since Johnson's efforts.

Like virtually every other public intellectual of his era, Ellison distanced himself from the one political movement most committed to doing something to redress the inequality of wealth in American life—an inequality that proportionally affects blacks more than any other group. Of course, Wright's experience in the Party only underscored for Ellison how expendable blacks were. By the time the Supreme Court said otherwise, the systematic destruction of the Communist Party in American had begun. Nonetheless, the ongoing fact of black poverty did not and does not mean that there were not opportunities for blacks never before possible in American life. Under King's symbolic leadership, blacks demanded and started to receive social equality, but this was only a start. Blacks also had to learn to occupy the seats that had been denied them (just as whites had to learn to move aside) and, in the process, help to create a working society different from Jim Crow, which had prevailed virtually since the Civil War.

Perhaps more than any other American intellectual, Ellison's work and public persona addressed the cultural and civic challenges that the new society raised. As I argued in the Introduction, Ellison's essays and speeches defined a post-*Brown* ethic of American cultural citizenship. Wherever pertinent, he argued against the premise that American life was irreducibly "black" *or* "white." Thus, he found himself revising his pre-*Brown* novel so that it spoke to and for the post-*Brown* society. His second novel, by contrast, did not allow for this kind of critical retro-engineering. Its symbolic focus was on the doomed effort of blacks to be heard by the U.S. government, and at its center was the assassination of a "white" U.S. senator. Yet insofar as masses of blacks still are not above the poverty line and are more likely to be educated in prison than in colleges, the second novel as well as the first illustrates the historical situation of blacks in America. In the second novel too blacks cannot find their way to "official" American society, and the most committed act of protest is violent action that only brings more grief on the protesters. Such also is the logic of the contemporary American prison system which is home to alarming numbers of black men.

Although Ellison, who understood the black bourgeoisie to be at odds with the black masses, might have chosen to become the kind of oppositional intellectual who calls attention to the fact that society is not doing enough to help its poor, and especially its black poor, he instead chose to position himself symbolically at the forefront of the changing post-*Brown* America. His 1953 address upon receiving the National Book Award announced his role as a black American public intellectual intent on having "influence upon how we think of ourselves and our relationship to what is truly valuable in this country" (*Collected* 196). In his lectures Ellison could have portrayed *Invisible Man* as an indictment of a racist, hypocritical American society and been true to the spirit in which he wrote the novel. Instead, he chose not to be known through the prism of black anger, and this choice became the defining one of his career. Ironically, when Amiri Baraka and Addison Gayle attacked him for being insufficiently militant, they did so from a position that Ellison had already occupied and moved past.

Ellison chose to represent himself and his novel according to a logic that King would affirm. To the questions posed in his 1967 address "Where Do We Go from Here," King answered that blacks had to continue to fight "the tendency to ignore the Negro's contribution to American life and to strip him of his personhood [that] is as old as the earliest history books and as contemporary as this morning's newspaper." Thus, "to upset this cultural homicide," King urged, "the Negro must rise up with an affirmation of his own Olympian manhood" (*I Have* 171). Ellison answered this charge and he worked to create a cultural context in which such heroic gestures, once affirmed, need not be made over and over again since the opportunities open to blacks would change as American society changed. In a 2007 interview Charles S. Johnson describes the arc of Ellison's ambition as a black American intellectual and also suggests how his success had changed what it now means to be a black (or white) intellectual:

> During the age of slavery, then the era of Jim Crow segregation, when whites separated themselves from blacks, they needed a black individual to tell them what black people thought, desired, needed, etc. (How else were they going to find out?) Often that person was the black community's minister; later writers served that purpose, from Richard Write to Ralph Ellison to James Baldwin. I personally think in the post–Civil Rights period a black person is wasting his (or her) time, the preciously few years of their lives, by devoting their energy—as a "spokesman"—to explaining so-called "black" things to white people. Whites can—and should—do their own homework. Read from the vast library of books on black American history and culture. Take a course, for God's sake, on some aspect of black history. Then black individuals can be free to pursue the whole, vast universe that awaits their discovery (as it does for any white person), leaving behind emotionally draining racial discussions to investigate astrophysics, DNA sequencing, cosmology, Sanskrit, the Buddhadharma, mathematics, nanotechnolgoy, everything in this university that remains such a mystery us us. (*M&C* 3)

Under Ellison's instruction *Invisible Man* became a novel about the American commitment to "equality" rather than Jim Crow anger, and, while always looking forward, he never stopped reminding his audiences that black experience had always been integral to American experience. For over forty years Ellison gave speeches, attended symposia, and wrote essays that depended on an elastic, flexible reading of his novel (the better to elucidate the elastic, changing meaning of American history) which kept the book's message fresh for each generation of new readers. In arguing for the universality of his narrator's experience, Ellison was extending King's message that white and black Americans were inextricably bound together through their past and by the present in which that past was being transformed into a more nearly equal society. Performing the changing meaning of *Invisible*

Man as the social realities around him changed, Ellison made himself into a living edition of his second novel—and maybe his third and fourth too.

Ellison's other tactic for capitalizing on King's gains and creating the society that Johnson describes, one that derived from the explicit lessons of *Invisible Man*, involved his astute analysis of how power circulates through institutions. Like C. Wright Mills's contemporaneous *The Power Elite* (1956), *Invisible Man* is a profound investigation into the ways that social institutions produce the range, a limited one, of individual choice. In this respect, the "Marxist" origins that Foley has found in Ellison's novel were never quite abandoned. When contemporary critics speak of novels that invite systems analysis, the works of Don De Lillo and Thomas Pynchon usually come first to mind. *Invisible Man*, however, despite its seeming affirmation of the heroic individual, actually demonstrates in a proto-Foucaultian manner the recognition that an individual's success within a given institution depends on his or her acts being structured within the range of possibilities sanctioned by the institution.

William James once remarked that "the most violent revolutions in an individual's beliefs leave most of his old order standing" (513). The same logic might be said to apply to revolutions in society and the institutions that define them. *Brown* made it possible for blacks to enter social arenas from which they had previously been denied a point of entry. This change of membership, as it were, did not necessarily mean that the logic of the institutions themselves would change. Rather, the people participating within these institutions changed. If blacks were suddenly to be allowed to participate in institutions that had previously prohibited their participation, then they were going to have to learn how to adapt to the logic of the institutions that now included them.

In this regard, Ellison was much shrewder than his narrator could be. To a certain extent, this is what Ellison himself did by becoming friends with Robert Penn Warren, serving as an adviser to President Johnson, and holding a position as a full professor at New York University, not to mention serving on numerous prestigious and influential boards and committees where his influence could be felt. Although Rampersad criticizes Ellison for this success, it shows that he had learned to "play the game, but play it your own way," as the Vet had advised Ellison's hero (*Invisible* 151). Many compelling readings of *Invisible Man* have involved at some level praising the hero's defiant individualism in the face of a clearly corrupt society, but the novel can also be read as critiquing the narrator's inability to function effectively within institutional structures. Ellison's narrator had opportunities to rise within a given structure, whether Bledsoe's machine or Brother Jack's Brotherhood, but he failed and called his failure success. One can well imagine him joining and then being ejected from both a Madison Avenue firm and the Communist Party. If you refuse to function within America's institutional structures (business, government, education), you may well end up in a basement, smoking pot, stealing power from a city you decline to recognize with your payments, listening to renegade forms of music, and generally jive-ass talking to yourself. Such was not Ellison's fate, and he might be understood as the version of his narrator who left his basement after *Brown* became law to challenge Americans to live up to the (new) reality that most Americans had spent their history denying.

When he was attacked in the 1960s and '70s by some black intellectuals, Ellison may have felt that he was talking to himself. Yet he persisted in his narrator's insistence that our American fate is to become many, not one, and that this fate is a matter of description, not prophecy. Ironically, the charge that was leveled against Ellison by his fiercest antagonists—that he advanced in American society at the expense of other blacks—can be leveled against most blacks (not to mention most whites) who have achieved success in post-*Brown* American society. From the perspective that Wright advanced in *12 Million Black Voices* or the one that drove Ellison to write *Invisible Man*, one can still ask, what constitutes success for blacks in post-*Brown* America? The answer is not obvious. Recent "successful" and highly visible black Americans such as Clarence Thomas, Colin Powell, Condoleeza Rice, Michael Steele, and Barack Obama might be seen as versions of what Ellison's hero could eventually have become in a post-*Brown* American society. Arguably, these people are representative Americans whose visibility probably depends less on their being "black" than on their ability to replicate in their own actions the logic of the structures that sanction them.

When prominent blacks such as Clarence Thomas and Shelby Steele argue that affirmative action has blighted the American ideal of equality and needs to be abolished, they are in effect declaring the Civil Rights movement over. Houston Baker underlines this point in *Betrayal: How Black Intellectuals Have Abandoned the Ideals of the Civil Rights Era* (2008). Speaking of the "resolutely middle-class" African American intellectuals who dominate most media discussions of what it means to be black in America, Baker argues that "the evolution of their relationship to the black majority during the past three decades can be summed up in a single word: good-bye!" (73). When Baker declares that African Americans have traded off the interests of the black masses for visibility within elite American culture, he is essentially replicating the critique of power structures that Ellison advanced in *Invisible Man*. What has changed since then is that blacks can now be seen as the face of power in a way that was impossible when Ellison was writing his novel.

In his searing 1967 critique of black intellectuals, *The Crisis of the Negro Intellectual*, Harold Cruse argued that black political advancement required political coalitions that consistently pushed forward collective Negro economic and cultural interests. He contended that the black intellectual is, "in the main, socially detached from his own Negro ethnic world" and that "the black creative writer as interpreter of reality or as social critic must wed his ideas to institutional forms"; otherwise, his ideas will fail (9, 37). Cruse also insisted that "without a literary and cultural critique of his own, the Negro cannot fight for and maintain a position in the cultural world" (105). *Invisible Man* provided a blueprint for the institutional critique that Cruse said was needed, just as Ellison, as an intellectual, advanced an explicitly Negro perspective when addressing American cultural issues. Arguably, King was part of a coalition that successfully challenged the "American cultural apparatus," which exists, Cruse said, "solely, and disproportionately, for the social supremacy, the group narcissism, and the idealization of the white Anglo-Saxon minority" (457). Cruse's argument, though, was that the legal sanction of equal rights for blacks would not be enough to overturn the de facto power of the white Anglo-Saxon minority. Instead, he prophesied, "when legal redress in civil rights reaches the point of saturation de jure, the civil righters are disarmed and naked in the spotlight of adverse power" (71).

Ellison compressed many possible novels into *Invisible Man*, and had he wished he could have constructed an entire, distinct novel from virtually every chapter. At almost any point after the Battle Royal the hero's story could end with his "success." The catch is that Ellison would have had to imagine his narrator developing his character within the existing social structure of that given chapter. Had the narrator been concerned only with augmenting his own personal power, he could have sacrificed his "race pride" and played the game according to the rules that Bledsoe or Brother Jack represented. He chooses (or claims to choose) to occupy a basement in a border region of Harlem instead. In a sense his situation is the reverse of Huckleberry Finn's at the end of his tale: instead of lighting out for the territory, he seeks a legitimate society he may join. None yet exists, so he remains invisible. The hard post-*Brown* lesson of *Invisible Man*, one that has not changed, is that advancing within a particular institutional structure—whether it is the U.S. Army, corporate America, the universities, or the political world—does not always translate into advancing the interests of the group that one represents except as a kind of symbol of the institution's power.

Though classic American novels rarely have their heroes collaborate with the existing structures of society (two notable exceptions would be the doomed heroes of *The Natural* and *The Great Gatsby*), American life endlessly encourages its ambitious sons and daughters not to do as Ellison's narrator does and to cooperate with the logic of institutional structures as soon and as often as possible. Thus, the "civil righters" that Cruse decried in 1967 now stand "disarmed and naked" in the sense that prominent, successful African Americans are obligated to support the "American cultural apparatus" in the guise of advancing "black rights." Read in this post–Civil Rights context, *Invisible Man* demonstrates that eliminating racism, to the extent that it is possible, from the way institutions work does not alter the fact that institutions still demand the selective maintenance and distribution of inequity in order to function. Powell or Rice would seem to confirm Cruse's arguments, since they are instances of a post–Civil Rights logic that isolates discrete African American individuals who have tried the spinning wheel of American success and won the game—for themselves only. Where conservative black intellectuals such as Shelby Steele might argue that figures such as Powell and Rice are to be viewed as proof that racism has diminished, since the U.S. government is willing to employ blacks at the highest levels to advance the U.S. interests as currently defined, Cruse or Baker would suggest that the success of these individual African Americans has not obviously advanced the political interests of the group. If blacks enter an institution of power previously closed to them—the army, the Supreme Court, or even the presidency of the United States—the fact of their inclusion does not necessarily change the logic of the structure. What changes is the color of some of the faces—and little else.

Powell, for instance, has stressed that his success was a consequence of affirmative action. Yet the tricky ironies of his claim are evident when one recalls his speech praising affirmative action during the 2000 Republican Convention, which would nominate a candidate who was against affirmative action. Isn't this a textbook example of a successful African American standing disarmed and naked in the spotlight of adverse power? An *Invisible Man* reading of Powell's career might suggest that he had merely affirmed the mission that *his* Brotherhood—the U.S. Army and the Republican Party—had assigned him. From this perspective, Powell is not so much betraying one group (African Americans) as he is dramatizing what virtually any American must do to be successful within an important segment of American society. Where wealth and opportunity are unequally distributed, one might argue, everybody with power is potentially selling somebody out. From the perspective of African American history, having a "black" face at the head of the United States armed forces was a remarkable achievement. But recognizing this fact only raises the question that Ellison's novel raises: what do such isolated instances mean for advancing the collective interests of African Americans?

Except for supporting Johnson, Ellison kept his political views to himself. Given that the Brotherhood works as a radical critique of all political parties in American life, Ellison was likely not very optimistic that American society would ever distribute its wealth equally. He did recognize, as Danielle Allen argues in *Talking to Strangers*, that in a post-*Brown* society Americans at the very least needed to hear arguments that encouraged or taught them "how to get along" with people who might seem strange. No better society was possible until Americans learned to accept each other as Americans. What made Ellison distinctive as a post-*Brown* black intellectual was his commitment to elucidating the social complexities of a culturally diverse society. His arguments in essays such as "The Little Man at Chehaw Station" and "Going to the Territory" imagined a society in which terms such as Negro and American could not remain stable. Ellison did not, obviously, want to eradicate the special meaning of a group's history, but neither did he want the history of the group to remain static. In this context, Powell's rise in post-*Brown* American society might be contrasted with that of Ellison's former teacher, Dr. Inman Page.

In "Going to the Territory," Ellison presents Page as an unlikely but inevitable consequence of democracy's capacity to unsettle its own structures and hierarchies. Ellison recalls that Page was a severe figure whose strict discipline and exacting standards moved his students "secret yearnings to possess some of his implicit authority" (*Going* 122). Many of Page's students, Ellison notes, "became teachers and community leaders." Although Page's work was mostly done in "segregated institutions and thus was overlooked by those who record the history of American education," his example was part of a collective, generational effort through which blacks achieved greater authority and influence within American life (122). Inman Page happened to be the first African American to graduate from Brown University, and his success there established a chain, Ellison suggests, that led to Ellison and the poet Michael Harper, who had invited Ellison to Brown to commemorate Page's life.

Here the point is not only that Page's work helped to bring forth one and two generations later two distinguished black American writers but also that Page's collaboration with the institutional structure of Brown University was part of the process by which future blacks could play larger roles in the shaping of American language and society. Ellison's tribute to Page is itself a kind of lesson in African American studies but one with the goal of revealing how African Americans working together and through the democratic institutional structures of American society can enhance everyone's sense of what it means to be American. Even if Page graduated from Brown to return to a segregated society, the fact of his graduating from Brown was part of a process that was dismantling segregation as a structure of American life. Page was making way for a future not like the life he had known and was himself the perfect example of Ellison's essay's theme: "the sheer unexpectedness of life in these United States" (*Going* 120). With Powell, however, the Ellisonian question is this: does his example further a process that helps African Americans rise in American society, or is he the end of a line? The answer is unclear.

I cannot stress too strongly that Ellison's ideal for understanding democratic cultural practices was in terms of something that "happens through a process of apparently random synthesis," or acts that require cultural mixing. Once the racial walls of Jericho fell, and different institutional mazes opened for ambitious African Americans to enter, the question for Ellison became how you should confront these puzzles when the prejudice against you was no longer legal. The answer that Ellison gave as he in his own way advanced the interests of his people was that when "we dread to acknowledge the complex, pluralistic nature of our society," we as Americans "misconceive our cultural identity" (*Going* 125). As he tried to tell us, *Invisible Man* can be seen as a version of this American cultural complexity even if it was written in response to the political and cultural disenfranchisement of Negroes. In music, a "seemingly random synthesis" may be what happens when Sonny Rollins interprets Cole Porter (though Ellison would disagree as a matter of taste, not syncretism). In politics, it may occur when Colin Powell advances to the upper echelon of a political party that does not otherwise obviously advance the interests of African Americans. In sports, one can point to the recent success of African American NFL coaches Tony Dungy and Mike Tomlin, who have led the Indianapolis Colts and the Pittsburgh Steelers, respectively, to Super Bowl victories in the sport that clearly reflects the dreams and aspirations of American corporate culture.

As the symbolic embodiment of American corporate culture, the NFL is to American society what ullamaliztli was to Aztec society. Thus, the success of Dungy and Tomlin is quite different from the "individual" success of Jackie Robinson, who integrated major league baseball as a player, precisely because they can be seen as management heroes whose actions oversee and dictate the success of others. They are not mere overseers, as some blacks were allowed to be over slaves, because they are responsible for a group action in which every member of the group works for and is committed to a shared goal. Only thirty years earlier, people had questioned whether blacks had the "leadership qualities" to play quarterback at the professional level. In the integrated NFL, blacks can assume a management position that requires them to lead and inspire and command excellence from a group of racially diverse men. Now week after week millions of Americans observe and cheer black men as examples of brilliant leaders. Such success does not eradicate racism and may only clarify the disparity that exists between the visible and the invisible in American society. But success and power in America no longer wears only a white face.

The lesson of Powell's rise in American society becomes more complex when applied it to Barack Obama, the first black U.S. president. On the surface, Obama's election seems to confirm Ellison's positive view of the possibilities for blacks (and for all Americans) in the post-*Brown* era. Ellison's arguments concerning the "seemingly random synthesis" enacted by democratic culture tacitly accepted that miscegenation was an integral and necessary component of American life. In Faulkner's work, the word figured as a form of dread. In the 1950s and '60s "miscegenation" was a fear-provoking label with which white segregationists hoped to stop the Civil Rights movement. The rise of Obama would seem to indicate that such prejudices no longer rule American life. Though Obama ran for president as a "black" candidate, he also stressed his mixed ancestry. Obama was officially nominated as the Democratic Party's candidate for president on the anniversary of King's 1963 "I Have A Dream" speech and inaugurated as president the day after the national celebration of King's birthday. For many, it was as if King's dream had been renewed and realized in the form of Obama. For other voters, Obama's mixed ancestry—his father was African (Kenyan) and his mother Caucasian (from the Republican state of Kansas)—signaled that the Jim Crow logic of American politics was giving way to a postracial logic in which the line between black and white could no longer be discerned.

Unless one wants to believe that race is no longer a decisive factor in American politics, Obama's election was less revolutionary than King's success in getting Johnson to pass the Voting Rights Act. Arguably, it was a logical consequence of that law.[1] In this respect, the possibility that Obama's election was yet another startling twist made possible by the ongoing post-*Brown* reconstitution of American society was hard to repress. The stunning symbolism of his election understandably overwhelmed harder political questions that would ask whose interests his election serves. More powerful than the assuagement of white guilt that Shelby Steele saw in Obama's appeal was the sense of affirmation experienced by blacks who said they had never imagined that this day would come. In the *New York Times* (20 Jan. 2009), Bob Herbert noted that "the holiday celebrating the birth of the Reverend Martin Luther King, Jr. became, in the midnight hour, the day that America inaugurated its first black president" and went on to wish that "the big four civil rights leaders of the mid-twentieth century"—King, James Farmer, Roy Wilkins, and Whitney Young, each of whom was interviewed by Robert Penn Warren—might have been present together to witness the fruits of their labor.

In this context, perhaps the most moving historical reunion—certainly the one with the clearest connection to Ellison—involved the Tuskegee Airmen, the members of the all-black pilot squadron who became the first black military pilots to serve in the U.S. armed forces, and some of whom were present at Obama's inauguration. These surviving pilots had flown missions during World War II as the 332nd Fighter Group in the U.S. Army Air Corps. Various political maneuvers had been undertaken to prevent them from ever leaving the ground; however, they prevailed and were trained at Tuskegee fewer than five years after Ellison had left the school. As Ellison once explained, during World War II "some of my friends were in the Air Force," and these "friends from college, friends from Tuskegee, had become pilots, combat pilots, and so on, and during that moment of the war, they were very active" (*Collected* 521). The distinguished combat record of the Tuskegee Airmen gave the lie to the U.S. policy of segregation within the armed forces and served as a source of inspiration to black Americans during World War II.

The Tuskegee Airmen had also inspired Ellison's creative imagination. "There had been a lot of political agitation on the part of Negro Americans because we were not being allowed to fight," Ellison once related to a West Point audience, "and those young men, those friends of mine, those pilots, were being withheld from duty, and that concerned me very much" (*Collected* 521–22). Ellison did not finish the novel he had intended to write about this situation, but did compose the extraordinary story "Flying Home." Named after a jazz song that featured a remarkable solo from Illinois Jacquet, it was also patterned on the experience of the Tuskegee Airmen before they were allowed to fight. In that story Ellison imagines an ersatz Tuskegee Airman "flying high" through a brilliant solo flight and dreaming of being recognized for his talent and the contribution he wants to make to a country that has refused to recognize him. The protagonist, Todd, does not find glory but instead crashes his plane, Icarus-like, into an Alabama field. He survives only to suffer the humiliation of wondering whether his failure would compromise his chance and the chances of others to fly in the war. At the heart of the story is his doubt about whether he was good enough to be the pilot he dreamed of being.

While Todd lies injured, dreading the machinery through which he will have to confront the consequences of his failure, an old black man with the ambiguous name of Jefferson happens upon him and tends to the young pilot's wounds. Jefferson discerns that Todd's most severe wound is psychological, and he quickly concocts a folk remedy in the form of a tale: the story of a one-winged black angel who tries to integrate heaven but is struck down for flying too high and with too much style. At first the Negro angel is granted two wings by St. Peter, but the other angels find his flying so audacious that St. Peter limits him to one wing. Jefferson's tale is meant to reassure Todd that in a segregated world he is doing the best he can and should not surrender his dream to excel, because if he keeps at it, he will succeed one day. Falling is the price one pays for learning to fly.

Despite the legal blocks put in the way of the Tuskegee Airmen, they represented their country with courage and honor. Their story might have become invisible to history (as Inman Page's story would have been were it not for his famous student), but Obama's election gave them a chance to have their remarkable feats recalled. Those voting for Obama may not have thought that the election of their candidate had anything to do with the forgotten story of these brave airmen, yet the unlikely success of those pilots was part of the story that made Obama's election possible. Their connection to the new president was not as direct as was the connection between Brown University's first African American graduate and Ralph Ellison, or even between the Airmen and Ellison, yet they are consistent with Ellison's contention in "Going to the Territory" that "our unknown history doesn't stop having consequences even though we ignore them" (*Going* 133). The obvious emotions that the Tuskegee Airmen experienced when seeing Obama inaugurated president affirmed for them, and many watching, the continuing importance of their heroic acts of more than half a century earlier. They were witnesses of and actors in an African American drama that changed how all Americans understood the meaning of their—our—history.

One need not belabor the point, but Obama himself seems to be aware of his connection to an Ellisonian politics. The opening to his *Dreams from My Father* clearly echoes the Prologue and Epilogue of *Invisible Man*. Like Ellison's narrator, Obama begins his story in a basement apartment located on a border region at the edge of Harlem. Obama is drawn out of his snug habitation by the news that his father, whom he did not know, has died. This phone call initiates Obama's quest for identity, which concludes, temporarily, with his arrival as an Illinois state senator. Whether or not Obama consciously adapted the logic of *Invisible Man* to order his political life, Ellison's work helps one to understand the origins and possibly the design of Obama's career—and not simply in the sense that as a politician Obama is obligated to manipulate to his political advantage other's misperceptions of who he seems to be. One might well imagine Obama's career as a response to the ambiguous conclusion of *Invisible Man*. Here an analysis of his meaning divides into two opposed questions that reflect the unresolved ending of Ellison's hero. Does Obama emerge from the basement to enact a new and more democratic society? Or must he become the symbolic "black" actor whose "blackness" masks the existing structures of social inequality and military imperialism?

Such questions cannot at this point be answered, but one reading does seem clear. When Barack Obama was inaugurated the forty-fourth President of the United States, with the surviving Tuskegee Airmen watching, Ellison was present in spirit too. In some vital sense, the nation had elected and was pursuing his vision.

Like that of no other American writer, Ralph Ellison's work continues to unfold before us.

Notes

Introduction

1. See Foley ("Reading," "Race," and "Rhetoric") and her *Wrestling*, which completes years of work on Ellison's early years. His legacy would be enhanced immeasurably were Foley (or someone) to edit an Ellison reader that emphasized his "Marxist" side. Given his lifelong distaste for the bourgeoisie, and his refusal ever to champion the spoils of American consumer culture (as his friend Bellow did), Ellison did not entirely reject his early Marxist premises. Nor did he scrub his novel of all of its Marxist underpinnings. The view of *Invisible Man* which I suggest in the Epilogue is tacitly Marxist in that it emphasizes Ellison's pessimistic critique of the institutions that sanction American society.

2. Foley's illuminating work, which uncovers an essential version of Ellison that has been missing from the Ellison canon and shows how fundamentally political his vision as a writer was, is particularly valuable in that it suggests that Ellison's career was one that he very much made and not one that "happened" to him. Even here, though, Foley's reading also plays into the narrative frame set out by the biographies: she laments Ellison's choice to distance himself from his Marxist origins and wishes for a version of *Invisible Man* that his artistic conscience simply could not authorize.

3. Despite his largely unsympathetic account of Ellison's life, Rampersad also states that no black writer has surpassed either Ellison's novel or his work of criticism. Rampersad says that Morrison's *Beloved* comes closest to his novel and that Du Bois's *Souls of Black Folk* comes closest to *Shadow and Act*. See Rampersad's interview with Amazon, http://www.amazon.com/Ralph-Ellison-Biography-Arnold-Rampersad/dp/0375408274.

4. "African American Thoreau" is one of Jackson's chapter titles. For Jackson, Ellison became Thoreau-like when he committed to being a fiction writer, but I would stress that as a fiction writer Ellison still sought, as he told Kenneth Burke, to demolish "the stereotypes and caricatures that white Americans used to keep the humanity of black Americans at bay" (Jackson, *Ralph* 326).

5. These numerous recent critical works confirm Ellison's continuing importance as perhaps the most consistently read and taught post–World War II American writer. Horace Porter's *Jazz Country* (2001) makes a strong case for the enduring appeal of Ellison's essays and the importance of his music criticism. David Yaffe's *Fascinating Rhythms* (2005) confirms Ellison's place as preeminent critic of jazz. H. William Rice's *Ralph Ellison and the Politics of the Novel* (2003) critiques Ellison's political vision.

6. For discussions of Ellison as a Cold War writer, see Schaub (1991) and Foley, *Wrestling* (2010).

7. This is a generalization. The most famous critic of Ellison as a black author is the white reader Irving Howe. Stanley Crouch, Charles Johnson, and Leon Forrest are black writers who valued Ellison greatly.

8. "Three Days before the Shooting" is not Ellison's title, so for the most part I refer to this work as Ellison's second novel. I understand that phrase to include all the fiction included in *Three Days* as well as the drafts left out of that publication.

9. Bradley and Callahan astutely make this comparison. Bolaño's book is five novels in one, though it still raises the question of whether the totality of the novel consists of five parts or if the five parts are divergent novels which together form a whole that is always fragmenting. Ellison, apparently, did not want to write such a book, but that is what he ended up doing. Were one to apply the aesthetic of *2666* to Ellison's second novel, that novel would no longer seem so incomplete. Its unfinished state would, paradoxically, only emphasize its totality.

10. Lawrence Jackson notes in *Ralph Ellison* (427–28) that "the least generous reviews of the book came from black readers and committed left-wing activists": Frank Lloyd Brown called Ellison "a 'Judas' alienated from black masses" in the *Baltimore Afro-American*; J. Saunders Redding said Ellison was a "writer of power" who used his power to describe the "diurnal life of gnats" in *Masses and Mainstream*; John O. Killens called the book "a vicious distortion of Negro life" in *Freedomways*; Abner Perry accused Ellison of using an "other worldly style to suit the kingpins of world white supremacy" in the *Daily Worker*.

11. Morris Dickstein calls *Invisible Man* "perhaps the single best novel of the whole postwar era" (146). A 1972 survey among American critics named *Invisible Man* the American novel "most likely to last" (Tracy 45).

12. See Parrish ("Ralph") for a discussion of Ellison's relationship to Burke.

13. Rosanna Warren to Ralph Ellison, 11 Aug. 1981, Ralph Waldo Ellison Papers, Library of Congress.

14. In 1945 Ellison asked Kenneth Burke for advice about the novel he was writing; he said wanted to combine the personal with the political, Freud with Marx. Burke suggested that Ellison frame the narrator's perspective as that of a Dostoyevskian idiot buoyed by the tradition of the Negro spirituals. Arguably, this is what Ellison did. In the end, Burke dubbed the novel a bildungsroman, a form concerned with the growth of an individual in society. See also Ralph Ellison to Richard Wright, Aug. 24, 1946, RWEP LC.

15. Shortly before his death, Leslie Fiedler, one of the great critics of American literature, said that of all post-Faulkner American writers, Ellison was the only one who would surely last. Fiedler also mentions Bellow as one who may last (Bauman).

16. See James T. Kloppenberg's discussion of Obama's debt to Ellison (*Reading*).

17. The philosopher Hannah Arendt and the historian Stanley Elkins revised their understanding of the civil rights protests and slavery, respectively, in light of Ellison's criticism. Danielle Allen's *Talking to Strangers* (2004), Leon Litwack's *Trouble in Mind* (1998), and Richard Kluger's *Simple Justice* (1977) rely on Ellison's work and indicate the range of his intellectual and cultural reach. If Litwack's *Trouble in Mind* identifies Ellison's work as the paradigm for understanding what happened to African Americans during the period between the Civil War and *Brown v. Board of Education* (1954), Kluger suggests the depth of *Invisible Man*'s context by using its key metaphor to convey the historical consequences of *Brown*: "The Justices had severed the remaining conditions of de facto slavery. The Negro could no longer be fastened with the status of official pariah. No longer could the white man look right through him as if he were, in the title words of Ralph Ellison's stunning 1952 novel, *Invisible Man*" (749). Between Litwack and Kluger, one sees how *Invisible Man* contains the past and predicts the future simultaneously.

18. As recently as 1999, the distinguished scholar Houston A. Baker Jr., who has held endowed chairs at elite and historically "white" universities such as Duke and Vanderbilt, complained that as "Civil Rights and Black Power became American—indeed global—realities," cool "Ellison reclined in butter-soft seats at exclusive clubs, explaining to whites why he could not take any active part in the Liberation Politics of black Americans" (Rampersad 548). Fifteen years earlier, in *Blues, Ideology, and Afro-American Literature* (1984), Baker had made Ellison the critical centerpiece of a work that integrated the white intellectual tradition figures such as Freud, Nietzsche, and Derrida with the blues tradition of Ellison, Wright, and Hurston.

19. Ellison is a guiding spirit in Posnock's groundbreaking history of black intellectuals after Du Bois (*Color and Culture* 2001).

20. Morris Dickstein also sees in Ellison "anti-essentialist notions of identity" (32).

21. Beth Eddy reinforces this point when she notes that for Ellison a democratic society requires "active virtue" on the part of citizens; thus, "active virtue is dramatic because it requires social cooperation and participation in social conflicts. This kind of virtue requires protest at crucial moments, but not just any sort of protest. It requires protest that aims at the transcendence of differences" (9). Walton Muyumba clarifies the implications of this stance when he notes that Ellison believed that "American cultural, social, and political practices demanded improvisation" on all levels of civic engagement (151).

1. Philip Roth's Invisible Man

1. David Yaffe notes that "the accusation that [Ellison] had merely fiddled with his typewriter while Harlem burned stayed with him, as did the Black Panther member's accusation that he was an Uncle Tom. Ellison was in no emotional state to tell him that *Invisible Man* was itself a civil rights statement" (65).

2. Contrast the Ellison-Roth position with that of Toni Morrison, who declared that her work must "fit first into African-American tradition and second of all, this whole thing called literature" ("Art" 118).

3. When the Black Aesthetic movement emerged in the late 1960s and early 1970s, Ellison's triumphant "integration" was seen as surrendering to white cultural agendas. *The Black Aesthetic* (1971), edited by Addison Gayle Jr., typifies this period of Ellison studies. On the shifting relationship between Ellison and his black critics, see Larry Neal's "Ellison's Zoot Suit." Robert Stepto's *From Behind the Veil* (1979) contains a probing discussion of Ellison's place in the canon of African American literature (163–94). In the 1990s Jerry Watts revived the Ellison-Howe debate and judged Howe the winner, whereas Ross Posnock connected Ellison to the African American pragmatist tradition of W. E. B. Du Bois and Zora Neale Hurston (*Color*).

4. When asked why those associated with "the Black Aesthetic crowd" had not written fiction, Ellison said: "To put it in the vernacular, I would think there's a heap of shucking going on and none of it stacks. They find it easier to issue militant slogans while remaining safely in the straight-jacket of racist ideology—the ideology that has been made of what they call 'Blackness'—than to deal with either the beautiful and confounding complexities of Afro-American culture or the difficulties that must be faced by those who would convert experience into the forms of the novel . . . which, after all, is a product of the *integrative* and *analytical* play of the imagination as it seeks to convert experience into forms of symbolic action" (*Conversations* 327–28, original emphasis).

5. His last words on the matter may as well be what he told David Remnick in 1994, "the truth is that the quality of Americanness . . . will always win out" over ethnic particularism (Remnick 401).

6. See "Change the Joke and Slip the Yoke" (*Collected* 110) and *Trading* (39).

7. This is a version of what happened to Ellison within his family of black readers. Lawrence Jackson speaks of Ellison's most successful period being when "he attained his moment of racelessness, his stature as an American icon to a nonblack audience, during the roughly fifteen-year time span following the release of the novel *Invisible Man*" ("Ralph Ellison's Politics," 173). Jackson also points to black intellectuals who have recently wondered "whether or not we ought or not continue to count Ellison as a Negro or black writer" (171).

8. See Ellison's "Extravagance of Laughter" for a remembrance of this period (*Collected* 659–75).

9. A significant portion of *Three Days* is told by a white narrator whose ability to comprehend

the "black" story his narrative frames is doubtful. This same narrator's affair with a black woman goes awry in an even more dramatic way than Coleman's affair with Steena does.

10. As early as 1948, Ellison was declining invitations to republish stories that to him no longer represented his development as a writer. He may have felt the same way about his second novel. Ralph Ellison to Richard Wright, Feb. 1, 1948, RWEP LC.

2. Richard Wright's Apprentice

1. Rampersad suggests that Ellison and Wright became friends because each had "grown more and more critical of black culture," and both were "especially disdainful of its political and religious leaders. This disdain was probably essential to the success of the two men" (97). Jackson says: "it would be difficult to exaggerate the importance of their friendship" and notes that their seeing each other so often limited the correspondence that might have better documented their friendship ("Ralph Ellison's Invented" 25). Rowley says: "Ellison was seeking a mentor and for a while Wright was it" (130). One of the most telling stories regarding the men's friendship concerns Wright's dedicated help to keep Ellison from being drafted into the Jim Crow army during World War II. Each was well aware of the harsh treatment black soldiers were receiving and viewed service in the army as a kind of treasonous act toward other blacks. See Webb 227–31.

2. For a discussion of Ellison's debt to Burke and this essay in particular, see O'Meally, ("On Burke"), Eddy (*The Rites of Identity* [2008]), and Parrish ("Democracy").

3. Daniel Y. Kim observes that Ellison's early essay "Recent Negro Fiction" is "a virtual hagiography" as it "canonizes Wright for living out in his own life and works the narrative of poetic development outlined in 'Blueprint'" (94).

4. In an early draft of the novel, Ellison had a character reflect in his diary that Nat Turner, rather than Frederick Douglass, was an appropriate model for black leadership (Jackson, *Ralph*, 415).

5. The most influential critic on the relationship between Wright and Ellison was Ellison himself. Howe's essay and Ellison's response in "The World and the Jug" canonized the critical divide between Wright and Ellison studies, and, as I suggest, most criticism has reinforced this divide. Michel Fabre's writings on Wright are crucial (see *The Unfinished Quest* [1993] and "From *Native Son*"). See Daniel Chin (*Writings* 105–9); Lawrence Jackson ("Birth"); Alan Nadel ("Integrated"); Larry Neal ("Ellison's Zoot Suit" 24–57); Brian Roberts ("CPUSA"); Robin Lucy ("Flying Home"); Joseph Skerret ("Wright Interpretation").

6. This essay, first published in 1971, may have been provoked by Constance Webb's 1968 biography of Wright in which the closeness between the two men was amply documented. Webb used Ellison as a source, and hence her account of their friendship was filtered through Ellison.

7. John F. Callahan used this designation as the epigraph for *Juneteenth*.

8. Hence, David Yaffe argues in *Fascinating Rhythms* that Ellison was America's preeminent jazz critic—that he founded the discipline of jazz writing.

9. See Gates (*Signifying*), Baker (*Blues*), Nicholls, and Lucy.

10. This of course is Du Bois's argument in *The Souls of Black Folk* (1903).

11. In *12 Million Black Voices*, Wright notes that Negroes invariably affirm whatever it is they think the white person wants to say.

3. Ellison, Warren, and Woodward

1. Posnock argues that Ellison's commitment "in the struggle for freedom" was viewed "skeptically by critics for whom 'political' functions as little more than a litmus test or moral

(read ideological) virtue" and that Ellison's sense of the political "recovers an almost classical sense of the word" (*Color* 9).

2. See Ellison, interview with Robert O'Meally (*Living* 265–88).

3. In *South to a Very Old Place* (1971), Albert Murray visits Robert Penn Warren and C. Vann Woodward and treats them as fellow-travelers. He notes with approval Woodward's observation that "as far as culture is concerned, all Americans are part-Negro" (19).

4. James Baldwin was inducted into the Century Club same year as Ellison.

5. For the reception history of *Origins*, see Johnson (1–20).

6. See also Woodward's *Strange Career* (154–63).

7. It was important to Warren that his former prejudices be acknowledged and forgiven. According to Joseph Blotner, Warren was "furious" when the *New Republic* suggested that his 1961 *The Legacy of the Civil War* repeated the "biases of *I'll Take My Stand.*" Blotner notes that Warren responded that he had explicitly repudiated that position and went on to endorse Martin Luther King as "a great man and great leader" (*Robert* 344).

8. Bayard Rustin compared his political stance to that of Ralph Ellison's efforts as "portraying human reality in all of its complexity" (332). Like Ellison, Rustin saw that after the success of King's movement there would be a need for a pluralistic coalition of blacks along with white labor and white liberal intellectuals to realize the Civil Rights protest movement.

4. *Invisible Man*'s Political Vision

1. Noting that the Bible and Declaration of Independence were his key texts, Sundquist argues that "King in no way rejected America's foundational values" and insisted that only when they were shared by all Americans "would they truly be America's foundational values" (*King's* 10).

2. During the protests that culminated in the march from Selma to Montgomery (which never crossed the bridge and thus began and ended in Selma), King faced dissension in his ranks. He agreed to lead a march across the Edmund Pettus Bridge but, in deference to Johnson, promised to try to get the marchers to turn around on the bridge rather than continue toward Montgomery and risk a violent encounter with Governor George Wallace's troopers. SNCC (Student Nonviolent Coordinating Committee) leaders, including James Forman, were disappointed in King; Forman pulled his staff out of Montgomery. When the Mississippi Freedom Democratic Party tried to seat its elected representatives at the 1964 Democratic National Convention, King again sided with Johnson and again angered other black leaders. Commenting on King's ability to bring fractious coalitions together during the 1965 Selma-Montgomery protests, however, J. L. "Ike" Chestnut said that "no one else [but King] could have unified the collections of ministers, gangsters, self-seekers, students, prima donnas, and devoted, high-minded people we had in Selma that winter" (Kotz 265; see also 250–77).

3. Loyal to Johnson, Ellison refused to join Robert Lowell when he organized a boycott of artists invited to attend a cultural function being hosted by Ladybird Johnson. King was criticized by other black leaders as well for risking Johnson's ire in protesting the Vietnam War.

4. Ellison appeared at a 1964 conference organized by SNCC and at a 1965 event staged by the NAACP's Legal Defense Fund, where he spoke on the meaning of the voting rights march in Selma.

5. Citing the political scientist Adolph Reed, Posnock argues that Booker T. Washington's role was as "a representative of black authenticity for elite whites" (*Color* 38).

6. Hence, Ellison would remark of King that his was a case of "martyrdom endowing the martyr with a hell of a lot more following than he had during his struggles." Ellison is not minimizing King's achievement but emphasizing the role played by all martyrs (*Conversations* 243).

7. King understood this role, as his many remarks predicting his own death by violence indicate.

8. For accounts of the Greensboro sit-in, see Branch *(Parting* 271–73) and Morris (195–97). For accounts of the Nashville sit-in, see Branch (*Parting* 274–81) and Morris (174–78; 205–13).

9. Fanny Lou Hamer became a national celebrity during the Mississippi Freedom Democratic Party's attempt to have their elected representatives seated at the 1964 Democratic Convention. On national television, with President Johnson watching, Hamer described how she and others were beaten by state highwaypolice because they were trying to register to vote. She described how a white man "walked over and pulled my dress down—and he pulled my dress back up. All of this on account we want to register, to become first-class citizens. And if the Freedom Democratic Party is not seated now, I question America" (Kotz 205, 202–6).

10. After Ellison made his remarks to Warren, Arendt wrote Ellison to say that she had been wrong and that "it was precisely this ideal of sacrifice which I did not understand" (Posnock, "Ralph," 201).

11. As Nicole Waligora-Davis argues, in the scene preceding the riot, where the narrator sleeps with Sybil, Ellison "marks his own nationalist project, his own rebirth of America: a dawning of racial consciousness on the part of black Americans who not only must concede their invisibility in American society, but also must concede their history, a history that renders them responsible for realizing America's democratic promise" (397).

12. Excellent accounts of this episode are to be found in Branch (*Pillar* 551–600), and Kotz (250–77).

13. King was presiding over the funeral of James Reeb, who had been killed during the Selma protests, and declined Johnson's offer to fly him to Washington. Although Reeb was white (he had not remained silent), King's presence at the funeral meant that he was enacting the role of mythic hero which was demanded of him according to the logic of ritual that Ellison advances in *Invisible Man*.

14. James Forman, anticipating how difficult it would be to realize in fact the "beloved community" that Johnson's words affirmed, bitterly remarked that Johnson had ruined a good song (Kotz 312).

Epilogue

1. This is the argument that one of Johnson's biographers, Robert Caro, makes in an essay published the day that Obama accepted the Democratic Party's nomination. "To me," Caro writes, "Barack Obama is the inheritor of Lyndon Johnson's civil rights legacy. As I sit listening to Mr. Obama tonight, I will be hearing other words as well. I will be hearing Lyndon Johnson saying 'We Shall Overcome.'"

Works Cited

Allen, Danielle S. *Talking to Strangers*. Chicago: U of Chicago P, 2004.

Baker, Houston A., Jr. *Blues, Ideology, and Afro-American Literature: A Vernacular Theory*. Chicago: U of Chicago P, 1984.

———. *Betrayal: How Black Intellectuals Have Abandoned the Ideals of the Civil Rights Era*. New York: Columbia UP, 2008.

Bauman, Bruce. "The Critic in Winter." *Salon*, 2 Jan. 2003. *http://www.salon.com /books/int/2003/01/02/fiedler*.

Bellow, Saul. *Ravelstein*. New York: Viking, 2000.

Benston, Kimberly W., ed. *Speaking for You: The Vision of Ralph Ellison*. Washington, DC: Howard UP, 1990.

Bloom, Harold. *Genius: A Mosaic of One Hundred Exemplary Critical Minds*. New York: Warner, 2002.

———, ed. *Philip Roth*. New York: Chelsea House, 1986.

Blotner, Joseph. *Faulkner: A Biography*. 2 vols. New York: Random House, 1974.

———. *Robert Penn Warren: A Biography*. New York: Random House, 1997.

Bolaño, Roberto. *2666*. Trans. Natasha Wimmer. New York: Farrar, Straus, and Giroux, 2008.

Boles, John B., and Bethany L. Johnson, eds. *"Origins of the New South": Fifty Years Later*. Baton Rouge: Louisiana State UP, 2003.

Bradley, Adam. *Ralph Ellison in Progress*. New Haven: Yale UP, 2010.

Branch, Taylor. *Parting the Waters: America in the King Years 1954–63*. New York: Simon and Schuster, 1988.

———. *Pillar of Fire: America in the King Years 1963–65*. New York: Simon and Schuster, 1998.

Burke, Kenneth. "Ralph Ellison's Trueblooded *Bildungsroman*." Benston 349–59.

Butler, Robert J. "Bibliographic Essay: Probing the Lower Frequencies: Fifty Years of Ellison Criticism." Tracy 233–61.

Callahan, John F. "Democracy and the Pursuit of Narration." *Carleton Miscellany* 18.3 (Winter 1980): 51–69.

———. "Frequencies of Eloquence: The Performance and Composition of *Invisible Man*." *New Essays on Ellison's* Invisible Man. Ed. Robert O'Meally. New York: Cambridge UP, 1988. 55–94.

Carby, Hazel V. "Ideologies of Black Folk: The Historical Novel in Slavery." In *Cultures in Babylon: Black Britain and African America*. London: Verso, 1999. 146–59.

Caro, Robert A. "Johnson's Dream, Obama's Speech" *New York Times*, 27 Aug. 2008.

Crewdson, Arlene, and Rita Thomson. "Interview with Ralph Ellison." Graham and Singh 259–71.

Crouch, Stanley. "Ralph Ellison's Endless Blues." *Daily Beast*, 6 Feb. 2010. *http://www .thedailybeast.com/blogs-and-stories/2010-02-06/ralph-ellisons-endless-blues/*.

Cruse, Harold. *The Crisis of the Negro Intellectual*. New York: William Morrow, 1967.

Dickstein, Morris. "Ralph Ellison, Race, and American Culture." In John F. Callahan, ed. *Ralph Ellison's Invisible Man: A Casebook*. Oxford; Oxford UP, 2004. 125–47.

Du Bois, W. E. B. *Black Reconstruction in America: An Essay toward a History of the Part Which Black Fok Played in the Attempt to Reconstruct Democracy in America, 1860–1880*. New York: Harcourt Brace, 1935.

———. *The Souls of Black Folk*. 1903. New York: Library of America, 1990.

Eddy, Beth. *The Rites of Identity: The Religious Naturalism and Cultural Criticism of Kenneth Burke and Ralph Ellison*. Princeton, NJ: Princeton UP, 2008.

Ellison, Ralph. *The Collected Essays of Ralph Ellison*. Ed. John F. Callahan. New York: Modern Library, 1995.

———. *Conversations with Ralph Ellison*. Ed. Maryemma Graham and Amrijit Singh. Jackson: UP of Mississippi, 1995.

———. *Flying Home and Other Stories*. Ed. John F. Callahan. New York: Random House, 1996.

———. *Going to the Territory*. New York: Random House, 1986.

———. *Invisible Man*. 1952. New York: Modern Library, 1992.

———. *Juneteenth*. Ed. John F. Callahan. New York: Random House, 1999.

———. Letter to Saul Bellow. 4 May 1956. Ralph Waldo Ellison Papers, Library of Congress (RWEP LC).

———. Letter to James L. Roark. 23 Nov. 1982. C. Vann Woodward Papers, Beinecke Library, Yale University.

———. Letter to Robert Penn Warren. 1 June 1963. RWEP LC.

———. Letter to Robert Penn Warren. 1971. RWEP LC.

———. Letter to Robert Penn Warren. 15 May 1940. RWEP LC.

———. Letter to Robert Penn Warren. 3 Nov. 1941. RWEP LC.

———. Letter to Robert Penn Warren. 5 Aug. 1945. RWEP LC.

———. Letter to Robert Penn Warren. 24 Aug. 1946. RWEP LC.

———. Letter to Robert Penn Warren. 1 Feb. 1948. RWEP LC.

———. *Living with Music: Ralph Ellison's Jazz Writings*. Ed. Robert O'Meally. New York: Modern Library, 2001.

———. "Recent Negro Fiction." *New Masses* 40 (5 Aug. 1941): 22–26.

———. "Richard Wright and Recent Negro American Fiction." *Direction* 4 (Summer 1941): 12–13.

———. *Shadow and Act*. New York: Random House, 1964.

———. *Three Days before the Shooting*. Ed. John F. Callahan and Adam Bradley. New York: Modern Library, 2010.

Ellison, Ralph, and Albert Murray. *Trading Twelves: The Selected Letters of Ralph Ellison and Albert Murray*. Ed. Albert Murray and John F. Callahan. New York: Modern Library, 2000.

Emerson, Ralph Waldo. *Essays and Lectures*. New York: Library of America, 1983.

Fabre, Michel. "From Native Son to *Invisible Man*: Some Notes on Ralph Ellison's Evolution in the 1950s." Benston 199–217.

———. *The Unfinished Quest of Richard Wright*. Urbana: U of Illinois P, 1993.

Fields, Barbara J. "*Origins of the New South* and the Negro Question." Boles and Johnson 261–77.

Foley, Barbara. "Race, Class and Communism: The Young Ralph Ellison and the 'Whole Left.'" *Radical Relevance: Toward a Scholarship of the Whole Left*. Ed. Laura Gray-Rosendale and Steven Rosendale. Albany: State U of New York P, 2005.

———. "Reading Redness: Politics and Audience in Ralph Ellison's Early Short Fiction." *Journal of Narrative Theory* 29.3 (Fall 1999): 323–39.

———. "The Rhetoric of Anticommunism in Invisible Man." *College English* 59.5 (Sept. 1997): 530–47.

———. *Wrestling with the Left: The Making of Ralph Ellison*. Durham, NC: Duke UP, 2010.

Frady, Marshall. *Martin Luther King, Jr.: A Life*. New York: Penguin, 2002.

Gates, Henry Louis, Jr. "The Passing of Anatole Broyard." *Thirteen Ways of Looking at a Black Man*. New York: Random House, 1997. 180–214.

———. *The Signifying Monkey: A Theory of African-American Literary Criticism*. New York: Oxford UP, 1988.

Gayle, Addison, Jr., ed. *The Black Aesthetic*. Garden City, NY: Doubleday, 1971.

Gilmore, Michael T. *Surface and Depth: The Quest for Legibility within American Culture*. New York: Oxford UP, 2003.

Graham, Maryemma, and Amritjit Singh, eds. *Conversations with Ralph Ellison*. Jackson: UP of Mississippi, 1995.

Hendricks, Randy, and James A. Perkins, eds. *Selected Letters of Robert Penn Warren: Volume Three*. Baton Rouge: Louisiana State UP, 2006.

Henrik, John, ed. *William Styron's Nat Turner: Ten Black Writers Respond*. Boston: Beacon, 1968.

Herbert, Bob. "I Wish You Were Here." *New York Times*, 20 Jan. 2009.

Hersey, John.. "A Completion of Personality: A Talk with Ralph Ellison." Benston 285–307.

———, ed. *Ralph Ellison: A Collection of Critical Essays*. Englewood Cliffs, NJ: Prentice-Hall, 1974.

Howe, Irving. "Black Boys and Native Sons." Hersey, *Ralph Ellison* 36–38.

———. "Philip Roth Reconsidered." Bloom, *Philip Roth* 71–88.

Jackson, Lawrence. "The Birth of a Critic: The Literary Friendship between Richard Wright and Ralph Ellison." *American Literature* 72.2 (June 2000): 321–55.

———. *Ralph Ellison: Emergence of Genius*. New York: John Wiley, 2002.

———. "Ralph Ellison's Invented Life: A Meeting with the Ancestors." Posnock, *Cambridge Companion* 11–34.

———. "Ralph Ellison's Politics of Integration." Tracy 171–206.

James, William. *Writings: 1902–1910*. New York: Library of America, 1987.

Johnson, Bethany L. "Introduction: C. Vann Woodward and the Reconstruction of the New South." Boles and Johnson 1–20.

Johnson, Charles S. *The M&C Interview*. *http://www.monstersandcritics.com/books*

/interviews/article_1308738.php/The_M&C_Interview_1_Charles_Johson
_6_07.

Johnson, Michael P., and James L. Roark. *Black Masters: A Free Family of Color in the Old South*. New York: Norton, 1986.

Kakutani, Michiko. "Confronting the Failures of a Professor Who Passes." *New York Times*, 2 May 2000.

Kim, Daniel Y. *Writing Manhood in Black and Yellow*. Stanford: Stanford UP, 2005.

King, Martin Luther, Jr. *I Have a Dream: Writings and Speeches That Changed the World*. Ed. James M. Washington. San Francisco: HarperCollins, 1992.

Kloppenberg, James T. *Reading Obama: Dreams, Hope, and the American Political Tradition*. Princeton, NJ: Princeton UP, 2010.

Kluger, Richard. *Simple Justice*. New York: Vintage, 1977.

Kotz, Nick. *Judgment Days: Lyndon Baines Johnson, Martin Luther King Jr., and the Laws That Changed America*. Boston: Houghton Mifflin, 2005.

Lewis, R. W. B. *The Jameses: A Family Narrative*. New York: Farrar, Straus, and Giroux, 1991.

Litwack, Leon. *Trouble in Mind: Black Southerners in the Age of Jim Crow*. New York: Knopf, 1998.

Lucy, Robin. "'Flying Home': Ralph Ellison, Richard Wright, and the Black Folk during World War II." *Journal of American Folklore* 120.477 (Summer 2007): 257–83.

Lyons, Bonnie. "Lies, Secrets, Truthtelling and Imagination in *The Human Stain*." *Studies in Jewish American Fiction* 20 (2001): 89–93.

Margolick, David. "The Day Louis Armstrong Made Noise." *New York Times*, 23 Sept. 2007.

Mills, C. Wright. *The Power Elite*. New York: Oxford UP, 1956.

Moore, Laurie. "The Wrath of Athena." Rev. of *The Human Stain* by Philip Roth. *New York Times Book Review*, 7 May 2000.

Morel, Lucas, ed. *The Raft of Hope: A Political Companion to Invisible Man*. Lexington: UP of Kentucky, 2006.

Morris, Aldon D. *The Origins of the Civil Rights Movement*. New York: Free Press, 1984.

Morrison, Toni. "The Art of Fiction CXXXIV." Interview with Elissa Schappel. *Paris Review* 129 (1993): 83–125.

———. *Beloved*. New York: Knopf, 1987.

———. *Jazz*. New York: Knopf, 1992.

———. *Song of Solomon*. New York: Knopf, 1997.

Mumford, Lewis. *The Golden Day: A Study in American Literature and Culture*. 1926. Boston: Beacon, 1957.

Murray, Albert. *South to a Very Old Place*. New York: McGraw-Hill, 1972.

Murray, Gilbert. *The Classical Tradition in Poetry*. Cambridge: Harvard UP, 1927.

Musil, Robert. *The Man without Qualities*. 2 vol. Trans. Sophie Wilkins and Burton Pike, New York: Knopf, 1995.

Muyumba, Walton. *The Shadow and the Act: Black Intellectual Practice, Jazz Improvisation, and Philosophical Pragmatism*. Chicago: U of Chicago P, 2009.

Nadel, Alan. "The Integrated Literary Tradition." Tracy 143–70.

———. *Invisible Criticism: Ralph Ellison and the American Canon.* Iowa City: U of Iowa P, 1988.

Neal, Larry. "Ellison's Zoot Suit." *Visions of a Liberated Future: Black Arts Movement Writings.* Ed. Michael Schwarz. New York: Thunder's Mouth, 1989. 30–56.

Nicholls. David G. *Conjuring the Folk: Forms of Modernity in African America.* Ann Arbor: U of Michigan P, 2000.

Obama, Barack. *Dreams from My Father: A Story of Race and Inheritance.* 1995. New York: Three Rivers, 2004.

O'Meally, Robert. *The Craft of Ralph Ellison.* Cambridge: Harvard UP, 1980.

———. "On Burke and the Vernacular: Ralph Ellison's Boomerang of History." *History and Memory in African-American Culture.* Ed. Geneviève Fabre and Robert O'Meally. New York: Oxford UP, 1994. 244–60.

Parrish, Timothy. "The End of Identity: Philip Roth's *American Pastoral.*" *Shofar* 19.1 (Fall 2000): 84–99.

———. "Ralph Ellison, Finished and Unfinished: Aesthetic Achievements and Political Legacies." *Contemporary Literature* 48.4 (2007): 639–44.

———. "Ralph Ellison, Kenneth Burke and the Form of Democracy." *Arizona Quarterly* 52.3 (Autumn 1995): 117–48.

———. *Walking Blues: Making Americans from Emerson to Elvis.* Amherst: U of Massachusetts P, 2001.

Pinsker, Sanford. "Climbing over the Ethnic Fence: Reflections on Stanley Crouch and Philip Roth." *Virginia Quarterly Review* 78.3 (Summer 2002): 472–80.

Podhoretz, Norman. "Bellow at 85, Roth at 67." *Commentary* 110.1 (July/August 2000): 35–43.

Porter, Horace A. *Jazz Country.* Iowa City: U of Iowa P, 2001.

Posnock, Ross, ed. *The Cambridge Companion to Ralph Ellison.* Cambridge: Cambridge UP, 2005.

———. *Color and Culture: Black Writers and the Making of the Modern Intellectual.* Cambridge: Harvard UP, 1998.

———. *Philip Roth's Rude Truth: The Art of Immaturity.* Princeton: Princeton UP, 2008.

———. "Purity and Danger: On Philip Roth." *Raritan* 21.2 (Fall 2001): 85–101.

Posnock, Ross. "Ralph Ellison, Hannah Arendt, and the Meaning of Politics." Posnock, *Cambridge Companion* 201–16.

Raglan, Lord. *The Hero: A Study in Tradition, Myth, and Drama.* 1936. Mineola, NY: Dover, 2003.

Rampersad, Arnold. Interview posted on Amazon.com, *Ralph Ellison: A Biography* webpage.

———. *Ralph Ellison: A Biography.* New York: Knopf, 2007.

Reid-Pharr, Robert. *Once You Go Black: Choice, Desire, and the Black American Intellectual.* New York: New York UP, 2007.

Remnick, David. "Visible Man." Graham and Singh 392–401.

Rice, H. Williams. *Ralph Ellison and the Politics of the Novel.* Lanham, MD.: Lexington, 2003.

Roberts, Brian. "The CPUSA's Line and Atmosphere: Did Ellison and Wright Walk It as They Breathed It as They Wrote?" *Journal of Narrative Theory* 34.2 (Summer 2004): 258–68.

Roth, Philip. *American Pastoral.* Boston: Houghton Mifflin, 1997.

———. *The Anatomy Lesson.* New York: Farrar, Straus, Giroux, 1983.

———. "Defender of the Faith." *Goodbye, Columbus 173–214.*

———. "Eli the Fanatic." *Goodbye, Columbus 261–313.*

———. *The Facts: A Novelist's Autobiography.* New York: Farrar, 1988.

———. *The Ghost Writer.* New York: Farrar, Straus, 1979.

———. *Goodbye, Columbus and Five Short Stories.* Boston: Houghton Mifflin, 1959.

———. *The Human Stain.* Boston, New York: Houghton Mifflin, 2000.

———. *I Married a Communist.* Boston: Houghton Mifflin, 1998.

———. Interview. With Charles McGrath. "Zuckerman's Alter Brain." *New York Times Book Review,* 7 May 2000.

———. *Operation Shylock: A Confession.* Simon and Schuster, 1993.

———. *Patrimony.* New York: Simon and Schuster, 1991.

———. *Portnoy's Complaint.* New York: Random House, 1969.

———. *Reading Myself and Others: A New Expanded Edition.* New York, Penguin, 1985.

———. *Zuckerman Unbound.* 1981. New York: Farrar, Straus and Giroux, 1981.

Rowley, Hazel. *Richard Wright: The Life and Times.* New York: Henry Holt, 2001.

Rustin, Bayard. *Down the Line.* Chicago: Quadrangle, 1971.

Schaub, Thomas. *American Fiction in the Cold War.* Madison: U of Wisconsin P, 1991.

Schwartz, Delmore. "The Wrongs of Innocence and Experience." *Partisan Review* 19 (1952): 354–59.

Skerret, Joseph T., Jr. "The Wright Interpretation: Ralph Ellison and the Anxiety of Influence." Benston 217–30.

Spillers, Hortense. "Ellison's 'Usable Past: Toward a Theory of Myth." Benston 144–58.

———. "'The Little Man at Chehaw Station' Today." *boundary 2* 32 (Summer 2003): 5–19.

Stepto, Robert. *From Behind the Veil.* 1979. Urbana: U of Illinois P, 1991.

Sundquist, Eric J. *King's Dream.* New Haven: Yale UP, 2009.

———. *To Wake the Nations: Race in the Making of American Literature.* Cambridge: Harvard UP, 1993.

Tracy, Stephen C., ed. *A Historical Guide to Ralph Ellison.* Oxford: Oxford UP, 2004.

Waligora-Davis, Nicole A. "Riotous Discontent: Ralph Ellison's 'Birth of a Nation.'" *Modern Fiction Studies* 50. 2 (Summer 2004): 385–410.

Warren, Kenneth W. "Chaos Not Quite Controlled: Ellison's Uncompleted Transit to *Juneteenth.*" Posnock, *Cambridge Companion* 188–200.

———. *So Black and Blue: Ralph Ellison and the Occasion of Criticism.* Chicago: U of Chicago P, 2003.

Warren, Robert Penn. *The Legacy of the Civil War.* 1961. Lincoln: U of Nebraska P, 1998.

———. *Segregation: The Inner Conflict of the South.* New York: Random House, 1956.

———. *Selected Letters*. Ed. Randy Hendricks and James A. Perkins. Vol. 3. Louisiana State UP, 2006.

———. *Who Speaks for the Negro?* New York: Random House, 1965.

Watts, Jerry Gafio. *Heroism and the Black Intellectual: Ralph Ellison, Politics, and Afro-American Life*. Chapel Hill: U of North Carolina P, 1994.

Webb, Constance. *Richard Wright: A Biography*. New York: Putnam, 1968.

Wilson, Edmund. *Patriotic Gore: Studies in the Literature of the American Civil War*. New York: Oxford UP, 1962.

Woodward, C. Vann. *The Burden of Southern History*. New York: Random House, 1960.

———. Letter to Ralph Ellison. 18 Mar. 1968. C. Vann Woodward Papers (MS 1436), Manuscripts and Archives, Yale University Library

———. *The Origins of the New South, 1877–1913*. 1951. Baton Rouge: Louisiana State UP, 1971.

———. *The Strange Career of Jim Crow*. 1955. 3rd rev. ed. New York: Oxford UP, 1974.

———. *Thinking Back: The Perils of History*. Baton Rouge: Louisiana State UP, 1986.

Wright, John S. *Shadowing Ralph Ellison*. Jackson: U of Mississippi P, 2006.

Wright, Richard. *Early Writings*. New York: Library of America, 1991.

———. *Later Writings*. New York: The Library of America, 1991.

———. *12 Million Black Voices*. 1941. New York: Thunder's Mouth, 2002.

Yaffe, David. *Fascinating Rhythms: Reading Jazz in American Writing*. Princeton: Princeton UP, 2005.

Index

TIMOTHY PARRISH is professor of English at Florida State University. He is the author of *Walking Blues: Making Americans from Emerson to Elvis* (2001) and *From the Civil War to the Apocalypse: Postmodern History and American Fiction* (2008). He is also the editor of *The Cambridge Campanion to Philip Roth* (2007) and, most recently, *The Cambridge Companion to American Novelists* (forthcoming, 2012). He has published widely on contemporary American literature in such journals as *Contemporary Literature, Modern Fiction Studies, Prospects, Studies in American Fiction, Texas Studies in Literature and Language*, and *Arizona Quarterly*, among others.